Gender in Campaigns for the U.S. House of Representatives

Barbara Burrell presents a comprehensive comparative examination of men's and women's candidacies for the U.S. House of Representatives in elections from 1994 through 2012. Analyzing extensive data sets on all major party candidates for 10 elections—covering candidate status, party affiliation, fund-raising, candidate background variables, votes obtained, and success rates for both primary and general elections—Burrell finds little evidence of categorical discrimination against women candidates. Women compete equally with men and often outpace them in raising money, gaining interest group and political party support, and winning elections.

Yet the number of women elected to the U.S. House has expanded only incrementally. The electoral structure limits opportunities for newcomers to win congressional seats and there remains a lower presence of women in winnable contests despite growing recruitment efforts. Burrell suggests that congressional dysfunction discourages potential candidates from pursuing legislative careers and that ambitious women are finding alternative paths to influence and affect public policy.

Barbara Burrell is a professor emerita at Northern Illinois University, where she was a member of the Political Science faculty and a faculty associate in the Women's Studies Program. She is the author of *A Woman's Place Is in the House: Campaigning for Congress in the Feminist Era* (University of Michigan Press, 1994), a landmark study of women candidates for the U.S. House of Representatives from 1968 through 1992.

CAWP Series in Gender and American Politics

SERIES EDITORS:
Susan J. Carroll, Rutgers University
Kira Sanbonmatsu, Rutgers University

TITLES IN THE SERIES:
When Protest Makes Policy: How Social Movements Represent Disadvantaged Groups
by S. Laurel Weldon

The Paradox of Gender Equality: How American Women's Groups Gained and Lost Their Public Voice
by Kristin A. Goss

The Changing Face of Representation: The Gender of U.S. Senators and Constituent Communications
by Kim L. Fridkin and Patrick J. Kenney

The Political Consequences of Motherhood
by Jill S. Greenlee

Gender in Campaigns for the U.S. House of Representatives
by Barbara Burrell

Center for American Women and Politics
Eagleton Institute of Politics
Rutgers University
www.cawp.rutgers.edu

GENDER IN CAMPAIGNS FOR THE U.S. HOUSE OF REPRESENTATIVES

Barbara Burrell

The University of Michigan Press
Ann Arbor

Published in the United States of America by
The University of Michigan Press
Manufactured in the United States of America
⊗ Printed on acid-free paper

2017 2016 2015 2014 4 3 2 1

A CIP catalog record for this book is available from the British Library.

Library of Congress Cataloging-in-Publication Data

Burrell, Barbara C., 1947–
Gender in campaigns for the U.S. House of Representatives / Barbara Burrell.
pages cm. — (The CAWP series in gender and American politics)
Includes bibliographical references and index.
ISBN 978-0-472-07231-6 (hardcover : alk. paper) — ISBN 978-0-472-05231-8 (pbk. : alk. paper) — ISBN 978-0-472-12051-2 (e-book)
1. Women—Political activity—United States. 2. Women legislators—United States. 3. United States. Congress. House—Elections. 4. Political campaigns—United States. 5. United States—Politics and government—1993–2001. 6. United States—Politics and government—2001–2009. 7. United States—Politics and government—2009– I. Title.

HQ1236.5.U6B868 2015
320.0820973—dc23

2014014530

Contents

Acknowledgments

A number of years and several elections have passed since I first contemplated examining the elections since the 1992 "year of the women" to assess the campaign experiences of female candidates and compare those experiences with that of male candidates in the more contemporary era. My goal was to both update findings from studies of earlier elections and to replicate and extend research that had developed and tested new hypotheses about gender in congressional elections across a larger number of elections to explore systematic trends and build on election-cycle-specific findings.

My effort to assemble such a data set and provide a comparative analysis of men's and women's campaigns across electoral seasons extended over more years than I had originally expected. As I worked, more elections passed and needed to be incorporated into the database and trends extended for the most thorough study that included the most up-to-date information. Over this time period many graduate students assisted in the construction of individual candidate campaign data into one file for analysis purposes. I thank them for their efforts and hope that they will see their contribution in this end product.

Melody Herr, the political science editor at the University of Michigan Press, has been extremely patient as I slowly completed a draft of this book and then worked to respond to the comments and suggestions of reviewers. I greatly appreciate her positive encouragement over time. The critiques of the readers of the drafts of this manuscript have also made it a much better product. I especially wish to thank my colleague and friend Richard Matland for his detailed reading of the chapters and his suggestions that have made the analyses much finer.

As always I appreciate the support and encouragement of Skip and Caroline, my husband and daughter, and hope that they are proud of my work. Finally, if all of the fine women had not taken the risk to run for a seat in the U.S. House of Representatives in these elections there would be no research to conduct. Their diverse efforts, victories, and defeats make both the study of American politics and the democratic process itself much richer.

ONE

Introduction

Some decades ago, a political puzzle stimulated my initial exploration into the comparative campaign experiences of male and female candidates for the U.S. House of Representatives: Why had so few women been elected to that body in the decades since the emergence of the second women's rights movement in the 1960s? Conventional wisdom had suggested that female candidates and their election to national office suffered primarily from voter discrimination against them, from political party organizational promotion of them primarily as "sacrificial lambs" for elective office in districts the party had little hope of winning, and from their deficiency as fund-raisers. Yet only a few political scholars had conducted studies to empirically investigate these ideas as explanations for the small number of women who had won congressional seats. Thus, I set out to examine systematically reasons for the continued gap in the number of women and men seeking and winning elective political leadership positions. The findings of this research were published in *A Woman's Place Is in the House: Campaigning for Congress in the Feminist Era* in 1994.

For the research reported in that book I constructed a database consisting of all of the primary and general election major party candidates for the U.S. House of Representatives from 1972 through 1992 covering 11 election cycles. The database included information about candidate status, electoral performance, financial resources, and demographic characteristics. My systematic analyses of men's and women's experiences in the campaigns of that era found little support for the conventional wisdom ideas cited in the preceding paragraph. The most general finding that emerged from that study and from several others in the same vein during that era was that "when women run, women win." (See also Seltzer, Newman, and Leighton 1997.) On average, the votes women obtained equaled that of their male counterparts, they won as often as men did, and by the late 1980s female candidates were raising the same amounts of money to finance their campaigns. Controlling for party and candidate status did not diminish these findings.

In the years since the publication of *A Woman's Place Is in the House*, a community of scholars has delved more deeply into political puzzles surrounding women's quests for national office. For example, Barbara Palmer and Dennis Simon's *Breaking the Political Glass Ceiling* (2006, 2008) notably developed and examined the idea of "women friendly districts" to account for variations in women's successful quests for seats in the U.S. House of Representatives. In addition, much scholarly research has examined the impact of female membership in the U.S. House and Senate on those institutions' agendas and policy-making processes. The collection of articles in *Women Transforming Congress* (Rosenthal 2002a) stands out in this domain of research along with Michele Swers's *The Difference Women Make* (2002) and Debra Dodson's *The Impact of Women in Congress* (2006). Further, scholars have begun to explore the question of political ambition, focusing on why women have not sought public office in greater numbers and extending our research into the precampaign stage of women's lives. Jennifer Lawless and Richard Fox's *It Takes a Candidate: Why Women Don't Run for Office* (2005) and *It Still Takes a Candidate* (2010) are the most prominent studies addressing gender and political ambition to date.

Since the 1992 "year of the woman" substantially increased their numbers in the U.S. House and Senate, female membership in the national legislature has grown slowly and incrementally across ten subsequent election cycles. And at the beginning of the second decade of the 21st century, female representation in the U.S. House still lags far behind the membership of women in many national legislatures in electoral democracies around the globe. Women have mounted a substantial number of campaigns for a seat in the U.S. House during this time period, however. The research presented in this volume takes advantage of those many candidacies to explore the contemporary nature of women's quests for national political leadership, to compare their experiences with those of the campaigns of male candidates over the course of these elections, and to better understand the incremental nature of gains in their numbers as U.S. representatives. A data set of all of Democratic and Republican candidates for the U.S. House in the nine election cycles from 1993 through 2010 has been constructed. In addition, since the 2012 election was held consequent to the analyses of these nine election cycles, I include a postscript on key factors from that election that add to the analyses that are at the core of this work.

This study revisits the research questions regarding conventional wisdom about women and politics that were central to my initial work. It asks whether female candidates have kept pace with their male counterparts, surged ahead perhaps, or, as some subsequent studies have suggested, had to overcome greater challenges than male candidates to achieve equal results. It also builds on the numerous additional research questions that other scholars have initiated in contemporary studies. Some of these research efforts have examined one aspect of the campaign process such as fundraising in more depth over a number of elections while other research has explored a number of factors focusing on a single election cycle in building our base of knowledge of women's campaign experiences. This study replicates a number of those efforts, addressing them from the vantage point of a large and longitudinal data set to more definitively show patterns and ongoing trends and to provide greater generalizability.

I further incorporate distinctive facets of contemporary campaigns. Special attention is given to the concept of "opportunity structure" in the various analyses undertaken in this work than has been done previously. Opportunity structures center on partisan contexts and electoral environments in assessing presence and performance. Chapter 3 particularly addresses questions of opportunity with a focus on open seats, the most opportune contests for newcomers to win seats in the House. This attention provides the opportunity to look beyond an examination of women's overall presence and take into account the strategic nature of women's entrance into races for seats in the U.S. House for an enhanced understanding of the incremental growth in their membership.

Throughout its chapters this study presents an appraisal of the gendered nature of contemporary elections for seats in the U.S. House of Representatives. I contend that the multitude of studies systematically analyzing a variety of research questions about the challenges male and female candidates have faced in recent elections principally show that gendered factors have greatly diminished in races for national office below the presidency. Not only do women win when they run, they run in the same ways and face the same obstacles as male candidates and voters respond to them in a similar ways.

Although numerical parity may be a long way off, gender parity as a distinctive concept may be much closer at hand. This distinction may be particularly notable if one takes into account opportunity structures and view women as strategic politicians. Further, female candidates have become masters of politicking. They have also advanced their power and influence in the national legislature, most notably in the historical election in 2007 of Nancy Pelosi (D-CA) to be Speaker of the U.S. House, the highest constitutional position in the legislative branch, which made her second in line for the presidency. She then lost the speakership in 2011 after the Republicans won back the House in the 2010 election but she continued as minority leader.

My perspective is that a continued emphasis on a gendered nature to these elections to the disadvantage of female candidates may be misplaced. Some features of campaigns that have been presumed to be gendered in nature disadvantaging female candidates may actually be more the result of the structure of election seasons. For example, the numbers of women seeking election to the U.S. House across the nine elections that form the core of this study may be primarily a factor of varied opportunity structures that each election has provided for newcomers based on the number of incumbents who have decided to retire in a particular election year, rather than women's lack of ambition and lack of recruitment being the key to their low numbers as candidates.

My proposed minimal "gender" perspective results from quantitative analyses of the campaign process that have tested hypotheses about the effect of sex through the systematic comparison of male and female candidates' presence and experience on the campaign trail. This approach, while extremely important for both descriptive and causal inference, minimizes the significance of anecdotal evidence of continued gendered based experiences. Certainly such incidences still are present, recorded by observers and on occasion expressed by women candidates themselves. These experiences will be interpreted, and properly should be, as evidence of a continued presence of sexism in the political process but how large of a factor it is needs to be discussed and put into proper perspective. Surely, the presidential campaign of U.S. Senator Hillary Clinton brought new life to the idea that our political process is still infused with gendered aspects (Lawrence and Rose 2010). Georgia Duerst-Lahti describes presidential elections as gendered spaces (2010). What are the gendered spaces of contemporary congressional elections? Sarah Palin's "mama grizzlies" certainly called attention to a new distinct aspect of gender politics in the 2010 election. I do not brush aside such pieces of data but the process has evolved to one in which few systematic distinctions between the sexes in their quests for political leadership have been found, at least in legislative elections as the research presented in the following chapters will show.

Problems do remain for achieving equity for women in the world of lawmakers and executives, however, and the importance of having women in these positions is substantial from normative perspectives of justice and fairness, for the symbolic nature of their presence as leaders, and from the substantive impact of the distinctive experiences of women's lives that they bring to the policy-making process. Continued close attention to the "complex world of women in U.S. politics" (Reingold 2008, 1) from a variety of lenses is important and a balance between anecdotal and systematic data analysis and normative perspectives is required in our examination of trends in men's and women's campaigns.

The Numerical Representation of Women in the U.S. House since 1992

In political lore, 1992 was the "year of the woman" in American politics. Women tripled their numbers in the U.S. Senate and nearly doubled their numbers in the U.S. House of Representatives. Many of the women who ran campaigned as "women," meaning that they highlighted their differences from the typical and traditional political leaders, principally men. Gender was a central frame of electoral politics that year, perhaps made most notable in Patty Murray's now famous (and successful) "just a mom in tennis shoes" Washington State race for the U.S. Senate. Ten national elections have occurred since that watershed year and the second decade of the 21st century.

As a result of the 1992 election, women increased their membership in the U.S. House of Representatives from 29 to 47 representatives, and advanced their membership in the U.S. Senate from two to six out of 100 Senators. Yet, that was still only a small minority of the membership, 10.8 percent of the U.S. House and 6 percent in the U.S. Senate.

After ten additional congressional elections since 1992 women have increased their membership to 17.9 percent of the House. In 2008, 74 women were elected to the House, the largest number ever, which decreased by one as a result of the 2010 elections but then increased to 78 in the 2012 election. Figure 1.1 shows the trend in the number of female members of the U.S. House of Representatives from 1994 through 2012, illustrating the incremental nature of their rise in numbers and a growing gap between the presence of Democratic and Republican women in that body.

Even though women's presence and influence in the United States Congress has grown during the contemporary era, from a numerical per-

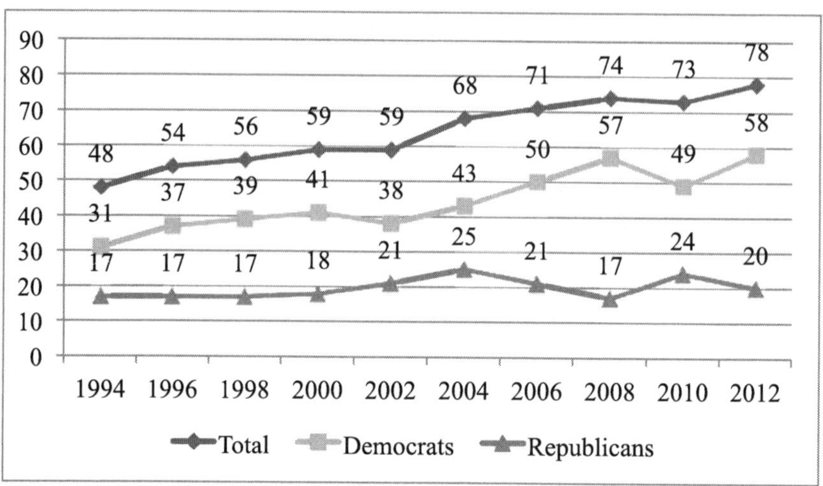

Fig. 1.1. Women Elected to the U.S. House of Representatives, 1994–2012. (Data collected by the author from the Center for American Women and Politics, Rutgers University.)

spective the United States lags behind the majority of democratic parliaments in the world in the percentage of women members in its lower house. Other countries have adopted procedures to enhance the presence of women among their elected political leaders, such as the use of fast-track quota strategies, which has moved them ahead of the United States. Out of 115 electoral democracies, the United States in 2012 ranked 62nd in the percentage of its members of parliament who were women.[1]

Electoral structures are key factors affecting the numerical representation of women in national parliaments. Electoral structures consist of such factors as the rules by which candidates get their names on the ballot, the role of party organizations in the electoral process, the votes it takes to win, and how many candidates for whom voters can cast ballots in particular districts. The United States has an electoral structure that is the least conducive to the election of women from a comparative electoral structure standpoint. List proportional representation systems do better when it comes to women's numerical representation. Proportional representation requires the use of electoral districts with more than one member. Under a list proportional representation system, each party or grouping presents a list of candidates for a multimember electoral district, the voters vote for a party, and the parties receive seats in proportion to their overall share of the votes (Larserud and Taphorn 2007). The candidates actually elected to the legislature depend on their placement on the list. The greater the magnitude of the seats a party can win, the better the opportunity for female candidates in such systems (Matland 1993; Schwindt-Bayer 2009).

The United States has constructed a very different system called a "first past the post" process in which the winning candidate is the one who gains more votes than any other candidate, even if the number of votes is not an absolute majority of valid votes. This system uses single-member districts in which voters cast only one vote and select a candidate, not a political party. In the United States, not only do voters only cast one vote but the parties only nominate one candidate. That means it is impossible for them to present a balanced slate because they have only one candidate. Also one of the crucial factors that makes the U.S. system distinctive from other first past the post systems is the limited power the party has to select and to veto candidates that run under its label. The U.S. system is much more candidate centered than in other majoritarian countries, which makes it much harder for the parties to increase representation even if they are interested in achieving that goal.

Further, the candidate-centered single member district system in the United States has contributed, among other factors, to incumbents being overwhelmingly advantaged. Also, because much of the history of the public realm has been a "men only" domain, their domination as incumbents has created a major drag on women making much numerical progress in Congress.

Twenty-six countries have also adopted national candidate quota laws, "fast track" mechanisms for increasing women's representation (Schwindt-Bayer 2009). A number of other countries have instituted voluntary party quotas for women nominees. Quotas are primarily a form of affirmative action to help women overcome the obstacles that have prevented them from entering politics in the same way as their male colleagues (Larserud and Taphorn 2007). Although the implementation of quota laws has achieved substantial success in increasing the number of women in parliaments, neither the American political culture nor the structure of its electoral system is conducive to the introduction of legal quotas as a method of boosting the representation of women in the U.S. Congress or in lower level offices. The educational and economic advances American women have made in the latter part of the 20th century suggest that the idea that they need this extra help, rather than achieving electoral office on their own merit, would most likely not receive widespread support among the American citizenry, perhaps even among liberal feminists.

The 1995 Fourth UN World Conference on Women held in Beijing,

China, adopted a Platform for Action that, among other things, called for the equal participation of women and men in governmental decision making. The goals of equality, development, and peace could not be achieved, the Platform declared, without the active participation of women and the incorporation of women's perspectives at all levels of decision making. Thus, the Platform declared that the underrepresentation of women in elective and policy-making positions was a problem. The Beijing Platform described "discriminatory attitudes and practices" and "unequal power relations" that led to the underrepresentation of women in arenas of political decision making. Attention was directed toward institutional and cultural mechanisms of exclusion that prevented women from obtaining an equal share of political positions in most political institutions in the world. It spoke of securing a "critical mass" of women in political leadership and of achieving the target the United Nations Economic and Social Council had endorsed in 1990 of having 30 percent women in positions at decision-making levels.[2]

The idea of a critical mass and as a goal to be achieved provides a context in which to assess the U.S. system.[3] A number of countries have surpassed that critical mass goal and are much closer to equity than the United States. But their national parliaments also vary in the degree to which they are independent policy-making centers in their national governments. The U.S. Congress is one of the most powerful legislatures in the world. The U.S. Congress is distinctive among national legislatures around the world in the extent of its independent powers regarding making national policy and the degree to which its members can affect the policy-making agenda by introducing and pursuing legislation (and having laws informally named after its members). It occupies the center stage in national policy making (Kernell and Jacobson 2003). Based on their comparative research Smith, Roberts, and Vander Wielen have concluded that "[n]o other national legislature has greater power than the Congress of the United States" (2007, 1). In most parliamentary systems the policy-making centers are solidly in the executive branch, which has a supportive majority in the parliament with limited powers and limited resources to pursue independent policy initiatives.

Thus, although women constitute a smaller proportion of membership of the U.S. Congress than do women in 61 other democratic parliaments, they at least have the opportunity to meaningfully affect public policy, more so than female members of many other parliaments. Not just numbers but capacity for influence is important in measuring the progress women have made as national public officials in a comparative context and should serve as a frame of reference in assessing the campaigns for and election of women to seats in the U.S. national legislature.

Gender Analysis

The concept of gender is central to the research undertaken in this project. A gender analysis requires one to examine the processes, practices, images, ideologies, and distributions of power in various sectors of society to determine how they differentially affect men and women, how men and women's performance in various activities and institutions are viewed and assessed differently, and how gender affects the presence of women in power positions (Acker 1992). Whereas sex is biological, gender is socially constructed (see Duerst-Lahti 2006 for a primer on gender). Gender analysis involves comparisons between men and women as they engage in the political, social, and economic realms and how those differences are perceived.

Scholars study the gendered aspects of political phenomena when they examine the ways in which men and women interact with the public world. For example, male and female candidates for public office may have had different experiences on the campaign trail because of their sex. The conventional wisdoms cited in the beginning of this chapter are examples of gender differences. Other examples include how candidates present their families in their campaigns. Female candidates' family lives have been scrutinized differently in the past. Gender stereotypes have infused our politics and affected the candidacies of women (see, for example, Dolan 2005).

Governing institutions are also gendered in that masculine behavior has been the norm. Sally Kenny has challenged researchers to explore the gendered nature of political institutions. Such work, she argues, should treat gender as a continuous, variable, and tenacious process, that, while usually leading to women's disadvantage, is challenged, negotiated, subverted, and resisted (1996, 463). Cindy Simon Rosenthal has shown that an integrative style of legislative leadership exists and is more visible in the committee behavior of women than men. An integrative style is distinguished from an aggregative style more characteristic of male legislative leaders according to Rosenthal. She describes an aggregative style as being explicitly transactional with participants calculating the consequences of different strategies and competing for advantage or a share of a decision (1999, 159–60). In studying political leadership, gender is a multifaceted aspect.

Continued Gendered Themes

How have scholars theorized about the continuing gendered nature of electoral politics since the 1992 "year of the woman"? Sue Thomas in her introduction to the second edition of *Women and Elective Office: Past, Present, and Future* published in 2005 states that institutional gendering, that is, persistent experiences of discrimination and structures designed to extend male privilege, continues to plague women in their quest for numerical equality and prestige in elective office at the same time that women have made substantial gains. She notes that women's progress has occurred slowly, and has been accompanied by significant challenges, by some setbacks, and by not inconsiderable costs. By costs, Thomas referenced more than the monetary financing of their campaigns. Costs included the personal and cultural challenges women faced compared with men when they sought elective office.

Susan Carroll and Richard Fox describe how they view elections as continuing to be gendered in nature in *Gender and Elections* (2006, 2010). According to Carroll and Fox, men still dominate political life, gendered language continues to permeate the political landscape, gender continues to infuse expectations about candidates' qualities, appearance, and behavior, and candidates employ distinctive strategies in reaching out to male and female voters. Thus, for example, campaigns were described as "battles waged from war rooms," creating harm and damage to the other side. It was a gladiatorial process. Nancy Pelosi has noted that when women have asked her for advice about entering politics, she has told them, "Don a suit of armor. . . . 'Campaign' is a battle term" (Dobbin 2002). Leaders must be tough, dominant, and assertive, all masculine descriptors. Sports' metaphors have dominated media coverage, such as the description of party leaders and staff "performing like football coaching staffs in hot pursuit of high school prospects, they are pulling together the lineups of the future" (Davidson 2009, 81). In 2008 the National Republican Campaign Committee initiated its Young Guns program, focusing resources on its most resourceful recruits for seats in the House.

A theme of much of the research on women candidates has been on the extent to which they have adopted masculine styles and whether such approaches are effective (see, for example, DaBelko and Herrnson 1997; Herrnson, Lay, and Stokes 2003). Carroll and Fox note that "candidates, both men and women, strategize about how to present themselves to voters of the same and opposite sexes" (2010, 4).

The 2010 special election in Massachusetts to replace U.S. Senator Ted Kennedy, who had died the year before from brain cancer, and then the general election contest that followed in 2012 for his seat provided recent references to masculinity and sports and political campaigning. Here the examples centered on affinity with the Boston Red Sox baseball team. Lack of passion for and knowledge of the team and not seeing its relevance to getting elected as a U.S. senator tripped up Democratic attorney general Martha Coakley, gaining her considerable negative publicity. She lost to Republican state senator Scott Brown in the special election. Then the successful 2012 challenger to Senator Brown, Harvard law professor Elizabeth Warren, had what the *Washington Post* called a "Red Sox test." Not only that, she had a "beer gap" (who would you most like to have a beer with) (Blake 2012).

Many studies of individual aspects of women's campaigning for Congress in recent elections have suggested a continued downside regarding women's increasing representation and movement up the power ladder. For example, the chapters in *Women and Congress: Running, Winning, and Ruling*, edited by Karen O'Connor (2001), show that women had failed to maintain the level of success in congressional open seats that was achieved in 1992 in the elections from 1994 through 1998 (Hoffman, Palmer, and Gaddie 2001); the growth in the presence of women in the electoral arena was disproportionately a Democratic phenomenon, at least since 1988 (Palmer and Simon 2001); that news media coverage disadvantaged women candidates in Senate races between 1988 and 1992 (Kropf and Boiney 2001); and the media engaged in a gender-centered view of women politicians as determined through a survey of press secretaries to female U.S. congresswomen (Niven and Zilber 2001).

More recently, Jennifer Lawless in the "Critical Perspectives on Gender and Politics" section of *Politics and Gender* concluded that gender stereotypes continue. Voters rely on "stereotypical conceptions of men's and women's traits, issue expertise, and policy positions when casting ballots," and that gender stereotypes "affect the manner in which the media assess women candidates" (2009). Further, female congressional candidates face more primary competition than do their male counterparts, "female candidates are more likely than men to report having been recruited to run for office," rather than being self-starters, and "that geographic differences facilitate women's election in some districts, but lessen their chances of success in others" (78–79). These studies all stress elections as gendered processes from a campaign perspective to women's disadvantage.

Emergence of Equality Themes

Opposed to these negative gendered stereotypic themes affecting women's campaigns, much recent research has shown that women have developed into formidable vote-getters and fund-raisers, being equally assertive, even as aggressive, as male contenders. They have benefitted from substantial independent party expenditures in close congressional races and have ascended to powerful positions within the U.S. House. In addition to Speaker Pelosi, for example, Louise Slaughter (D-NY) chaired the Rules Committee in the 110th and 111th Congresses, the most prestigious and particularly powerful House committee, and female representatives and senators have chaired both parties' campaign committees. In 2011, U.S. Representative Debbie Wasserman Schultz was elected chair of the Democratic National Committee, another first.[4] Female candidates have even proven to be as negative campaigners as male candidates (Bystrom et al 2004). Media presentations of their candidacies and campaigns have become primarily indistinguishable (Sapiro et al. 2011).

Women and politics scholars have often invoked the concept of a double bind and incorporated it into their studies to characterize the impossible situations would-be female political leaders find themselves in when they have attempted to achieve public office. For example, Herrnson and Lucas introduce their research on male and female candidates' perspectives on the use of negativity in advertising with a focus on the lack of parity in the political arena and cite as one explanation for the lack of women in office "the role of gendered voter stereotypes and the 'double bind,' whereby female candidates must carefully balance masculine and feminine traits" (2006). The double bind is also central to Lawrence and Rose's study of Hillary Clinton's presidential race in 2008 (2010).

Kathleen Hall Jamieson brought this concept to the forefront of political studies in her 1995 work *Beyond the Double Bind*. She chronicles many different double binds women have faced historically. However, it is important to note her title and consider how we have moved "beyond" the double bind. Jamieson evokes a perspective on women's history that

> differs from that of those who argue that liberation for women is an endless war in which small battles are won only to be met with violent repression. . . . Women's progress has been thwarted by double binds that, when surmounted, have in fact been replaced by other double binds, as I will show here. But as women have conquered the no-win situations confronting them, they have marshaled resources

> and refined aptitudes that have made them more and more capable of facing the next challenge, the next opportunity. At the same time, they have systematically exposed the fallacious constructs traditionally used against them, and changed and enlarged the frame through which women are viewed. Although the result is not a steady move toward equitable treatment of women, it is a world in which progress is certainly sufficient to justify optimism. (6, 7)

In her conclusion, Jamieson highlights ways of overcoming double binds. Her ideas include "asserting control over the language through which we see ourselves is consequently an indispensable move in vanquishing the vestiges of the binds that tie. Reframing, recovering, reclaiming, recounting, and confounding the stereotypes are the tools being used to clear them away." The "bad old days" are gone, according to Jamieson. "The times . . . are a changing," women are being "seen and heard," and "have overcome" (197). Understanding the changing nature of gendered features of contemporary campaigns for national office, in particular for the U.S. House of Representatives, is central to this study.

Normative Perspectives on Women in Political Leadership

Political theorists have cited a number of normative concerns about the underrepresentation of women in political leadership positions and empirical scholars have tested these concerns in the contemporary political world. Regarding survey findings, public opinion scholars have studied evolving public perceptions of women as political leaders as they have expanded their presence as candidates and officeholders over time.

The normative stimulus for studying women's quests for political leadership stems from ideas about justice and fairness, perspectives on women's symbolic importance as political leaders, and thoughts on women's substantive impact on policy making. Justice and fairness arguments demand that we be concerned with the unequal distribution of men and women in leadership positions. In addition, women's presence among political leaders may have a symbolic importance for constituent women and girls. The invisibility of women as role models among our leaders would discourage girls and young women from envisioning themselves in such positions. Women may ask why they should pay attention to politics, state their opinions, and join in political campaigns if people like themselves are not visible as policy makers. A further philosophic perspective focuses on the possible substantive importance of having a critical mass of women present as public policies are being made. Female lawmakers may bring distinctive policy preferences and ideas to the legislative agenda, to policy debates, to problem solving, and to policy outcomes.

A number of normative theorists have proposed and hoped that greater numbers of women in political office would have a variety of positive effects on the political system such as compensating for past and present injustice, providing a voice for overlooked interests, and contributing to the overall legitimacy of a democratic system (see, for example, Wolbrecht and Campbell 2006). Justice requires that one-half of the population not be excluded from political leadership. Symbolic significance centers on the importance to constituents of women's presence among the political leaders. Difference and substantive perspectives hold that women would bring new issues to the legislative agenda and unique orientations to public policy debates based on their distinctive life experiences.

The justice argument centering on ideas about fairness demands that men and women be present in roughly equal numbers among political elites. The gender, ethnicity, and race of elected representatives serve as evaluations of democratic political institutions. Implicit in these evaluations is the assumption that democratic political institutions that lack any representatives from historically disadvantaged groups are unjust and perceived as illegitimate. It is "grotesquely unfair for men to monopolize representation," Anne Phillips has argued in laying out the justice argument for gender parity in representation. She asks "by what 'natural' superiority of talent or experience could men claim a right to dominate assemblies" (1998, 232). Phillips maintains that descriptive representatives are needed to compensate for past and continued injustices toward certain groups. According to this argument, past and present betrayals by privileged groups create a belief that trust can be given only to descriptive representatives. The presence of descriptive representatives partially compensates for those betrayals.

Jennifer Lawless, too, has recently summarized this normative perspective, stating that "many scholars conclude that there appears to be something wrong with a political system that produces governing bodies dominated by men, when, in fact, women comprise the majority of the population" (2004, 81). Structural discrimination has kept women from pursuing political leadership positions on an equal basis with men. Many historical examples exist of the prejudices women have faced when they stepped out of their traditional roles in the home and sought a place in the public sector. Indeed, it took over 70 years of campaigning for women just to get the right to vote.

Justice and fairness arguments stress that the presence of women among political leaders is important regardless of how different women's perspectives and interests are from those of men's. But we know that those interests have not been the same in the past: otherwise, why would women have organized, marched, and lobbied for an Equal Rights Amendment; why would they have sued in court for equal rights, have needed special laws regarding violence, job security, and so on. The distinctive experiences of women's lives have also not been incorporated into the agenda of policy making and not been heard in legislative debates without the presence of women to express them (see, for example, Hawkesworth 2003 and Dodson 2006).

Further, the symbolic argument advanced in support of the idea of descriptive representation is that female politicians serve as role models, inspiring other women to political activity and greater political competence. They perform a symbolic representation function. This perspective emphasizes that women running and serving in high public office would have an impact on their female constituents, stimulating greater interest and involvement in the electoral process on their part. Female leaders may affect people's attitudes toward government and their ability to influence it, seeing it as more accessible and open as it becomes more diverse. Their presence may especially influence women, helping to close their deficit vis-à-vis men on political factors such as efficacy, interest, knowledge, and general political participation. These possible effects on women's engagement in the political process merge together descriptive and symbolic representation concerns in advocating for more women in political leadership positions.

Jane Mansbridge (1999) has written that the descriptive representation of having women as candidates and elected officials (along with members of minority groups) contributes to a "construction of social meaning that members of these groups are capable of governing. Their very presence as candidates and office holders signals to the public that politics is no longer exclusively a male domain." Mansbridge also suggests that this altered social meaning of the nexus of "political" and "woman" lends increased "de facto legitimacy" to the polity itself (1999). According to researchers Atkeson and Carrillo, "A representative body that shares physical characteristics with its constituency symbolically appears more open to input from more citizens and appears better able to understand citizen interests.

Female citizens, therefore, may perceive that their own opinions will have greater value when larger proportions of female representatives are present" (2007).

Empirical Studies of Symbolic Representation

The two philosophical perspectives that highlight symbolic and substantive representation as normatively important to women's presence as political leaders have been the subject of empirical analyses. I take up questions about the substantive impact of women representatives in contemporary congresses on the legislative process via agenda setting, distinct policymaking perspectives, and leadership in chapter 8 after exploring their experiences on the campaign trail. Here I summarize the empirical research on aspects of women's symbolic representation, namely their function as role models. Consider, for example, the symbolic significance of Nancy Pelosi as Speaker of the House of Representatives sitting behind President Bush for the first time as he gave his State of the Union address in January 2007. Consider also the scene on the floor of the Capitol as TV cameras spanned the audience for the president's address with white women and men and women of color prominent as members of the nation's political leadership. These images speak to the empowerment of previously excluded groups from political leadership and serve as important symbols.

The presence of women as elected officials surely should raise the ambitions of girls, increase women's interest in political campaigns, and expand their engagement in political discussions, theorists suggest. Note, for example, the tremendous excitement Hillary Clinton's campaign for the presidency generated among women, especially older women who argued it was their time and who worked hard to get her elected. Sarah Palin energized a whole different group of women who believed that feminists had not been speaking to their interests when she was nominated for vice president in 2008. These women running for office in the presidential domain stand as a catalyst for other women to become more politically engaged.

Female elected officials act as symbols or role models when their presence leads women in the general public to feel more politically efficacious, believing that they too can influence the political process. If their presence as elected officials stimulates more interest in and knowledge about the political process among women and encourages more women to run for public office themselves, then they are symbolically important. Is there empirical evidence of these types of connections?

Scholars have found some evidence that the presence of women candidates has an effect on the behavior of voters at the individual level, from both a dyadic and a collective perspective. Dyadic representation refers to relationships in which women are directly represented by female legislators or executives. Collective representation centers on national trends as women increase their numbers among elected leaders. Dyadic representation examines how well a specific member of a governing body represents his or her constituents. Collective representation pays attention to how well the institution as a whole represents its citizens.

Empirical studies have shown that the effect on female citizens of having female representatives seems to vary with the context of the election, however. In the 1992 "year of the woman" election, women living in areas with a female candidate for governor or the U.S. Congress had significantly increased involvement in the election compared with women in election contexts with no female candidates (Sapiro and Conover 1997). Women in states with female U.S. Senate candidates had higher levels of political interest and a greater ability to recall the names of the Senate candidates than those living in states without women candidates. They were also more likely to engage in political proselytizing, that is, convincing others to vote (Koch 1997). However, these relationships were not found in other election years.

Other research has found that the density of women politicians, (i.e., the number of statewide female political figures in the respondent's state) influences the gender gap in psychological orientations to politics, generally by increasing the involvement of women (Burns, Schlozman, and Verba 2001). The Burns et al. study found that the more women who vie for or hold important political offices in a respondent's congressional district or state, the more likely a female respondent was to be interested in politics and political campaigns, to follow the campaign in the media, and to be able to express likes and dislikes about the majority party candidates for the House of Representatives (2001, 347). They also demonstrated that female respondents in the American National Election Studies (ANES) from 1990 to 1999 were significantly more likely than male respondents to mention a female candidate's sex as a reason to evaluate her positively. Female respondents who lived in states with competitive female candidates had higher levels of political efficacy and knowledge and were more likely to discuss politics than women who lived in states with noncompetitive female candidates in general (Atkeson 2003).

Evidence of a symbolic impact goes beyond female voters. Campbell and Wolbrecht (2006) have found that the presence of visible female role models increases the propensity for girls to express an intention to be politically active. Further, female incumbents, at least at the congressional level, tended to foster additional female candidates in their district both within their party and within the challenging party (Palmer and Simon 2008). As Palmer and Simon conclude, "successful women candidates inspire other women to run. . . . [their] victory serves as a cue signaling that a woman can overcome the hurdles and compete successfully in [those] districts" (148).

However, Lawless in her examination of ANES data found little evidence of the independent symbolic effects scholars had typically ascribed to women's presence in Congress (2004). Nor does the presence of female candidates appear to act as a mobilizing effect on voter turnout as evidenced through an extensive analysis of ANES data from 1990 through 2000 for both Senate and House races (Dolan 2008). Scholars who have worked to empirically test aspects of symbolic hypotheses have been hindered in that the general election studies that they have had to depend on to research symbolic effects have not been constructed with such questions in mind. Thus, they have only allowed for tenuous correlations rather than providing for a more focused in-depth analysis. The lack of proper measures has left the question of symbolic effects open for greater empirical study.[5]

Public Perceptions of Women as Political Leaders

Stereotypes or stereotyping is an important aspect of a gendered perspective on political campaigns. In this arena, stereotyping refers to ideas about women candidates based on perceptions about women possessing certain characteristics or approaching politics in a particular way because of their nature. These perceptions may have little basis in empirical reality but they govern voters' thinking about what women would do in office and affect the likelihood of voting for them. Stereotypes have been the subject of much empirical research on female candidates including both experimental and survey data.

Contemporary research has measured various aspects of gender stereotyping regarding men and women in politics. One domain of survey questions has centered on the public's basic support for women in politics and general comparative perceptions of men and women as political leaders. I present three contemporary examples of this research to provide a summary of the survey findings and a contemporary picture of the public's views on women as political leaders.

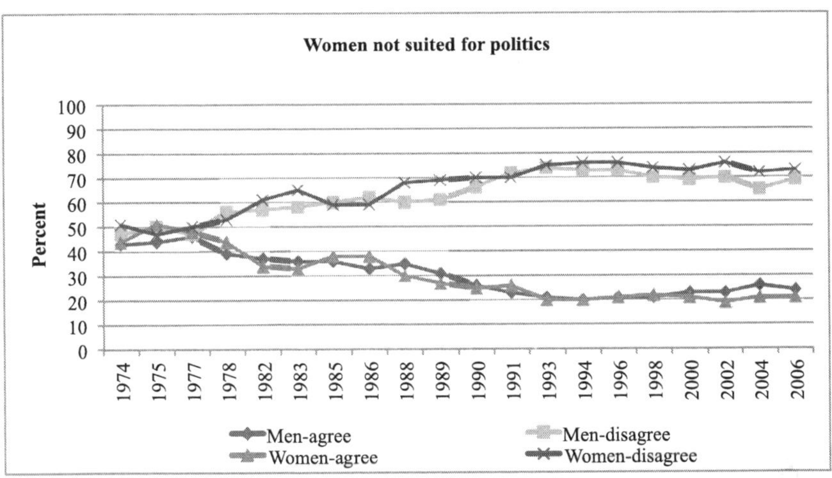

Fig. I.2. Most Men Are Better Suited Emotionally for Politics than Are Most Women. (Data from General Social Survey, NORC.)

Suitability for Political Leadership

First, for over 30 years the National Opinion Research Center at the University of Chicago in its General Social Survey has asked a national sample of respondents whether men are better suited emotionally for politics than most women. Figure 1.2 shows trends in men's and women's responses to this question. In 1991, just before the famous "year of the woman" election, 72 percent of men and 70 percent of women disagreed with the statement that men were better suited emotionally for politics than most women. In 2008, the most recent data point available, 66 percent of men and 71 percent of women disagreed that men were better suited emotionally for politics than most women. Disagreement has held quite steady at approximately 70 percent since the "year of the woman." At the same time, nearly one-quarter of the male respondents (26%) and over one-fifth (24%) of the female respondents agreed that men are better suited for politics. The fact that about one-quarter of Americans express this perspective should give us pause.

Second, in 2007, Kathleen Dolan conducted a national study that queried whether respondents had a baseline preference for candidates of one sex or the other. Respondents were asked "if two equally qualified candidates were running for office, one a man and the other a woman, do you think you would be more likely to vote for the man or the woman?" Sixty percent opted for the male candidate while 40 percent opted for the female candidate. This 20 point male advantage should also give us pause in reflecting on a diminishing aspect of gender in elections for public office. However, respondents were not given an option of saying the sex of the candidate would make no difference to them, which might have resulted in a lesser divergence. But when forced to choose in this study, they were substantially more likely to select the male candidate, especially the male respondents (72% to 28%) while female respondents split their likely vote nearly evenly between the male (49%) and female candidate (51%) (2010).

Third, the Pew Research Center in 2008 asked a national sample who they thought would make better political leaders: men or women. Here respondents were provided with a third option that men and women were equally good political leaders. A substantial majority, 69 percent opted for the statement that in general men and women make equally good political leaders, while 21 percent replied that "men generally make better political leaders than women" and 6 percent said that "women generally make better political leaders than men" (Taylor et al. 2008).

Leadership Performance

In a second domain of public opinion questions, the public has been queried about its perceptions of male and female political leaders' performance in different policy areas and their personality traits. In 1999, Roper Starch Worldwide conducted the 8th *Virginia Slims' American Women's Opinion Poll.* In this study a national sample of adults were presented with 13 public policy areas and asked whether for each area women would do a better job, a worse job, or just as good a job as men in public office. Table 1.1 shows the distribution of responses of men and women to this set of questions.

The extent to which respondents believed that women would do a better or a worse job in areas of public policy indicates the degree to which stereotyping continues to pervade women's quests for political leadership. With the exception of two items, both men and women tended to respond that women would do just as good of a job as men in public office. But on no issue were the male and female respondents unanimous or nearly unanimous that women would do just as good a job. Stereotyping was present both to the advantage and disadvantage of women seeking political leadership positions and it confirmed findings of other studies for the most part. Women were particularly advantaged when it came to improving the health care and educational systems and dealing with the concerns of the elderly. Perhaps somewhat indicative of movement away from women being disadvantaged were perspectives on "strengthening the economy" where approximately two-thirds of both men and women saw no difference and over one-quarter of the female respondents thought women would do a better job.

In the foreign policy area, the study asked about conducting diplomatic relations with other countries and about directing the military. In this area,

TABLE 1.1. When it comes to [*read first item on list*], do you feel that women in public office would do a better job than men, a worse job than men, or just as good a job as men in public life? (responses in percentages)

	Women Better		Women Just as Good		Women Worse		Don't Know	
	Respondents							
When It Comes To:	Male	Female	Male	Female	Male	Female	Male	Female
Improving Our Educational System	45	53	48	42	6	4	2	2***
Changing the Educational and Health Care Systems	45	53	46	42	7	3	2	2***
Dealing with Concerns of Seniors (e.g., Social Security, Medicare, housing)	44	50	49	44	6	4	2	2**
Encouraging the Arts	41	45	52	48	5	4	3	3
Improving Justice for Minority Groups	34	40	55	52	8	5	3	2***
Protecting the Environment	31	39	58	54	8	5	3	2***
Maintaining Honesty and Integrity in Government	31	47	57	46	9	4	3	3***
Conducting Relations with Other Countries	19	28	56	57	20	12	5	4***
Strengthening the Economy	16	27	67	64	14	6	3	3***
Developing Policies and Programs to Reduce Crime	14	25	60	61	22	11	4	3***
Strengthening the Internet and High Tech Industries	11	12	63	67	17	12	10	8**
Improving the Country's Infrastructure (such as highways and bridges)	9	12	54	61	31	22	6	6***
Directing the Military	7	9	36	49	52	34	2	2***

Source: 8th Virginia Slims American Women's Opinion Poll, 2000, available at the Roper Center, Public Opinion Archives, University of Connecticut, www.ropercenter.uconn.edu.

$^{*}p < .05$; $^{**}p < .01$; $^{***}p < .001$.

while women were predominantly viewed as performing as well as men or better, 20 percent of the male respondents and 12 percent of the women said women would do a worse job in conducting diplomatic relations. Few male or female respondents opted that women would do a better job directing the military but large gender gaps emerged regarding doing the same or a worse job. Female respondents were much more likely to say that women would do the same job as men while male respondents were more likely to say women would do a worse job. So here we see some lingering negative stereotyping occurring as far as women leaders are concerned, but it is definitely overwhelmed by either a sense of equality or of women being advantaged. Findings of no difference among the public in how well they believed male and female candidates would do across public policy domains is a primary measure of diminished gender stereotypes.

Personality Traits

The Dolan and Pew Research Center studies also queried the public about their perceptions of the personality traits of political men and women. Dolan asked her respondents when they thought about political candidates and officeholders did they think men or women were more likely to be assertive, compassionate, consensus builders, and ambitious, or did they think there was no difference between the sexes on each of these traits. She reports that "on three of the four traits (assertive, consensus-builder, ambitious), either a plurality or majority of people saw no difference between women and men in the likelihood of possessing that trait. Only on the variable measuring compassion did a majority of respondents (71%) hold the expected stereotype, which is assuming women would be more compassionate than men." At the same time, between 20 percent and 40 percent of respondents are willing to say that they see men as more likely to be ambitious or assertive.

In the Pew study, women in politics were rated as more honest, intelligent, compassionate, outgoing, and creative than men. Men were rated as being more decisive and men and women scored equally on ambition and being hard-working. Summarizing the results of these questions on personality traits, the Pew Center researchers highlighted a paradox. Even though women were rated more highly on political leadership traits than men, they were not seen as making better political leaders. According to the report's authors, "[T]he paradox embedded in these survey findings is part of a wider paradox in modern society on the subject of gender and leadership. In an era when women have made sweeping strides in educational attainment and workforce participation, relatively few have made the journey all the way to the highest levels of political or corporate leadership" (Taylor et al. 2008).

Reasons for Numerical Inequality

Finally, in this summary of scholarly attention to diverse aspects of gender stereotyping among the public, a second set of questions from the Virginia Slims study are examined. Why do people think there is a paucity of women in high political office? Respondents in this survey were presented with ten possible reasons for why few women were political leaders. They were asked whether they thought each one was a major reason, a minor reason, or not a reason. Table 1.2 shows the distribution of responses of men and women to this inquiry.

Responses to this inquiry are intriguing. First, there is support for the belief that it is the "public's fault." A majority of both men and women agreed that the fact that Americans were not ready to elect a woman to higher office was a major reason for the paucity of women in such offices. What were they thinking? What does it mean to be ready to elect a woman (or a Black or a Hispanic) to high public office? Even though women were scarce as governors and U.S. senators, women had been serving in a variety of high political positions for a number of years at the time of survey. Both senators representing California and Maine were women. Ann Richards had served as governor of the state of Texas and the majority of states had had women as their U.S. representatives. In addition, at that time Elizabeth Dole was seeking the Republican Party nomination for president. What thought process was stimulating people's response to the notion that Americans were not ready to elect a woman to higher office? Were people thinking of a woman as president in response to this question, perhaps?

This type of question has often been used as a "third person" effects' measure, viewed as an indirect way of gauging an individual's own attitude and to overcome the social desirability effect of asking individuals how supportive they are of some socially complex issue. That may or may not be the case here. But it is problematic that in 1999, after 30 years of the women's movement and women being elected to a variety of high level offices, even if in much smaller percentages than men, a majority of the populace still believed that Americans were not ready to elect a woman to higher office. Responses to such a question deserve more in-depth scrutiny.

Such questions continued to be asked throughout the 2008 presidential nomination process as Senator Hillary Clinton mounted a long and strong campaign for her party's nomination for the presidency.

Women particularly rejected the idea that it was "women's fault" for the paucity of women in high office, a second proposed reason presented in this set of questions in the Virginia Slims survey. Sixty-two percent

TABLE 1.2. As you may know, our country only has 3 women governors out of 50, and only 9 women senators out of 100. There may be many reasons that there are so few women in high political offices. Here is a list of some of them. For each, please tell me whether you think it is a major reason, a minor reason, or not a reason why there are so few women in politics. (responses in percentages)

	Major		Minor Respondents		Not a Reason	
Reason	Male	Female	Male	Female	Male	Female
Many Americans aren't ready to elect a woman to higher office	55	56	30	31	14	12
Women who are active in politics get held back by the "old boy" network	41	45	36	35	17	14
Young girls are not encouraged to aspire to careers in politics	37	42	36	36	23	20
There are very few women in high political office to inspire others	36	40	47	43	16	15
Since fewer women hold leadership positions in business, the professions, and the military	33	33	47	43	19	22
Women are discriminated against in all areas of life, & politics is no exception	30	36	39	39	29	23
Men are better suited emotionally for politics than are most women	27	17	32	27	39	54***
Women are mostly given the detailed dirty-work chores in politics, while men hold the real power	26	32	37	37	32	25***
Women just aren't as interested in going into politics as men	24	23	46	45	26	30*
Women's responsibilities to family don't leave time for politics	24	23	44	40	31	35
Generally speaking, women don't make as good leaders as men	23	13	23	24	47	62***
Generally speaking, women aren't tough enough for politics	18	13	31	30	48	56***

Source: 8th Virginia Slims American Women's Opinion Poll, 2000, available at the Roper Center, Public Opinion Archives, University of Connecticut, www.ropercenter.uconn.edu.

* $p < .05$; ** $p < .01$; *** $p < .001$.

rejected the idea that women do not make as good leaders as men (compared with 47% of the men), 56 percent did not believe women were not tough enough for politics (compared with 48% of the men), and 54 percent did not believe men were better suited emotionally than are most women compared with 39 percent of the men. Otherwise, men and women were pretty much aligned in their perspectives on the reasons why few women held high public office.[6]

The ultimate standard on the extent to which the public has egalitarian perspectives on women's performance in national leadership centers on responses to queries about men and women as president. In February 2007, the White House Project commissioned a national survey to determine Americans' perspectives on a woman as president. Among other things, respondents were queried about the comparative performance of men and women as president in five issue areas. Here, too, stereotypes continued but more to the advantage than to the disadvantage of women, as table 1.3 shows. A woman president is perceived as doing a better job in the areas of health care, human rights, and education by a majority of the female respondents, and a substantial plurality of male respondents agreed. A large gender gap existed in dealing with the economy though both men and women are positive about the job a woman would do as president in this area. If an election centers on foreign policy, women candidates run into some problems, particularly among men, although in general they are seen as performing similarly at least from a generic research focus. Furthermore, the summary of public opinion polls on the issue competency and personality traits of Hillary Clinton as a presidential candidate that I have presented elsewhere shows that she did not suffer from gender stereotypes regarding masculine characteristics or policy areas (Burrell 2008a). It remains to be shown how the campaigns of Clinton and Palin in 2008 have affected images of women as president as we move forward in future presidential elections. No national surveys have yet replicated the 2007 White House Project's study or some variation of that study.

The various ways in which survey researchers have queried the American public about gender stereotypes in recent years show continued distinctions in how male and female political leadership are perceived. Men are still advantaged on some dimensions while women in politics hold other advantages. Lingering but limited bias against women candidates in generic terms and as officeholders shows up in surveys among a minority of the public and affinity gaps continue to show up and perhaps have grown between men and women as they consider candidates for political leadership positions. At the same time, recent studies of gender stereotyping in real election environments suggest that stereotyped beliefs are diminishing in the public mind (Dolan 2011). Dolan concludes, based on her survey of voters in the 2010 elections, that "these data support the hypothesis that gender stereotypes are not major, permanent, unwavering forces, but instead are, like many things, context-bound and episodic, appearing as significant in some races, but not others. Too, when stereotypes do have an impact, they are still not likely to override the importance of traditional political variables like party and incumbency" (11). All of these studies provide valuable context for the continued study of life on the campaign trail for male and female candidates and for women in public office that this book presents.

Looking Ahead

Chapter 2 examines the contexts of elections from 1993 through 2010 in which women have sought seats in the U.S. House of Representatives since the "year of the woman" election. There I present an overview of women's movement from the pool of eligible citizens to candidates. Chapter 3 then begins an assessment of women's movement from candidates to U.S. representatives through an analysis of their presence and performance in primary elections, the first crucial stage for newcomers to win a seat in the House and especially open seat primary elections, the most opportune situations. In chapter 4 the focus turns to general election outcomes. I determine whether women have continued to win at the same rate as men in similar candidate situations, that is, as incumbents, incumbent challengers, and open seat contenders. Would there be any reason to expect that

TABLE 1.3. Do you think a female president would be better, worse, or no different than a male president handling each of the following issues? (responses in percentages)

	Better		No Different		Worse		Don't Know	
	Respondents							
Issue	Male	Female	Male	Female	Male	Female	Male	Female
Health Care	48.6	61.5	44.4	33.0	5.6	4.6	1.3	.8
Education	47.4	52.7	48.3	43.0	3.1	3.7	1.2	.6
Human Rights	43.8	52.6	49.6	41.6	5.4	4.9	1.2	.9
The Economy	27.8	42.3	58.0	48.3	12.7	7.7	1.5	1.8
Foreign Policy	21.4	26.8	52.7	55.4	22.8	15.6	3.1	2.2
Homeland Security	18.4	27.5	55.8	52.3	23.5	17.9	2.3	2.2

Source: The White House Project, www.thewhitehouseproject.org/culture/researchandpolls/Roper2007.php. The original data are not available for analysis to determine statistical significance.

women would do worse than their male counterparts in any of these elections? Would we expect them to continue to outpace male candidates? Or perhaps the electorate has become indifferent to a candidate's sex, contributing to gender becoming a minimal factor in elections for the U.S. House at least as far as comparative results are concerned. It may also be that any finding of equal success between male and female candidates is still based on a gendered campaign process in which women candidates have had to be better in order to achieve at an equal rate with men candidates.

Chapter 5 assesses trends in women candidates' fund-raising prowess. Given the central importance to this study of the concept of gender at each stage of analysis, careful comparisons of the experiences of female candidates with those of male candidates are made. But, in addition, this presentation is enhanced on occasion with stories of the women who have overcome stereotypes to seek and sometimes achieve national political leadership. Chapter 6 explores political party organizational efforts to get their female candidates elected, chronicles the movement of women into leadership positions with the parties' congressional campaign organizations, and shows the extent to which women's groups have sought to close the "encouragement gap" between men and women as potential candidates and provide training and resources for female candidates.

Having systematically examined life on the campaign trail for male and female candidates from 1993 through 2010, I investigate the demographic characteristics of the winners in chapter 7. I explore the background of the men and women who have become members of the U.S. House of Representatives during this time period. A significant question centers on how the backgrounds women have brought to national leadership positions have diversified Congress. Chapter 8 then centers on the question of the substantive difference women in the U.S. House have made and chronicles the movement of women into leadership positions within the body and the growing polarization between Democratic and Republican female members. Finally, in chapter 9 I provide a postscript on the 2012 election and reflect on the questions I have raised in this introduction about gender in contemporary elections, consider some normative questions about the nature of recent elections and life in the U.S. House for advancing the number of women's candidacies and progress toward numerical equity in Congress, and ponder whether the feminist era continues or whether women's quests for political leadership in the most recent nine elections have occurred in a new, distinctive era regarding women and politics. The data, stories, and trends reported in these chapters address the overarching goals of this work: updating the comparative experiences of men and women seeking national public office and performing as national legislators since the publication of *A Woman's Place Is in the House;* consolidating and assessing recent scholarship on women's quests for these offices; and reflecting on the gendered nature of campaigns for national office at the millennium and the subsequent decade. Throughout these chapters I also suggest research questions about women's campaign experiences that remain for scholars to examine in the future. I hope that this study will stimulate even further research on the gendered aspects of quests for national public office.

TWO

Women's Campaigns for the U.S. House of Representatives beyond the "Year of the Woman"

Every election season since 1996 the Center for American Women and Politics (CAWP) has tracked and reported on the number of women running for Congress. Drawing on these reports, pundits have chronicled the ebbs and flows in the number of female candidates across these elections as a measure of their ambition for political leadership and as an assessment of a particular election's environment for their candidacies. John Fortier's 2008 assessment in Politico.com looking at early CAWP numbers of women who had become congressional candidates in that year's election is an illustration of such commentary. Fortier observed that "in Congress, where the number of women has increased each election for the past 30 years, that rise may come to a halt in November. . . . 2008 does not look like a banner year for women. Fewer women are running in primaries, and there are fewer likely female nominees. In 2006, 211 House women filed for primaries. That number will drop below 200 this year." (His early assessment turned out to be wrong.) Often these assessments are made in comparison with the 1992 election reflecting on the likelihood of whether a particular year would be another "year of the woman."

Although the presence of female candidates may have become quite common, the tracking of their numbers and subsequent commentary about their campaigns emphasize a continued curiosity with women seeking national public office. Tracking the overall numbers of female entrants in congressional elections is important, but assessing women's presence as candidates requires a consideration of partisanship, electoral swings, and opportunity structures, particularly in terms of the number of open seats and issue contexts of the various election cycles under examination. These factors are all important ingredients in any analysis of the numbers of women contending for seats in the U.S. House as indicators or measures of equity gains in the political process.

Thus, this chapter begins this book's longitudinal comparative analysis of male and female campaign experiences by tracing the presence of Democratic and Republican women in each of these election cycles, taking into account their candidacy status. I also present an overview of how the political context of each electoral cycle potentially affects the experiences of female candidates and media attention to them. Political scientists quite routinely note the importance of context in studying elections and election campaigns. Women and politics scholars have also stressed the contextual nature of our various election cycles from a gendered perspective. To illustrate, Kathleen Dolan concludes that her 2010 election study data "support the hypothesis that gender stereotypes are not major, permanent, unwavering forces, but instead are, like many things, context-bound and episodic, appearing as significant in some races, but not others" (2011).

To provide a snapshot of the gendered context of the nine election cycles that form the core of this study, I conducted a search of media commentary from each election, first using Lexis-Nexis, seeking news articles containing the key words "women's campaigns" and "elections" for each election year. Online articles discussing the prospects for women candidates from such sources as Politico.com, The Hill.com, and Womensenews.org supplemented the Lexis-Nexis search as they became prominent in the election media scene. The presence of perspectives on whether an election cycle appeared to be or appeared not to be another "year of the woman" was also spotlighted. Such an exercise is limited in terms of conducting a systematic quantitative analysis of media assessments of women's candidacies over the course of these election cycles due to changes over time in media sources. Thus, the sense of an election from a woman candidacies' perspective is based on a qualitative overview of coverage as documented in Lexis-Nexis, supplemented with other source articles such as Congressional Quarterly's articles in 1994 described below.[1]

Congressional election candidacies consist of six types of entrants: incumbents, incumbent primary challengers, opposition party challengers, open seat candidates, special election candidates, and a few others who were nominated by their party in postprimary situations involving incumbent deaths, scandals, and retirements. In the elections since 1992 women have mounted numerous campaigns for a seat in the U.S. House of Representatives, a total of 1,343 nonincumbent and 505 incumbent reelection attempts.[2] Female candidacies have become quite commonplace although they have only been a fraction of male candidacies. Including special elections from 1993 through the 2010 general election a total of 12,930 candidacies for the House were undertaken, including 9,354 nonincumbent candidacies and 3,576 cases of incumbents attempting to keep their seats.[3] Women comprised 14.4 percent both of all candidacies and 14.5 percent of all nonincumbent candidacies during this time period. Their proportion increased marginally from 13 percent to 16 percent over time due to the incremental increase in the number of women incumbents seeking reelection rather than an increase in nonincumbent female candidates.

Figure 2.1 shows the Democratic and Republican female candidates' entrance patterns in each of the election cycles from 1994 through 2010 and figure 2.2 presents summary figures on their entrance patterns. As the figure 2.1 columns indicate, female Democrats have been numerically more active than their Republican counterparts. In some election cycles they had a substantially greater presence. In 2010, however, they barely outpaced Republican female candidates. Their greater incumbency status resulting from their distinctive success in 1992 (although a substantial proportion of the female Democratic first-termers lost in the 1994 Democratic rout) has advantaged them. In addition, in six of the nine elections Democratic women have been more frequent opposition party challengers than Republican women. Given the fairly close partisan division in the House during most of these election cycles, the greater Democratic female opposition party nomination seekers can only be partially explained by a greater number of opportunities to run against incumbents of the other party. But Republican women rather dramatically increased their challenges in 2010 as part of the Tea Party wave.

Few women in either party have mounted primary challenges against their own party's incumbents. Their presence as open seat contenders, small in number, has been a function of the limited opportunities presented in the various elections of this time period based on incumbents voluntarily leaving office and partisan leanings of open districts. More Democratic women have taken advantage of the opportunities open seats created than Republican women in each of the election cycles except 2010. Open seats are the focal point for groups seeking to increase their numbers. Twenty-two of the 24 women who entered the U.S. House in 1993 as a result of the 1992 election ran for open seats. Thus, the presence and success of female

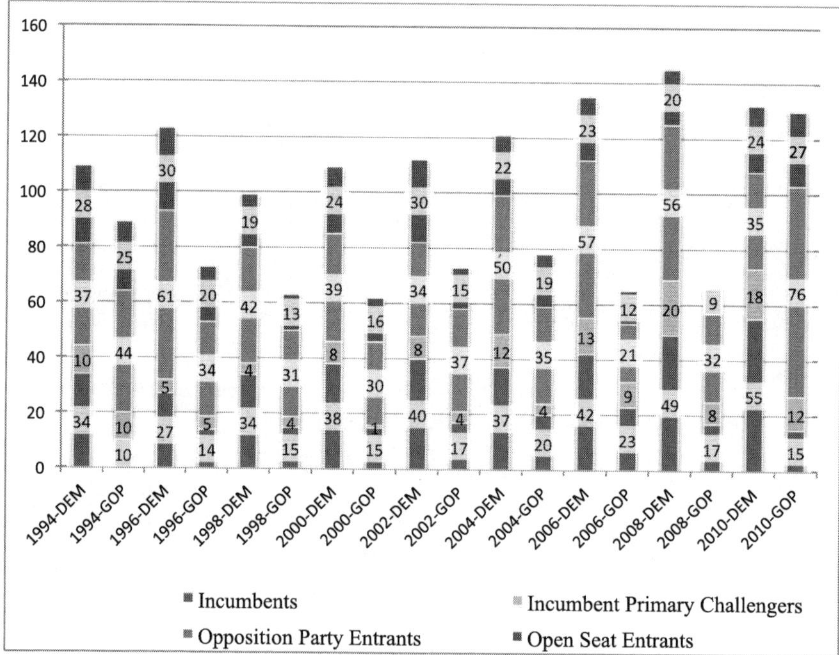

Fig. 2.1. Women's Candidates for the U.S. House of Representatives, 1994–2010 by Party. (Figure constructed by the author from data compiled by the Center for American Women and Politics, Rutgers University.)

candidates contending for open seat nominations and election since 1992 receive special attention in chapter 3.

Electoral Contexts

Each of the election cycles had its own particular political context while at the same time being part of a distinct overarching political era. In the contemporary period, the Republicans ended 40 years of Democratic rule in the U.S. House in 1994. They maintained control until 2006, when the national tide turned and the Democrats won back the House even though operating at a distinct structural disadvantage, and they narrowly gained control of the Senate with the help of independents Bernard Sanders of Vermont and Joseph Lieberman of Connecticut who caucused with the Democrats. The Democrats expanded their gains in the 2008 elections only

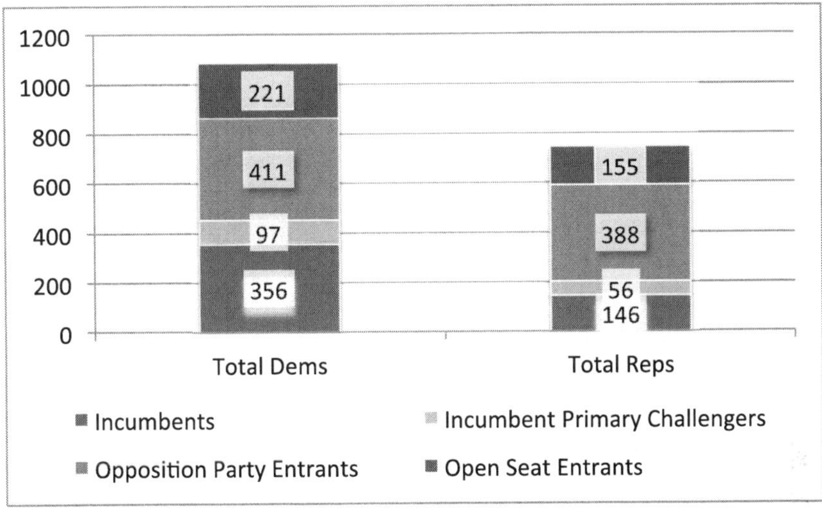

Fig. 2.2. Total Number of Female Candidates by Party and Candidate Status, 1994–2010. (Figure constructed by the author from data compiled by the Center for American Women and Politics, Rutgers University.)

to suffer a large reversal in 2010 when the Republicans retook the House of Representatives and substantially narrowed the Democratic advantage in the U.S. Senate. Thus, these nine elections span a period of Republican takeover of the Congress and Democratic resumption of control for two congresses and a swing to divided government at the end of the first decade of the new millennium.

Polarized Context

Intense polarization characterized the congresses of this period. Three pieces of empirical data provide evidence of the polarized nature of the U.S. House during this time. First is the distance between the parties on partisan votes, that is, the percentage of all recorded votes on which a majority of Democrats voted against a majority of Republicans. It was low in the 1970s; on about two-thirds of recorded votes in the House (and three-fifths in the Senate) majorities of Republicans and Democrats voted on the same side. In the House, party voting, a further measure of polarization, went up significantly in the 1980s and then increased even more in the 1990s to where in over one-half of the votes majorities of Republicans and Democrats voted on opposite sides. (Sinclair 2006, 6–7). Second is the frequency with which the average member of each party voted with his or her party colleagues, a measure of party cohesiveness. Since 1991, members of Congress have voted with their party colleagues on average between 85 and 90 percent of the time. As Sinclair states, "When we talk about party voting in the 1990s and beyond, we are really talking about almost all Republicans lined up in opposition to almost all Democrats" (2006, 7).

A third measure is the ideological distance between members of the two parties as reflected in the ideological consistency of their voting scores. Trend analysis has shown that the ideological distance between Democrats and Republicans has grown over the course of the 1990s and into the millennium (Sinclair 2006). At the end of 2008, *CQ Politics* reported that President George W. Bush had "presided over the most polarized period at the Capitol since Congressional Quarterly began quantifying partisanship in the House and Senate in 1953."[4] It became even more polarized in the first two years of the Obama administration. During the 2010 session, Senate Democrats voted together a record 91 percent of the time. In the House, the average Democrat voted with the Democratic Caucus 89 percent of the time, close to a record according to *CQ Weekly*, and the average House GOP lawmaker supported its caucus 88 percent of the time (Zeller 2011, 32).

Varying Issue Contexts

The issues that dominated in each election varied and the extent to which local or national issues received the most attention differed, affecting opportunities for newcomers. These elections encompass a period of an economic upswing and then retrenchment, a partial shutdown of the government, an impeachment trial of a president, the worse terrorist attack on American soil in the nation's history, and a nation at war in the last five elections. The concluding two elections took place during a massive economic downturn. The country was also described as being in a culture war during this period (Fiorina 2005; Brewer and Stonecash 2007). In the following descriptions of each election season I summarize its general context and the character of the attention paid to female candidates to construct a framework for analyzing women's presence and performance as candidates over time.

The diverse issue context of the elections also was deemed to variously affect women's candidacies based on stereotypes about women as political leaders as described in chapter 1. For example, Jennifer Lawless, examining survey data about voters' perceptions, has argued that the emphasis on terrorism in the 2002 election hurt women's candidacies (2004). Political consultant and pollster Celinda Lake argued during the 2010 election that economic downturns make it risky for political entities to nominate women. According to Lake, "It's always been tougher for women to get elected in a tough economy because voters tend to think women aren't as good on the economy. They don't want to take risks in a bad economy, and they perceive women as being riskier" (Page 2010). Conservative female candidates in 2010, however, challenged that idea. They ran on platforms that "moms" were the knowledgeable, sensible, and tough ones when it came to economic issues and making hard monetary decisions. Therefore, they were implicitly challenging any idea that electing them was risky.

The 1994 Election

In great contrast to the "year of the woman" theme of the 1992 election, "the year of the angry white male" became one of the dominant postelection themes of the 1994 midterm elections. But during the 1994 campaign season the angry white male theme was not particularly visible. Indeed, the attention that was paid to women candidates as a group tended to focus on speculation about an extension of the 1992 "year of the woman" theme. At the same time, the opportunity structure was more restricted than in 1992 given the much smaller number of open seats, 47 compared with 65 in 1992. Further, to have made gains in the political landscape of 1994, women would have had to run disproportionately as Republicans as Democrats dominated the House. The 1992 election was sometimes referred to as the "year of Democratic women in American politics." For example, 19 Democratic women but only three Republican women won open seat races for the U.S. House in 1992 and the four new female U.S. senators were Democrats. Republicans in turn were much advantaged by their "outsider" status in 1994.

In September 1994, the National Women's Political Caucus released a report that analyzed women's presence and success as candidates since 1972 for the U.S. House and for state legislatures since 1986 titled *Perception and Reality: A Study of Women Candidates and Fundraising*. The report showed women winning as often as men. This report stimulated a number of media stories summarizing its results. David Broder of the *Washington Post*, for example, featured the study in his September 8 nationally syndicated column with the headline "Key to Women's Political Parity: Running." According to Broder, "The report throws cold water on a slew of clichés, ranging from the belief that the odds are stacked against female candidates to the notion that 1992 was a breakthrough 'Year of the Woman.' . . . When male incumbents were compared to female incumbents, men running for open seats to women running for open seats, and male challengers to female challengers, women won as high a percentage of their races as men. . . . The main reason the percentages are so low, the study concluded, 'is not that women candidates don't win elections but so few women have run'" (Broder 1994a).

"Storm clouds," however, were also mentioned along the way in that year's election commentary focusing on women candidates' prospects. Several articles stressed the importance of crime as a central issue in that year's election and how it might have a negative effect on women candidates. For example, writing about three governor races in June in a different lens from that noted in the previous paragraph, David Broder focused on the extent to which the male candidates were stressing crime as "the hot-button issue that can best throw their women opponents off-stride" (Broder 1994b). All three female gubernatorial candidates lost. "If 1992 was the year of the woman in politics, 1994 is the year of living dangerously for the record number of women elected to Congress two years ago," reported Dahl and Thomas in the *St. Petersburg Times* (1994). They spotlighted that about half of the women on the National Women's Political Caucus's endangered list were being challenged by hard-right candidates and their allies.

In addition to the major newspapers' take on women candidates, *Congressional Quarterly Weekly Report* weighed in with three analyses on women's candidacies during the 1994 campaign season. Female incumbents need to prove their staying power and protect the status quo was the theme of the first article in May, which stressed the difficulty the newly elected female members of the House and Senate would have defending their seats (Connolly 1994a). In August, the journal focused on the losses women were experiencing in high-profile primaries, most losing to "white men with extensive Washington experience" (Connolly 199b). Then in October the Report declared "1994 Elections Are Looking Like the 'Off Year' of the Woman" (Rubin 1994). The "off year" prediction was attributed to the "relative lack of prominence of so-called women's issues such as abortion that can draw large number of women to the polls," and that "the successful challengers of 1992 are now freshman incumbents, a historically vulnerable position." *Congressional Quarterly Weekly Report* predicted a net gain of five to eight seats for women and that Republican women appeared more likely to boost their numbers than did their Democratic counterparts.

Postelection commentators highlighted that after 1992's "year of the woman," 1994 would be recorded as the "year of the angry white male." *USA Today* led the commentary with its November 11 headline, "ANGRY WHITE MEN, Their Votes Run the Tide for GOP, Men Want to Torch Washington" (Edmonds and Benedetto 1994). "As many as 4 million white men changed their votes and took out their frustration—plus their fears about crime, jobs and the economy—at the ballot box," the article noted. To produce the first Republican House in 40 years, men voted Republican by 54 percent to 46 percent, whereas women, especially unmarried women, favored Democrats. White men voted 63 percent for Republicans, and by about 70 percent in the once-Democratic South.

Eleven women were newly elected to the U.S. House, seven Republicans and four Democrats.[5] (In comparison, 70 Republican and 12 Democratic men won seats during this election cycle.) At the same time, nine female Democratic incumbents were defeated including seven first-termers elected in 1992. Two lost to female Republican challengers. With retirements added to the mix, the number of female U.S. representatives grew by one as a result of the 1994 election, the most minimal of increases.

The 1996, 1998, and 2000 Elections

In an analysis of the 1996 election, political scientist Marjorie Hershey concluded that voters endorsed the status quo and the "media spotlight did not shine on congressional races" in that year's elections (1997, 218). Political scientist Gary Jacobson has described the 1996 and 1998 congressional elections as appearing "positively mundane" after the upheavals of the 1992 and 1994 elections (2001, 185). The 2000 elections also took place in a positive political environment, one that was clearly advantageous for congressional incumbents. In his analysis of the 2000 election, Jacobson determined that short-term electoral forces favored neither party that year so the outcomes reflected the underlying partisan balance in the electorate with unusual clarity (2001). This environment advantaged incumbents, giving little incentive for potentially well-qualified challengers to come forward. *CQ Weekly*'s November handicapping of the 2000 races listed only nine of the four hundred seats that incumbents were defending as being either toss-ups or leaning toward the challengers, a remarkably small number.

As far as attention to women's campaigns as a group was concerned, in 1996 they were seen as "no longer a novelty," as Jo Mannies (1996) reported in an article titled "This Election Year 'Politics as Usual' Means

That Women Are Everywhere." In a *New York Times* piece titled "A Good Year for Running; More Women, Fewer Causes," Adam Nagourney (1996) reported that women's candidacies were not "attention-grabbing political phenomena."

This theme continued in media coverage of women's campaigns in 1998. Coverage of female candidacies as a political phenomenon was at a minimum. In January 1998, Lawrence Goodrich in a *Christian Science Monitor* piece did suggest that 1998 looked like a good year for women running for office. In his evaluation, he stressed themes that were becoming prominent in news analyses of women's candidacies in post "year of the woman" elections: more experienced women candidates and more women incumbents. In an October *Boston Globe* article reviewing the presence and status of women candidates in that year's statewide and national elections, the storyline centered on movement away from running as a woman in successful female campaigns. In this article, Democratic political consultant Jennifer Burton was quoted as describing women as no longer being "the campaign novelty that they once were, and they will lose if they portray themselves simply as female messengers. They have to be message-deliverers because women voters have moved on to connect with the issues" (Leonard 1998). The Goodrich piece also quoted one political scientist as noting early on that it is "a wonderful year to be an ambitious Republican woman." But only 45 nonincumbent Republican women entered primaries in search of a seat in the U.S. House of Representatives, compared with 64 Democratic women, as the total number of nonincumbent female candidates fell to 109.

Commentary about female candidates during the 2000 election cycle focused on similar themes, stressing their gains and their prowess as candidates rather than the hurdles they faced. "Hear Them Roaring at the Ballot Boxes; Female Candidates Take a Giant Leap to Heights of Power," ran the headline for Martha Ezzard's 2000 commentary on the election results in the *Atlanta Journal and Constitution*. *Washington Post* columnist Juliet Ellperin commented that "2000 marks the coming of age for female candidates." She noted in August that half the Democratic House candidates in the dozen most competitive contests were women. She also noted that female candidates were "excelling in fundraising, once a strictly male domain: Among the 12 nonincumbent Democrats who raised at least $1 million this election, eight of them are women" (2000). Her fellow *Washington Post* journalists Richard Morin and Claudia Deane added that "women candidates are not disadvantaged when running against men. . . . female incumbents raise just as much money and win just as often as male incumbents. . . . Women challengers are just as successful as men in collecting cash, unseating incumbents or winning open seats" (2000).

In each of these three elections incremental gains were made in female U.S. House membership (six in 1996, two in 1998, and three in 2000). By the 107th Congress (2001–02), the number of female representatives had climbed to 59, 13.6 percent of the members. Of the female membership, 41 were Democrats and 18 were Republicans.

The 2002 and 2004 Elections

The contexts of the 2002 and 2004 elections were quite different from that of the preceding three national elections coming after the September 11, 2001, terrorist attacks. In their aftermath the economy faltered and the country entered into a "war phase." The dominance of war rhetoric and foreign policy concerns played to stereotypes that have traditionally advantaged men. Thus, media perspectives suggested that women candidates might be hurt because the focus of the 2002 election was on war in the aftermath of the 9/11 tragedy. Pollster Celinda Lake noted early in that campaign season that "a lot of women who were thinking about running see a tougher environment now. It's already a risk to elect women, and now there is going to be less risk-taking" (Leonard 2002). The 2002 election was a redistricting election following the 2000 Census, which usually is considered a good opportunity for newcomers, as it certainly was in 1992. But that turned out not to be the case in 2002. Twelve new seats were created in eight states but the partisan redistricting process dampened competition for House seats (see Jacobson 2003). The limited number of competitive races and the loss of several women incumbents due to retirements and redistricting meant that gains for women candidates would be difficult in 2002 beyond suggestions of a tough environment based on stereotypes. The 2004 election for the House also featured few competitive races.

Women gained only one seat in the U.S. House during the 2002 election cycle and that was in a special election. No gain was made in the general election. Summing up the contests, columnist Ellen Goodman stressed that the "double bind" theme negatively affected women's candidacies in that election. The number-one double bind is the experience bind, Goodman told us. She quoted Kathleen Hall Jamieson: "Women have long been told they didn't have enough experience but now that women have gained experience, they are told they have lost their outsider status and integrity." The second bind involves being too aggressive: "It is unbecoming." A third double bind, according to Goodman, is that "it's apparently easier now to run negative ads against a woman candidate. She ought to be 'tough enough' to take it. But it's still dicey for a woman to go negative" (2002). One should keep in mind that these statements are media messages and only rarely are based on having engaged in or even read any systematic empirical research.

Women as congressional candidates received little media attention in 2004. One article did have the upbeat message that it might be a historic election as far as women candidates were concerned. In a *Washington Post* piece in October, the headline on Peter Slevin's article was, "For Women, A Year to Make History; Number of Candidates on National, State Ballots Reflects a Rise in Aspirations" (2004). His focus was on their numbers, not on some favorable political context playing to strengths based on stereotypes.

On the other hand, former Vermont governor Madeleine Kunin struck a more somber note. In a guest editorial in the *Boston Globe* she bemoaned the lack of progress the United States had made in electing women to political leadership positions. Placing the United States in a comparative context similar to that described in chapter 1, she called for a "new wave of political pressure on the political parties in our own country. The process must start in the primaries. For every office at the state and federal level, we must begin to demand that an equal number of women and men candidates stand for the nomination of their party" (2004). And columnist Ellen Goodman chimed in, reflecting on the vice-presidential politics of that year. She noted that we needed more risk-taking politicians, including female politicians (2004).

The chapters that follow will examine whether systematic data analysis confirms the notion that women were disadvantaged in terms of their presence and voter response in these elections or whether these commentators were working from outdated stereotypes. Women did make gains in the 2004 election. They increased their numerical representation by eight. In the 109th Congress (2005–06), the number of female representatives increased to 15.6 percent of the membership.

The 2006 and 2008 Elections

In 2006 a national political tide resulted in the Democrats taking control of both chambers of Congress and then expanding their majority in 2008.

The main source of the pro-Democratic tide was public unhappiness with the Iraq War and disapproval of President George Bush who had initiated it (Jacobson 2007). Support for the Iraq War and belief that it would make Americans safer from terrorist attacks had gradually declined since the presidential election of 2004. By election day 2006, less than 40 percent of the public believed that the Iraq War was going well. Public discontent with the lack of productivity in the Republican-controlled Congress and a series of scandals also fueled the pro-Democratic national tide. Congressional approval ratings averaged only 27 percent in the month before the election. Scandals involving financial relations with convicted lobbyist Jack Abramoff, the indictment of majority leader Tom Delay, and other improper personal behavior, particularly that of Republican Rep. Mark Foley of Florida with House interns, hurt Republicans. Republican leaders had not sought to investigate allegations of Rep. Foley's activities, which brought scorn upon them in the latter days of the 2006 election. These problems provided Democrats with a major campaign theme of urging rejection of the Republicans' "culture of corruption." Even though the economy was rebounding, Democrats and independents did not acknowledge the upswing (Jacobson 2007).

According to Gary Jacobson's analysis:

> The national climate of opinion gave the Democrats their main campaign strategies: Attack Republicans for loyally supporting the President and his misconceived war and for sharing a 'culture of corruption' in Congress, emphasizing the latter especially in states and districts where the incumbent's personal record gave the charge local resonance. Frame the choice in national terms, urging voters to use their franchise to express their unhappiness with the Republican regime and, most particularly, its leader. Aside from criticizing the war, emphasize making health care more accessible, raising the minimum wage, and protecting Social Security—issue domains in which majorities consistently trust Democrats more than Republicans. (2007, 13)

Republicans tried to replace the war in Iraq with terrorism and homeland security as the dominant electoral focus. At the same time, *CQ Weekly* rated 364 of the 435 seats (84%) as being safe for the incumbent party of the district.

The context of the 2006 election had the potential of being a positive year for women as congressional candidates. Media accounts during the campaign season illustrate the perception of a positive climate for women candidates. On October 22, the *San Francisco Chronicle* headlined "Big Election Predicted for Female Candidates; Seen as Honest Outsiders, They Could Have Best Showing since '92" (Holland 2006). The theme of change ran throughout political analyses that discussed the prospects for women candidates in that year's elections. Scandals and war weariness were making the public attracted to change in national leadership, and women continued to be viewed as agents of change at least from the perspective of activists and media folks. According to one pundit, "This year's emphasis on unethical behavior by members of Congress. . . . helps female candidates. . . . When ethical issues or what we call 'scandals' are center stage that advantages female candidates because they are seen as outsiders, not part of the regular power structure" (Nichols 2006). The Center for American Women and Politics at Rutgers University also issued a press release in late September in which its director, Debbie Walsh, stated, "When people think the system is broken, it's good news for those who don't look like the congressional candidate from central casting—and that includes women" (Walsh 2006). Allison Stevens's assessment in the online Womensenews also noted this theme: "This time scandal and foul moods are affecting the GOP, which bodes well for women because more are running as Democrats" (2006a).

Pundits considered whether it might be another "year of the woman" similar to 1992 although the number of competitive races was much smaller so that at most it would only be a "mini" year of the woman if female candidates were especially successful (see, for example, Bar-Lev 2006; Stevens 2006c). Writing in the *New York Times* in March of that year, Robin Toner noted: "If the Democrats have their way, the 2006 Congressional elections will be the revenge of the mommy party. Democratic women are running major campaigns in nearly half of the two dozen most competitive House races where their party hopes to pick up enough Republican seats to gain control of the House. Democratic strategists are betting that the voters' unrest and hunger for change—reflected consistently in public opinion polls—create the perfect conditions for their party's female candidates this year" (2006). This theme was repeated throughout media reports of that year's election campaigns. Women candidates were also viewed as running strong races. In perhaps a self-promoting statement, Ramona Oliver, spokesperson for EMILY's List, told Womensenews that "I can definitely say we have one of the best groups of women candidates we have ever fielded, both in terms of its size—we have twice the number of candidates running for the House as we did last year—but also qualitatively. They're running bigger, stronger races and raising more money" (Stevens 2006a) Twelve women were newly elected in that cycle, three Republicans and nine Democrats. They increased their membership by four to 72, inching up to 16.6 percent of the House.

The 2008 election was distinctive from a gendered perspective in that U.S. Senator Hillary Clinton nearly won the Democratic nomination for president and Alaska governor Sarah Palin received the Republican nomination for vice president. Senator Clinton was considered to be the front-runner for the Democratic nomination for president throughout much of the campaign season but faltered in the end through a combination of campaign mistakes, sexism among the media, and the compelling nature of nominating the first black person, Senator Barack Obama, for the presidency. Senator Clinton's quest for the White House certainly put gender in the forefront of national politics. Her quest should have empowered women. At the same time her ultimate loss of the nomination created great anger among millions of women who were drawn to her campaign.

Commentators saw Senator Clinton's campaign as both a boost for women and as a warning. Allison Stevens, writing in Womensenews.org, focused on the idea that "Clinton's campaign will inspire more women to run for office and hasten the day when women reach parity in government." She quoted women's rights activists as seeing Clinton's run as "a visible statement of women's competence" and as showing "more women and girls that anything is possible, and that they can shoot for whatever they like, including the presidency" (Stevens 2008).

On the other hand, Caryl Rivers, also writing in the *Womensenews.org*, stressed that "the presidential campaign of Sen. Hillary Clinton has some disturbing messages for uppity women in the United States. . . . Some women worry that regardless of how the election turns out, . . . the resistance to Senator Clinton may embolden some men to resist women's efforts to share power with them in business, politics, and elsewhere" (Rivers 2008). In May, CBS News asked a national sample of adults whether they thought Hillary Clinton's candidacy had made it easier for other women to run for president in the future, made it harder for other women, or had no effect on other women running for president. Over-two thirds (69%—60% of men and 76% of women) responded that her candidacy had made it easier. Only 9 percent believed it had made it harder, and 21 percent said that it had no effect (Feldman 2008a).

The Clinton and Palin campaigns absorbed much of the attention the media devoted to women candidates in the 2008 election, leaving little consideration to the "other" campaigns for national office. A search of

Lexis-Nexis using the key words "women candidates" and "election" in major newspapers and wire services produced little analysis and commentary about women's campaigns in the 2008 election beyond the presidential race. Other media sources such as Politico.com, *The Hill*, *CQ Politics*, and *Womensenews* also produced only a few stories about women candidacies beyond the presidential race.

Earlier, in August 2007, the Cook Political Report had declared "Women's March into Office Slows" (Kronholz 2007) and that theme continued when, in March 2008, John Fortier concluded in Politico.com that "2008 Will Not Be a Banner Year for Women," as mentioned in this chapter's opening segment. Looking at the national legislature he noted that "fewer women are running in primaries, and there are fewer likely female nominees." Examining the competitiveness of races with women candidates and vulnerable incumbents, he concluded that "the bottom line is that the seats House women will gain and lose are likely to be fewer than 10 in each category, and the net gain is likely to be close to zero" (Fortier 2008). Contrary to his gloomy analysis, by the end of the primary season, which runs until September nationwide, the largest number of women ever had entered these races for the U.S. House.

Former New Jersey governor Christie Whitman chimed in with a widely distributed editorial bemoaning the "plight of women seeking elective office." Watching the Clinton campaign reminded her "of the challenges that women candidates still face in this country. . . . The challenges women candidates face remain very different from those of their male counterparts" (2008). Those challenges, she enumerated, were whether women with business backgrounds would be considered qualified for public office, attention to what they wore, questions about toughness to govern, and "male pundits bemoaning the idea that women voted for a woman candidate because she was a woman" (in reference to Hillary Clinton's run for the presidency). "These same commentators have been voting for men for years and never found that to be a problem. When will they understand that, when all other things are equal—positions held, experience earned and competence—it is acceptable to vote for the woman because she is a woman?" (2008).

In June, Gilda Morales, a researcher at the CAWP, summarized that "[s]o far, the 'Hillary Effect' on the pipeline hasn't been realized. Women have not filed statements of candidacy in unusually high numbers, and women are not expected to break the record set in 1992, the 'Year of the Woman,' when women nearly doubled their ranks in Congress" (Stevens 2008). At the end of the election, the *Christian Science Monitor* concluded that "[w]omen make modest gains in Election 2008: More women serve in state legislatures, but the United States is far behind many other countries. . . . In Congress it would be business as usual" (Feldman 2008b). Even though 15 women (13 Democrats and two Republicans) were newly elected, the largest number since 1992, their membership only increased by one due to Republican women incumbent losses and retirements.

The 2010 Election

The 2010 election was striking overall and in terms of women and their campaigns. It was a tumultuous affair in general and was peppered with raucous "gendered moments." After the Democrats regained control of Congress in 2006 and expanded their numbers in the House and the Senate in 2008 as well as capturing the White House, the Republicans gained 63 seats in the 2010 congressional election to regain control of the U.S. House, an unprecedented number in the contemporary era. They also increased their numbers in the U.S. Senate but not by enough to gain the majority in that institution. In addition, they made substantial gains in gubernatorial and state legislative races. The rise of the Tea Party movement, a conservative, populist outpouring of anger at the Obama administration and federal government spending and programs, fueled many campaigns to oust incumbents and install a different type of legislator in office. American election campaigns have traditionally been negative events but the vitriol in the 2010 campaign reached particularly high levels. In many ways, it recalled the 1994 election, often characterized as the "year of the angry white male" after the 1992 "year of the woman," although it was even more of a revolt and more contentious with women being active players and leaders in the Tea Party movement, under the leadership of former governor of Alaska and Republican vice-presidential candidate Sarah Palin and with liberal female Democrats being targeted along with their male counterparts.

A number of contradictory themes focusing on opportunities for women candidates were played out in the media as the election cycle progressed that year. It was dubbed potentially as the "year of the woman outsider," the "year of the conservative woman," and the "year of the Republican woman." Media commentary on women's candidacies in this election cycle began on a rather somber note, especially regarding any prospect of Republicans reversing the growing gap in female membership in the parties' legislative caucuses that had left the GOP far behind the Democrats and fighting a perspective of being "anti-woman." On May 10, 2009, for example, Politico.com led off with a piece titled "GOP Women: A Minority in a Minority" (Lovley 2009) and it followed up with a November piece, "The GOP's Women Problem" (Shiner and Thrush 2009). In March 2010, *CQ Politics* asked, "Where Are the Women GOP House Candidates?" (Toeplitz 2010). In his blog, David Bernstein of the *Boston Phoenix* ruminated about the "GOP's Glass Floor" for women candidates (2010).

The problem was described primarily as being the dominance of strident conservatives who opposed moderate female candidates within the party and the lack of visible women in the party's leadership. In response to the Democrats' Red to Blue program initiated in 2004 in which the DCCC recruited, advised, and funded strong candidates to challenge Republicans in traditionally GOP-leaning districts, in 2008 the NRCC established their own Young Guns counterpart program. Of course, the name itself was not particularly inviting to would-be female challengers, as some media commentators noted. As the 2010 campaign commenced, few women had been recruited into the program. Although commentary continued regarding the seeming lack of support on the part of party leadership as the election season progressed, it also began to highlight a new theme as the number of Republican women entering congressional contests grew. The *Washington Post* noted this trend in a May 2010 piece "Record Numbers of Republican Women Are Running for House Seats" (Franke-Ruta 2010). Their increase was part of an overall rise in Republican candidates fueled in part by the Tea Party movement and in part by the prospect of it being a very good year for Republicans as unemployment remained high and the economy continued in a recessionary mode.

The other pessimistic picture regarding women making any numerical gains in the national legislature was the growing possibility of substantial numbers of female Democratic incumbents losing to Republican challengers. In August 2010, Lisa Mascaro in the *L.A. Times* warned "Women in Washington, Your Seats Are at Risk." She pointed out that "[i]f large numbers of Democratic incumbents lose in November, as expected, many women could be replaced by men. Female candidates tend to do better in Democratic years, and 2010 is shaping up as a successful year for Republicans" (Mascaro 2010). She also noted that just four women were among the GOP's 46 "Young Guns."

Although gender was not the main theme of the election dominated by the rise of the Tea Party movement, there were certainly "gendered moments" in the campaign, some of the more infamous ones even being initiated by female candidates such as when Nevada Republican Senate candidate Sharron Angle told her Democratic opponent, Senate Majority Leader Harry Reid, to "man up." Colorado Republican Senate candidate Jane Norton attacked her opponent, Ken Buck, in the Republican gubernatorial primary by saying he wasn't "man enough." He responded at a public event that Coloradans should vote for him, "Because I do NOT wear high heels." Having successfully baited Buck, Norton went on to fund-raise with the tagline, "Ken Buck may think a woman's place is in the house. We know a woman's place is in the Senate." Karen Handel, running in the Republican primary for governor of Georgia, told her male opponent Nathan Deal that "[i]t's frankly time to put the big boy pants on" (*Hotline* 2010). From the male candidate side, U.S. Representative Betty Sutton (D-OH) was told to go back to the kitchen by her male Republican opponent Tom Ganley. His campaign sent mailers to voters telling them to "take Betty Sutton out of the House and put her back in the kitchen."

In some instances, the "gender" moments were actually female candidate on female candidate barbs. Perhaps most noteworthy was Carly Fiorina's "God, what is that hair? Soooo yesterday" comment regarding her opponent U.S. Senator Barbara Boxer's hair. Mary Fallin, Republican nominee for governor in Oklahoma, played what commentators have called the "Mommy card" when asked what set her apart from her opponent. She replied, "being a mother, having children, raising a family." Lt. Gov. Jari Askins, the Democrat nominee, had never been married and had no children (Marcus 2010).

The most notorious gender aspect to the election was undoubtedly Sarah Palin's clarion call to "mama grizzlies" to rise up. She issued a warning that a herd of "pink elephants" were stampeding to Washington with an "e.t.a. of November 2. "You don't want to mess with moms who are rising up. If you thought pit bulls were tough, you don't want to mess with mama grizzlies," she intoned at a Susan B. Anthony List fund-raiser in May. "Mama grizzly" candidates became part of the Republican campaign landscape in that election with Palin endorsements and characterizations of a number of the female candidates as "mama grizzlies," tough conservative women. "She brought to the Republican Party what some members had once complained did not exist: a concerted effort to tap female candidates for promotion and lift them out of obscurity," Anne Kornblut noted in the *Washington Post* (2010).

In a London *Daily Telegraph* piece commenting on the "mama grizzly" phenomenon, Alex Spillius (2010) highlighted both their boldness on the campaign trail in their policy presentations and their dress. He quoted Siobahn Bennett, president of the bipartisan, liberal Women's Campaign

Forum, as describing the "mama grizzlies" as "mini-Palins—conservative in values but bold in their willingness to step out and be heard." Bennett added, "So many women running this year have adopted a more feminised look on the campaign trail. Sarah Palin is making it clear she is a woman. Her look says 'I am confident in my femininity'." Following up on this idea, Spillius notes that they stood out

> for dressing with style. They have challenged the conventional thinking that female politicians should dress in a businesslike manner that reduces the risk of chauvinistic comments and increases the chances of being elected. Gone are the flat shoes and sober trousersuits that Hillary Clinton made her own during her 2008 bid for the Democratic presidential nomination. The grizzlies tend to favor high heels, skirts above the knee, figure hugging two-pieces and hairstyles straight from the pages of the latest magazines. (2010)

One might consider this commentary just another "hemline" story singling female candidates out in a sexist-oriented fashion (pun intended) but it could be calling readers' attention and signaling researchers to something different and of consequence happening among female candidates on the campaign trail.

Nine Republican women were newly elected to the U.S. House in the 2010 elections and the Republican Party capitalized on their success. In the days following the election, ten Republican female members of the U.S. House issued a press release trumpeting 2010 as the "year of the Republican woman." They highlighted the record-breaking number of Republican women who had mounted campaigns for the House, their success, varied backgrounds, and areas of the country from which they came. The press release noted that "these are the stories that made 2010 the year of the Republican woman. They're about farmers, attorneys, teachers, nurses, doctors, small-business owners, law enforcement officials, entrepreneurs, wives and mothers. They're the stories of the dynamic and driven women who will be sworn in as members of the 112th Congress" (Politico.com 2010).

They also credited the Republican establishment with efforts to recruit and support female candidates. Whether the results of this election represented a turning point in the party gap would have to await further elections. They might have been a harbinger of change although as the postscript on the 2012 election presented at the end of this book shows the partisan gap trend favoring Democratic female representatives returned two years later.

Female Republican candidates ran strong campaigns in both conservative Republican districts and more competitive but leaning GOP districts. At the same time nine Democratic female members of the House lost their reelection bids while four female Democrats were newly elected, all minority women. Even though it was touted as a good year for female Republican candidates, the number of female representatives in the U.S. House actually declined by one from 74 to 73 due to the female Democratic incumbent losses and retirements. This result was the first backward movement in women's quest for numerical equity. Perhaps, in somewhat of a partisan comment, DCCC vice-chair Debbie Wasserman Schultz suggested the results were "a hiccup" on the path to numerical gender equity in the Congress. Women made no gains in the U.S. Senate either in the 2010 election. The number of female senators remained at 17 with the Democrats losing one female incumbent, Blanche Lincoln of Arkansas, and the Republicans gaining one member with Kelly Ayotte's victory in New Hampshire. Looking back, only nine of the 25 women newly elected to the U.S. House in the "year of the woman" surge of 1992 were still members at the beginning of the 112th Congress in 2011 (36%) and one was serving as a U.S. senator, Maria Cantwell (D-WA).[6]

Conclusion

In the post-1992 elections no surge has occurred in the numbers of women seeking a seat in the U.S. House nor did women decrease their presence relative to men's presence. Women's presence as candidates marginally increased as their numbers among incumbents seeking reelection slowly climbed. A walk through these election cycles suggests a story based in part on women being strategic in undertaking a campaign for a House seat, but perhaps not maximizing their presence when positive opportunities presented themselves, as chapter 3 will examine.

Good opportunities for newcomers have been few in all of these elections, even given the diversity of the political environment across them, as noted in the contextual stories told in this chapter. Democratic women were more proactive than Republican women in mounting campaigns for a place in the national legislature, with the exception of 2010, even taking into account the fact that they would have had more opportunities to challenge incumbents because of their party's minority status in seven of the nine elections. On the other hand, the contexts of these elections suggest a more positive environment for Republicans in most of the electoral cycles, but Republican women did not take advantage of them until 2010. But even then they were a small minority of that party's candidates. Chapter 3 begins a more systematic analysis of the women's trek through the campaign process. Its focus is on the first step in the campaign process: seeking a party nomination by running in primary elections, highlighting open seat primaries. Open seats are the prime opportunity for newcomers to gain a seat and the best chance for increasing diversity among the membership.

THREE

Men's and Women's Presence and Performance in Primary Elections for the U.S. House

"I'm in, I'm in, I'm in, I'm in, I'm in," California state senator Gloria Negrete McLeod stated as she announced her candidacy on June 10, 2011, for an open congressional seat in the 2012 election. She looked at a newly redistricted seat in which no incumbent lived and reported that "I saw the map. That's mine" (Goldmacher 2011).[1]

How characteristic among potentially ambitious women was Senator Negrete McLeod's response to a political opportunity for national public leadership? Are women taking ownership of such opportunities in the contemporary era, asserting their qualifications and competencies and entering as candidates? This chapter systemically examines questions about women's presence and performance in congressional primaries in the nine elections that form the core of this study. What do their entrance patterns look like as incumbents seeking reelection, as challengers to incumbents of one's party, as seekers of an opposition party nomination, and as open seat candidates?[2] How successful have they been in winning primary contests, the first stage of the election process, especially open seat primaries, the most advantageous situations for newcomers? How does their presence and success compare to that of male candidates, which addresses questions of the contemporary gendered nature of this stage of the campaign process?

Women's presence and performance in congressional primary elections is an understudied aspect of the campaign process. "Scholars have virtually ignored the gender dynamics of the congressional primary process," Jennifer Lawless and Kathryn Pearson asserted in the introduction to their longitudinal analysis of gender in primary elections (2008). To overcome this void, they compiled a data set of all U.S. House candidates in primary elections from 1958 to 2004. They found that women comprised only 8 percent of the total U.S. House primary candidates, but the number of women running in congressional primaries had increased markedly since 1958 to where in 2004, the most recent election of their time series, women were 16 percent of all candidates. They also show that women running in congressional primaries in recent decades have disproportionately been Democrats, as the data in this study also show.

Turning to performance, Lawless and Pearson have shown that in the first three decades of their research male candidates won their primaries more often than female candidates did, particularly among Democrats. However, between 1992 and 2004, Democratic women had a higher success rate than Democratic men in every election cycle and Republican women had a higher success rate than Republican men since 1996. For the most part, Lawless and Pearson did not separate women's presence and performance data by candidate status, thus we do not know the extent to which incumbent status, which has grown in particular, affected their findings. A few other studies have taken candidate status into account in examining the relative performance of male and female candidates, providing a somewhat more nuanced analysis of gender factors.

In analyzing the reelection terrain for male and female incumbents, Barbara Palmer and Dennis Simon (2008) have suggested that while having reelection rates comparable to those of male incumbents, as empirical research has shown, female incumbents have had to work harder to retain their seats. This conclusion was based on research on reelection contests from 1958 through 2006. Female incumbents faced a more competitive environment, measured by primary competition and multiple candidacies in opposition party primaries. Since their data also were not divided by decades or periods, it remains to be determined whether this situation holds in recent elections. We might suspect that ideas of greater vulnerability, even for female incumbents, may be diminishing, paralleling growing fund-raising prowess and increased prominence in congressional leadership positions (see Burrell 2005, 2010, and chaps. 6 and 8 in this study).

Richard Matland and David King (2002) have added to our knowledge of female candidates' experiences in open seat primary elections from 1990 through 2000. Open seat primary contests within the Democratic Party were far more likely to have female contenders than the Republican Party, and Democratic voters showed a higher propensity to choose a female candidate in these elections (Matland and King 2002). It is important to update their findings through the first decade of the millennium and enhance their research by controlling for opportunity structure.

Even though open seats may be "where the action is," to quote Ronald Gaddie and Charles Bullock (2000), that is, where uncertainty and change are likely, not all open seats provide the same opportunity for both parties' would-be U.S. representatives' ultimate election to Congress. Female candidates may have had a higher success rate in Matland and King's study if these women had disproportionately run in districts unfriendly to their party, generating little nomination competition. An important political question is in what type of districts did they run related to their success rates? Clearly, a number of political puzzles remain to be addressed about the first stage of the campaign process and the role gender has played in it in contemporary elections.

An overarching puzzle concerns the question of whether female candidates face a more difficult terrain in primary elections. The equitable performance data that Lawless and Pearson found in their longitudinal research are important positive findings regarding women's electoral prospects. But on a contrary note, Lawless and Pearson also suggest that "primary competition is more difficult for women than it is for men," continuing a gendered primary process detrimental to women's advancement in national public office (2008, 68). Their evidence for such a conclusion centered on women on average having been more likely than men to have had an opponent in primary elections and that contests with a female contender had a larger pool of candidates than male-only primaries.

Lawless and Pearson's analysis has quickly been adopted as nearly conclusive evidence of a gender-biased election process in primary elections. Before this frame becomes defined as conventional wisdom, however, I believe it is important to take another look at primary elections to see if alternative hypotheses can plausibly explain their results and whether approaching competitiveness from a different lens might suggest an alternative perspective regarding a relationship between gender and difficulty. In this chapter I employ an alternate measure of competition—the number of competitors the average female and average male candidate in open seat primaries have—and adopt a more positive interpretation of the implications of Lawless and Pearson's findings for women's candidacies.

It is also important that primary contexts be disaggregated as suggested in this chapter's introduction to completely assess these authors' greater difficulty thesis for women candidates. Lawless and Pearson's negative findings, which actually only involved quite minor sex differences in having an opponent in some candidacy status groups, have received perhaps undue emphasis as evidence of a continued gender biased election process unfavorable to women candidates. (See Lawless 2009; Branton 2009; and Fowler and Lawless 2009 for examples of this greater difficulty frame becoming a common perspective, even perhaps the conventional wisdom.)

The analyses conducted in this longitudinal study include data on the population of candidates. The data are not a random sample of a population. Thus, tests of statistical significance that measure the confidence with which one can attribute the findings and relationships among a random sample of the population to the population are not particularly relevant or necessarily appropriate. Thus, such tests are minimized in this study. I instead call attention to the actual similarities and differences between the men and women who have run for a seat in the U.S. House since 1993. Correlational statistics and tests of statistical significance will be presented, however, where they help to highlight substantive differences and similarities throughout this study.

Figure 2.1 began a systematic presentation of trends in women's presence as congressional contenders after the 1992 election. It showed the number of female Democratic and Republican candidacies for a seat in the U.S. House of Representatives in elections from 1994 through 2010, broken down by the types of situations in which they have mounted electoral efforts. Figures 3.1 and 3.2 and table 3.1 add information to that picture of trends in women's candidacies for a more comprehensive view of their presence.

Figure 3.1 shows the overall trend in the total number of women entering primaries for a U.S. House seat and the numbers for Democratic and Republican female candidates. As figure 3.1 shows, women have only incrementally increased their presence as candidates for the U.S. House over the course of these nine elections. The number of Republican female candidates in 2010 did substantially boost women's presence. It was the first time that the number of female Republican candidates increased beyond their presence in 1994. At the same time their lack of numbers across the elections, much more so than that of female Democrats, has contributed to women not making a greater presence as congressional candidates.

Figure 3.2 and table 3.1 add a gender lens to women's candidacies during this time period. They present the total number of female candidacies within each status group and their candidacy status as a percentage of all candidates within each party. As the data show, women did not exceed 20 percent of any candidate status group except in Democratic special elec-

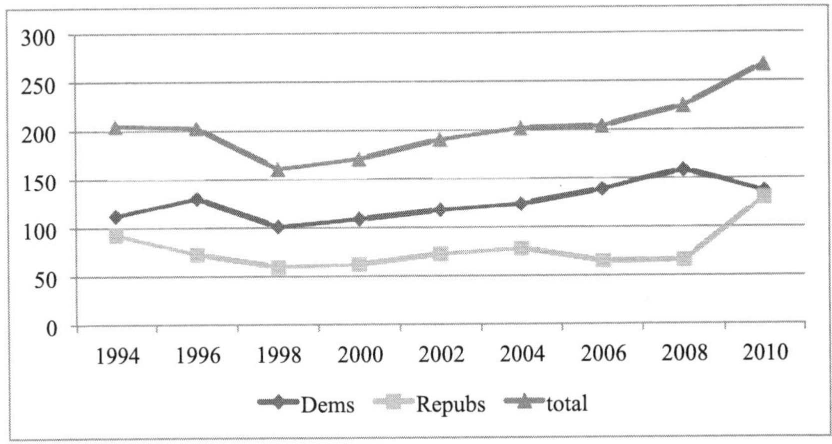

Fig. 3.1. Number of Female Primary Entrants by Party, 1994–2010. (Data compiled by the author from the Center for American Women and Politics.)

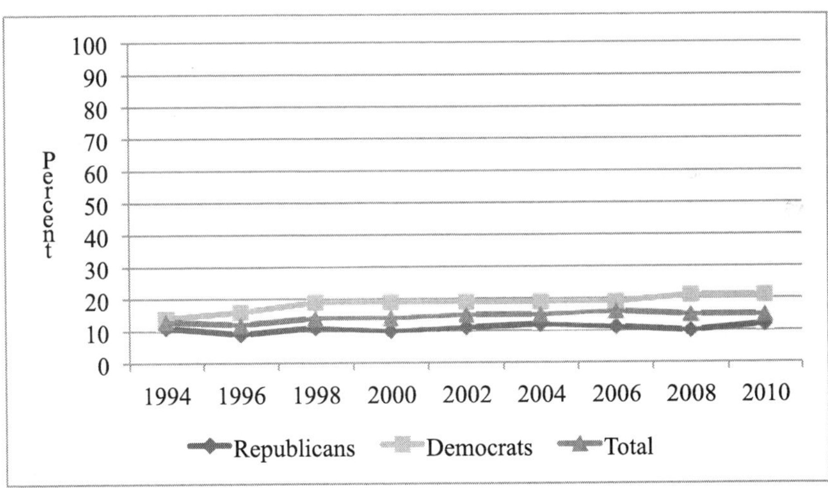

Fig. 3.2. Democratic and Republican Women as a Percentage of Primary Candidates, 1994–2010. (Data compiled by the author.)

tions. Democratic women reached a high of 20 percent among incumbents and open seat candidates. Women never surpassed 12 percent of Republican candidates in any candidate status group. Although Republican women increased their numbers in 2010, male Republican contenders surged even more.

Incumbents and Primary Challenges

I begin this investigation into the primary phase of this set of contemporary U.S. House elections from the perspective of incumbents. The vast majority of female and male incumbents run for reelection. Chapter 7 chronicles the post-initial election paths leading to reelection, defeats, retirements, and upward quests for all of the newly elected male and female U.S. House members elected in the post-1992 era. This chapter's concern is with the primary election environment and the extent to which fellow partisans challenge incumbents and whether the environment differs for male and female incumbents. Its main question centers on whether female incumbents in recent elections have had to face primary challengers to a greater extent than male incumbents. More widespread challenging of female incumbents in their party's primary would suggest a greater sense of vulnerability.

Defeat by a fellow party member in a primary is a rare event for female or male incumbents. Of the 3,576 major party incumbency reelection candidacies in these nine elections, only 28 representatives have suffered primary defeats, less than 1 percent for each of the sexes. Five female incumbency reelection bids out of 502 such contests ended in primary defeats.

TABLE 3.1. Summary of Women's Candidacies and Percentage of all Candidacies by Candidate Status and Party

	Democratic Women	Democratic Women, % of all Dem Candidacies	Republican Women	Republican Women, % of all Rep Candidacies
Incumbents	356	20	146	8
Incumbent Primary Challengers	98	15	57	10
Opposition Party Entrants	412	17	342	12
Open Seat Entrants	217	20	157	12
Special Elections	49	23	24	10

Note: The parties in a number of cases selected individuals to replace nominees who dropped out after a primary. For accounting purposes in this table individuals selected to replace incumbents are included as open seat candidates, which was their post-primary status.

One of those defeats occurred in 2002 when Rep. Lynn Rivers was defeated by Rep. John Dingell in a redrawn district due to reapportionment after the 2000 census.

Their renomination rates indicate little vulnerability at this stage of the process for female incumbents. But they may still be perceived to be weaker officeholders and thus more likely to face one or more primary challengers. Indeed that possibility was a stimulus for one aspect of Palmer and Simon's work (2008). As noted earlier, they stressed that an aura of greater vulnerability, even within general election outcomes indicating gender parity, may have produced more competition for female incumbents including facing a primary opponent. However, they found little difference between male and female incumbents incurring primary opponents in election cycles from 1956 through 2006; 31.7 percent of female incumbents had primary challengers compared with 29 percent of male incumbents (2008). Among Democratic incumbents, men and women were equally likely to face competition, 36 percent of men and 34.6 percent of women. Republican incumbents faced a less contentious primary arena than their Democratic counterparts over this long time span. But within their less contentious party arena female Republican incumbents were more likely to have a primary challenger than their male counterparts, 26.1 percent versus 19.7 percent (2008, 151).

As noted earlier, Palmer and Simon did not present their 50-year analysis by decades to determine whether any earlier gender difference indicative of female vulnerability may have diminished or grown in more recent elections. Table 3.2 provides a breakdown of primary challenges across the elections of the contemporary era. This analysis of the presence of a primary opponent in the nine elections of this study shows that differences across the parties and gender differences within the parties have become slight. In total, 22 percent of male incumbents and 23 percent of female incumbents faced a primary opponent in this set of elections. Within the Republican Party, 21 percent of the districts with male incumbents standing for reelection had contested primaries (335 of 1,596 contests) compared with 29 percent of the districts with female incumbents standing for reelection (43 of 146 contests). The especially small number of female Republican incumbents seeking reelection in each election cycle means that a minor increase or decrease in primary challenges could result in a large percentage change. Indeed, they had the widest variation across election cycles of all the incumbent groups from 9 percent to 47 percent (although it was only marginally greater than that of Republican male incumbents). Within the Democratic Party, in districts with male incumbents 24 percent had contested primaries (352 of 1,476) compared with 21 percent of the districts with female incumbents (75 of 358). These figures on internal party primary competition show little evidence of greater vulnerability on the part of contemporary female incumbents.

Looking at the process from the opposite lens—that of incumbent primary challengers—the high levels of successful incumbent renomination suggest that little incentive exists for would-be House members to challenge an incumbent of their party in a primary, yet over the course of these nine elections 1,220 individuals have mounted such campaigns with a low of 82 individuals undertaking such challenges in the 1998 election to a high of 236 incumbent primary challengers in 2010. Democrats, both male and female, were somewhat more active incumbent challengers than Republicans but the partisan differences were not substantial.

The biggest gap has been between male and female primary incumbent challengers. As figure 2.1 showed, few women have seen it in their interest or perhaps been bold enough to undertake campaigns against incumbents of their own party. Challenging incumbents of one's party has been much more a "guy thing" over the course of these election cycles. Men have also dominated in the other candidate status groupings, but challenging an incumbent seldom has little party organizational support, tending to make such a move a risky individual undertaking. Republican women were only 10 percent of all of the Republican incumbent primary challengers and Democratic women were 15 percent of all of the Democratic incumbent primary challengers over the course of these nine elections.

Only four women, all Democrats, won a seat in the House through a

TABLE 3.2. Incumbency and Contested Primaries by Party and Sex, 1994–2010

	Democratic Males		Democratic Females		Republican Males		Republican Females	
Year	*N*[a]	%	*N*	%	*N*	%	*N*	%
1994	70/194	36	11/34	32	37/148	25	4/10	40
1996	37/141	26	4/28	14	38/200	19	6/14	43
1998	20/154	13	3/34	9	22/197	11	4/15	27
2000	31/164	19	4/37	11	24/185	13	4/15	27
2002	30/159	19	10/40	25	42/184	23	4/17	24
2004	34/153	22	8/37	22	38/192	20	5/20	25
2006	37/149	25	10/43	23	34/189	18	2/23	9
2008	40/180	22	7/50	14	39/156	25	8/17	47
2010	53/182	29	18/55	33	61/145	42	6/15	40
Total	352/1,476	24	75/358	21	335/1,596	21	43/146	29

Source: Data compiled by the author from election result sources.

[a]The numbers in the numerator are the number of incumbents having a primary challenger, and the denominator is the total number of incumbents seeking reelection.

campaign process of winning a primary challenge and then winning the general election. Carolyn Cheeks Kilpatrick (D-MI) beat Barbara Rose Collins in 1998, California state senator Hilda Solis beat 18-year incumbent Matthew Martinez in 2000, Denise Majette (D-GA) ousted Cynthia McKinney in 2002, and Donna Edwards (D-MD) successfully ousted Albert Wynn in her second try in 2008. Her campaign against Rep. Wynn is chronicled in chapter 7.

Opposition Party Primary Challengers

Given the historically high reelection rates of incumbent U.S. House members, one might wonder about the size of the pool of opposition party candidates seeking nominations to challenge them in the general election. Democrats had more opportunities in six of the nine elections given Republican House majorities in those years but it was not always the case that Democrats had a greater presence in these primaries, as table 3.3 shows. From a gender perspective figure 2.1 showed that the number of women entering primaries to challenge an incumbent of the opposition party varied within a fairly small range over the course of these nine elections. Table 3.3 shows that more Democratic women than Republican women entered opposition party primaries in six of the nine elections. In total women were 14 percent of opposition party primary contenders. In no election cycle were women as much as 20 percent of the pool of their partisans seeking to oppose an incumbent of the other party. Ambitious women may be less likely to be risk takers, accounting for their smaller presence in opposition party primaries or, given incumbent advantage, their lesser involvement may also be strategic in nature. They have tended not to mount such campaigns given the knowledge that only about 5 to 10 percent of such efforts per election are successful.

Women's percentage of all opposition primary entrants varied from a low of 11 percent in 1996 to a high of 18 percent in 2004. Between 1994 and 2002, only minimal differences existed between the presence of Republican women and Democratic women in opposition party primaries. Beginning in 2004 and continuing through the 2008 election, the gap grew substantially with Democratic women expanding their presence while Republican women constricted theirs. For example, in 2004, 54 Democratic women mounted opposition party primary campaigns, 23 percent of all such Democratic efforts, compared with 28 Republican women, 13 percent of all Republican candidate efforts.

Within the Democratic Party when women entered these nomination contests they were more likely to win than their male counterparts. Overall, they had a 76 percent success rate compared to 59 percent for Democratic male opposition party contenders. The success rates for male and female Republicans were somewhat more evenly balanced. Overall, their female contenders outperformed the male contenders 60 percent to 54 percent.[3] The high percentage of victors in these opposition party primaries throughout these election cycles suggests a small pool of contenders facing few opponents such that female candidates did not face a more competitive environment as measured by larger candidate pools within the opposition party.

Given the overall lesser presence of Republican women as candidates and elected representatives during this time period, the spike in the number of GOP women seeking nomination in opposition party primaries in 2010—76 contenders—piques our interest as to their status in these contests. The previous high point had been 43 Republican women in 1994, another good year for Republican challengers in general as chapter 2 indicated.

The political environment in 2010 certainly favored Republicans and

TABLE 3.3. Presence and Performance, Opposition Party Primaries by Party and Sex, 1994–2010

	Democrats			Republicans		
Year	Men	Women	% Women	Men	Women	% Women
1994	190	38	17%	360	44	11%
% Win	54%	76%		53%	57%	
1996	283	61	18%	294	34	10%
% Win	58%	71%		47%	65%	
1998	194	42	18%	213	31	13%
% Win	63%	76%		56%	74%	
2000	196	40	17%	227	30	12%
% Win	68%	83%		63%	70%	
2002	158	34	18%	191	37	16%
% Win	75%	91%		70%	62%	
2004	258	50	16%	233	35	13%
% Win	50%	84%		59%	69%	
2006	299	57	16%	180	21	10%
% Win	56%	72%		69%	67%	
2008	240	56	19%	291	32	10%
% Win	51%	63%		58%	59%	
2010	160	35	18%	569	76	12%
% Win	69%	77%		35%	40%	
Total	1,976	413	17%	2,541	340	12%
%Win	59%	76%		54%	60%	

Source: Data compiled by the author.

the Tea Party movement stimulated candidates outside the more formal party structure, creating raucous primary contests within the Republican Party. Tea Party women were an especially distinctive political group, making questions focusing on gender of particular interest in these primaries. For example, CeCe Heil was one, and the only woman, of 11 Republican primary contenders competing to oppose Democratic Rep. Jim Cooper (TN) in the general election. She had the notoriety, if not the advantage, of gaining Sarah Palin's endorsement. In her endorsement, Palin described Heil (who had previously run for a seat in the House) as "another tough 'mama grizzly' with the experience, passion, and integrity to restore some common sense to Washington. As a small business owner, attorney, constitutional scholar, and proud mother of two, she will fight tirelessly to protect our freedoms and rein in the excesses of an out-of-control federal government that seems set on spending away our children's future" (Heil campaign website). Heil came in third in the primary, 5 percentage points behind the winner. A large gap existed between the top three contenders and the other eight men. None of the top three candidates had held elective office. Rep. Cooper won reelection.[4]

On a more systematic note, there was at least one female candidate in 64 of 232 GOP primaries to oppose a Democratic incumbent in the November election, 28 percent of the contests. As table 3.3 shows, they had a higher success rate than their male counterparts in achieving nominations but they had been more successful as a group in earlier primary elections. Further, in the vast majority of the contests they entered, a female candidate had the distinction of being the only woman in the contest. Only nine of these 64 contests had more than one female contender. In 12 primaries a woman was the sole candidate seeking nomination. To the extent that voters may have used sex as a cue in making their voting decision these female candidates were more likely to have been advantaged than disadvantaged.

Female Republicans were also not disadvantaged by being more likely to enter contests to oppose stronger Democratic incumbents. Using the percentage of the vote of the Republican presidential candidate, John McCain, in a district in 2008 as a measure of the potential competitiveness of the district, no difference existed in the partisanship of districts in which male and female Republicans chose to run to oppose an Democratic incumbent in the general election; the average Republican presidential vote was 41 percent for both sexes. Using district as the unit of analysis, districts with a woman seeking the Republican nomination had a slightly higher Republican presidential vote than districts without a female Republican contender (40% to 37%). Nor do we find a difference in the partisan character of the districts in which male and female candidates were primary victors to oppose a Democratic incumbent. The average Republican presidential vote was 37 percent for both male and female victors. These rather detailed findings are from only one election cycle and only for a subset of primary entrants, but they do present a piece of evidence of a growing assertiveness on the part of women candidates and minimal problems based on their sex at the primary stage of the campaign process.

An analysis of the character of all of the districts based on presidential vote in which women entered opposition primary campaigns over the course of these nine elections compared to that for male contenders shows a small difference between the sexes. The percentage of the Republican presidential candidate's vote was slightly lower on average for Democratic female candidates than Democratic male candidates—49.6 percent to 51.2 percent—suggesting that women sought such nominations in slightly more friendly environments. The opposition situation was present for Republican female opposition party contenders when all election cycles are included in the analysis. The average Republican presidential vote was 36.6 percent for the female candidates and 38.6 for the male candidates.

Summary

Presence is the key gender factor in contemporary primaries involving incumbents either directly through a renomination challenge or indirectly through contesting opposition party primaries. Within both Democratic and Republican parties women continue to be much less likely than men to undertake such campaigns. At the same time, gender has come to matter little for incumbents in terms of facing renomination challenges. Overall female incumbents are not more likely than male incumbents to have a primary challenger although the overall similarity masks some opposing partisan gender differences. A larger percentage of Republican female incumbents have faced opposition in their renomination attempts than their male counterparts while a lower percentage of female Democratic incumbents have faced primary opposition than their male counterparts. But they seldom have suffered defeats. Women have also entered opposition party primaries on a much smaller scale than men. When they do enter them, they have been more likely to win. Their greater success rates appear not to have been a consequence of running in more hopeless situations than male candidates.

I now turn attention to the most opportune primary contests regarding women's quests for national political leadership: open seat primaries.

Districts in which incumbents decide not to run for reelection, either retiring from public office completely or seeking higher office, dramatically increase the chances for potential new members to win a seat compared to incumbent challengers. Investigating women's presence and performance at the primary and general election stages in this subset of contests is central to an empirical analysis of a gendered nature to contemporary U.S. House elections and an assessment of the incremental nature of the increasing presence of women in that legislative body.

Open Seat Primaries

Although open seats may be "where the action is," not all open seats provide equal chances of ultimate victory for Democratic and Republican male and female candidates. As many scholars have noted, it is important to take context into account (e.g., Fowler and Lawless 2009; Ondercin and Welch 2009). To what extent have women taken advantage of these opportune situations, entering them strategically, that is, selectively running where chances of ultimate victory are greatest for their party? Have the women who have entered these contests been more likely to have had prior office-holding experience than their male counterparts, suggesting that women have perceived a need to be better or more qualified before seeking such offices? And has office-holding experience been more prevalent in female candidates' success? Also, what should we make of Lawless and Pearson's contention that the primary context has been more difficult for female candidates based on the size of the pool of candidates in races women have entered compared to male-only contenders? The difficulty hypothesis is best tested in open seat primaries.

Lawless and Pearson's greater difficulty thesis that female candidates faced a larger field of contenders in primary elections than occurs in male-only contests may have been the result of one of two distinct processes. It may have been the consequence of the perception of women's vulnerability as candidates, which Lawless and Pearson stress. But I propose another, more positive, perspective regarding the relationship between the size of candidate pools and the presence of female candidates in open seat races. It may be that women, being strategic actors just as men are, tend to enter more promising primaries, which in general would attract a large cast of participants regardless of any gender factors. Female nonincumbent candidates may be strategic in deciding what primaries to enter, focusing on those campaigns where the prospect of ultimate victory is greatest, especially open seat primaries in districts favorably disposed toward their party. If this process is the case, then women would tend to be contestants in primaries that are more attractive to strategic male candidates as well. Thus, this process would lead to the seemingly more difficult primary environment for female candidates, being based on the number of candidates in strategic races, than on a process stemming from women being perceived as vulnerable candidates.

This latter process turns the traditional notion that women are more likely to be "sacrificial lambs," that is, encouraged to enter races where the chances of victory for the party is miniscule, on its head, so to speak; it is an outmoded idea at best, in any case. It suggests women are less likely to enter primaries for "unwinnable" seats. The idea of women acting strategically in the political realm has become the default perspective of women and politics' scholars (e.g., Palmer and Simon 2001; Gertzog 2002; Fulton et al. 2006; Ondercin and Welch 2009). In their study of women's candidacies in the 1990s, Ondercin and Welch reported that "[t]he presence of open seats, a key opportunity factor, is strongly, positively, and significantly related to the presence of women candidates for both Democrats and Republicans" (2009, 603), supporting the idea of ambitious candidates weighing the costs and benefits of a candidacy.

I build on Lawless and Pearson's primary election analyses in this work through an extensive examination of the open seat primary election contests in the contemporary era. Lawless and Pearson did not single out the distinctiveness of these races for women gaining seats in the House, nor did they include political opportunity structure variables as explanatory factors in women's presence. The inclusion in this study of a more concentrated analysis of this key subgroup of elections and inclusion of opportunity structures enhances our understanding of the incremental nature of the growth of women's representation in the U.S. House and refines ideas about the gendered nature of contemporary political contests.

To answer more detailed questions about the emergence of women in contemporary open seat elections and to compare their performance with that of male candidates within partisan contexts, I assembled two data sets. The district is the unit of analysis in one data set. For each district with an open seat election during the primary season from 1994 and 2010, the number of Democratic and GOP male and female candidates running in it, a ranking of its competitive nature, and whether it was a southern district were entered into the data set. In the second data set, candidates are the unit of analysis. Information was included on candidates' party affiliation, prior office-holding experience, percentage of the vote obtained in the primary, and whether one was running in the South.

A total of 335 seats were opened during the primary seasons of the nine elections of this time period, varying from a high of 50 in 1996 to a low of 27 in 2006 (table 3.4). As an aside, the tumultuous election of 2010 did not produce a disproportionate number of open seats. Rather, its 38 open seats fell in the middle of the distribution. A total of 2,349 candidacies competed in these primaries.[5] To measure political opportunity, *CQ Politics* October rating of competitiveness immediately preceding the November election was used. Districts were coded as competitive if CQ rated them as either toss-ups or leaning in one or the other party's direction.[6] Districts rated as favoring one party or considered safe for the party were coded as either noncompetitive Democrat or noncompetitive Republican depending on their partisan leaning. For these nine election cycles, 53 percent of the seats were rated as competitive, 16 percent were likely or safe Democratic seats, and 31 percent were likely or safe Republican seats. Partisan distributions bounced around from election to election with no particular trend toward competitiveness or partisan advantage for one party or the other. The 2010 election was somewhat distinctive, however, with 58 percent of the contests (n = 22) being rated as likely or safe Republican seats.

I include a South/non-South variable since Palmer and Simon's construction of a district woman friendliness index showed that the South has not been a particularly friendly region for female candidates. Their classification of districts as southern is based on being in one of the 11 Confederate states. I follow their classification in this analysis. Core Democratic districts electing women have been nonsouthern districts. Districts that have elected Republican women have primarily been outside the South, their analysis shows (2008, 196, 198). Of the 335 open seat districts in this analysis, 114 (34%) were in the South. Southern districts were also somewhat more likely to be GOP-dominated districts than nonsouthern districts (37% to 28%). It is important to keep in mind when considering the emergence and performance of female candidates in this study that I am analyzing primary and not general elections. Thus, while women may have been less likely to have been elected to Congress from southern districts,

TABLE 3.4. Male and Female Candidates in Open Seat Primaries, 1994–2010

	1994	1996	1998	2000	2002	2004	2006	2008	2010
# of Districts	47	50	34	32	44	30	27	34	37
# Dem Men	154	169	80	61	113	53	77	74	67
# Dem Women	28	29	19	19	30	20	23	20	24
# GOP Men	159	182	97	108	146	92	89	103	159
# GOP Women	22	19	14	16	15	17	12	9	28

Source: Data compiled by the author.

we have not determined if this result stems from women not contesting primaries in such districts or contesting but not winning primaries in them.

Women's Presence in Open Seat Primaries

Women's standing as open seat primary candidates is evaluated from three vantage points or lenses for a comprehensive assessment of the impact of this first stage in the campaign process on women's ultimate representation in a legislative body. Vantage point 1 centers on their overall numbers as candidates. Vantage point 2 focuses on the extensiveness of their presence across races as indicated by the proportion of districts in which women have run, and vantage point 3 takes into account the partisan opportunity structure of districts, examining women's presence in seats considered winnable for their party.

Vantage point 1 centers on questions of the number of Democratic and Republican female partisans who have been candidates in these primaries overall and whether their presence has increased over time. But then many women may run, but if they cluster in only a few primaries voters have little opportunity to cast their ballot for a woman across the contests, diminishing the likelihood of increasing their numbers in the national legislature, which is vantage point 2's focus. Further, taking partisan opportunity into account, if women disproportionately contest seats where their party has little chance of being successful, then they would not be considered strategically minded politicians basing their decision to run on the likelihood of ultimate success. Vantage point 3 focuses on the presence of Democratic and Republican women in primaries in competitive districts and districts considered relatively safe for their party. I consider each of these vantage points in order in the following analyses to provide an overall assessment of women's strategic presence in open seat U.S. House primaries in the nine elections of this study and their competitive status and then turn to questions of their open seat primary performance.

The Overall Presence of Female Women Candidates in Open Seat Primaries

Table 3.4 shows the number of open seats and the number of male and female Republican and Democratic candidates contesting them in each of the 1994 to 2010 election cycles. The partisan breakdown consists of 212 Democratic women and 848 Democratic men, 152 Republican women

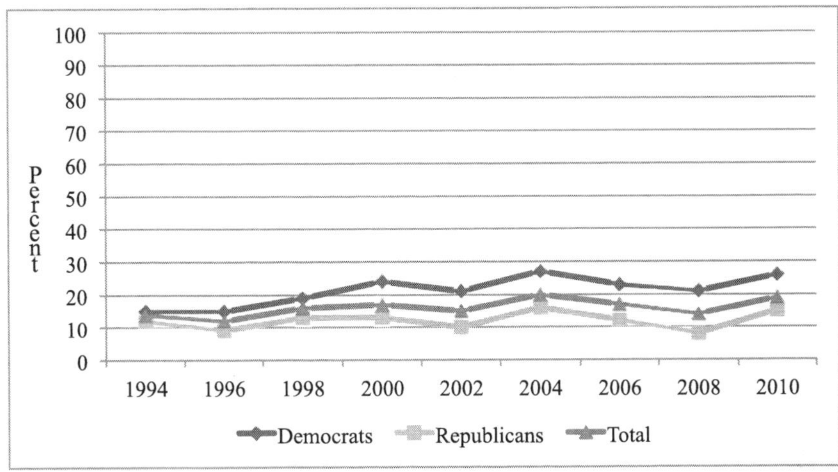

Fig. 3.3. Women as a Percentage of Open Seat Primary Candidates, 1994–2010. (Data compiled by the author.)

and 1,135 Republican men. Figure 3.3 presents the percentage of all party open seat primary contenders who were women over these election cycles. Women were 15.5 percent of the total candidate pool, 364 of the 2,349 open seat primary candidacies. Overall, women comprised 20 percent of Democratic candidacies and 10 percent of Republican candidacies. These percentages are slightly higher than found in my earlier study for open seat primaries from 1972 through 1990. However, in 1992 women were 16.4 percent of open seat primary contenders (Burrell 1994, 43).

As table 3.4 and figure 3.3 show, in each election cycle more Democratic women than GOP women have run in open seat primaries except in 2010 and have been a larger percentage of their party's candidates throughout this era. Although Republican women expanded their numbers in the open seat primaries in 2010 relative to Democratic women, their presence relative to Republican men, whose numbers surged that year, remained lower than that of the female Democrats among their partisan open seat candidates. Female candidates' overall share of the pool of candidates remained at a fairly low percentage over the course of these elections within either party. Democratic female contenders did increase their presence somewhat at the turn of the century and have maintained a slightly more substantial presence; in two elections Democratic women surpassed 25 percent of all party candidates. GOP women's high point was 16 percent in 2004.

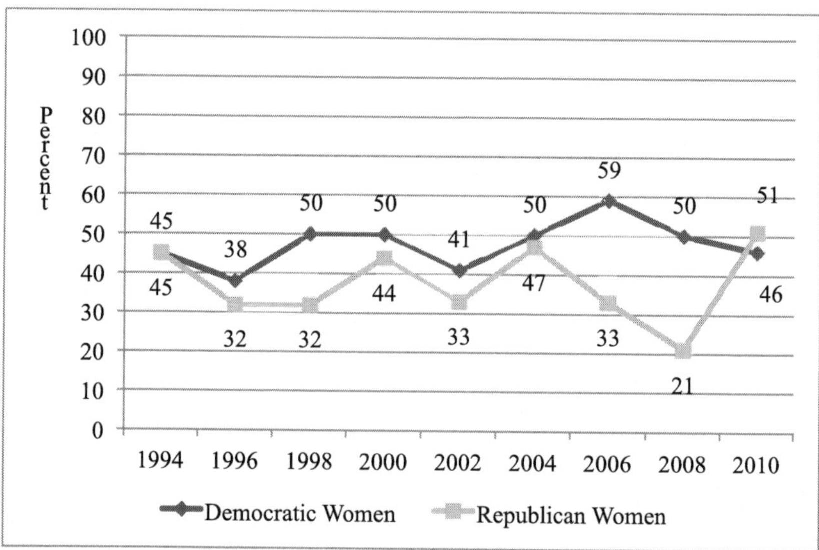

Fig. 3.4. Percentage of Open Seat Primary Races with at Least One Female Candidate, 1994–2010. (Data compiled by the author.)

The Extensiveness of Women's Presence

Table 3.4 and figure 3.3 have provided an overview picture of women's presence as open seat primary contenders in each party. An investigation of vantage point 2, which shifts attention from total numbers and percentages to the extensiveness of women's presence across races, requires taking a district focus, that is, an examination of the proportion of districts in which a woman candidate has run. The majority of open seat contests had no female candidates. In the GOP primaries, 63 percent had no female candidates, and no woman made a bid in 53 percent of the Democratic primaries over the course of these nine elections. Figure 3.4 illustrates the extensiveness of their presence across the elections. It shows that in six of the nine election cycles approximately one-half of the Democratic Party primaries had a female contender but only in 2010 was a woman present in one-half of the Republican Party primaries. In five of the election cycles no more than one-third of the GOP primaries had a woman among the pool of contenders.

These data show that voters have not been provided with a great many opportunities to select a woman as their party's nominee if they so desired in recent open seat primaries, with the Republican Party being less accommodating in this domain than the Democratic Party. Although no longer seen as unusual, women are still entering barely one-half of the Democratic Party open seat primaries and a much smaller percentage of Republican Party open seat primaries. This pattern of entry parallels Lawless and Pearson's findings of a "low entry rate" for women generally in primaries for seats in the U.S. House. Few women run. (Although once opportunity structure within open seat primaries is taken into consideration this conclusion is a slight oversimplification as far as Democratic female candidates are concerned.) From the very first stage of the most viable opportunities for making gains in their representation in the U.S. House, GOP female partisans have especially lagged behind. Although chances for ultimate victory were greater within the Republican Party during this era across the open seats, Republican women did not take much advantage of them, with 2010 being an exception. Whether 2010 represents a turning point in women contesting Republican Party open seat primaries or an anomaly will require more data points from future elections.

The analyses of women's emergence as candidates presented to this point, however, ignore an important consideration for a comprehensive assessment of their candidacies. The variation in their presence across these election cycles indicates the importance of controlling for the partisan nature of the open seat districts, which is the focus of vantage point 3 as indicated earlier. What would be the incentive for potential female candidates (and male candidates as well) to enter primaries in districts dominated by the other party? Had more of the districts, for instance, been competitive for the Democratic Party might there have been a greater pool of female candidates in them? Was the low rate of participation by Republican women a matter of their being particularly uninterested in entering contests with a slim likelihood of ultimate victory? The next section explores the strategic nature of women's open seat candidacies.

Opportunity Structures

Strategic politicians, Irwin Gertzog tells us, are "calculating and rational. The chances of their securing their party's nomination are carefully considered, and entry into a race is based on the likelihood of success. They calculate how victory or defeat will affect their careers and, more often than not, they wait for an incumbent to retire or otherwise leave an office before seeking the office" (2002, 103). If women are acting strategically then their numbers should be positively related to prospects of ultimate victory for their party in the general election.

Indeed, primary contests in districts seemingly unwinnable for their party attracted few Democratic and Republican women in the elections between 1994 and 2010. Focusing on women's presence, only 17 percent of the GOP primaries in safe Democratic districts had a female contender. Female Democrats were more active in contesting primaries in safe GOP districts. They ran in 31 percent of them. At the other end of the opportunity spectrum, 41 percent of Republican primaries in Republican dominated districts had at least one female contender while 72 percent of Democratic primaries in Democratic dominated districts had a female contender. The latter percentage is substantial and serves as a counterpoint to the overall "low entry rate" of female candidates. Of the 53 Democratic Party dominated districts, women entered primaries in 38 of them and won 16 of them, 42 percent of the contests they entered. In competitive districts women contested 41 percent of the GOP primaries and 48 percent of the Democratic primaries.

Moving from a district perspective to a candidate perspective, table 3.5 shows first, as one would expect, that the average number of contestants increases as one moves from an open seat in districts the other party dominates to districts that one's own party dominates. Both male and female candidates conform to this aspect of strategic presence. The average number of Democratic female candidates increased fourfold in moving from safe Republican districts to safe Democratic districts, which a strategic focus would predict. But their numbers were still just a fourth that of male Democrats in dominant Democratic districts. On average four men contested these most opportune elections compared to just over one woman per district.

Republican female candidates doubled their presence as one moved from safe Democratic districts to safe Republican districts but still less than one woman per race was a candidate. Their presence in these most opportune situations is miniscule compared to that of their male counterparts, who averaged over four candidates per race, and to the presence of Democratic women in safe Democratic districts. Indeed, their presence was no greater than in competitive districts in keeping with Palmer and Simon's description of Republican female candidacies in "women friendly" districts, which tend to favor Democratic Party candidates. According to their findings, "[F]emale Republican House members tend to win election in districts that are less conservative, more urban, and more diverse than those electing male Republicans; they come from districts that are 'less Republican.' . . . The districts that have elected Republican women are strikingly similar to the districts that have elected Democratic men.

The districts where Republican women are most likely to win the primary because they are female are the districts where they will have a hard time winning the general election because they are Republican" (2006, 152).

As noted earlier, region may be a factor in the growing partisan gap in the numerical representation of women in the U.S. Congress and the lagging presence of women in dominant Republican district open seats. As Elder has shown, Republicans have made inroads in the South, the region of the country least hospitable to women's candidacies (2008). As cited previously, open seat districts most favorable to the Republican Party during this time period have been in the South. However, the Republican-favored open seat districts in the South were not less likely than such partisan districts in other regions to have female contenders in their primaries. Essentially no difference existed between southern and nonsouthern regions in the presence of a Republican female candidate; at least one woman was a candidate in 38.6 percent of southern districts and in 36.4 percent of nonsouthern districts. The differences were not statistically significant. Further, 44 percent of safe Republican districts in the South had a female contender compared with 39 percent of safe Republican districts outside the South. Thus, the regional realignment of the parties does not appear to account for the lesser presence of Republican female members in the U.S. House at least from the perspective of their contesting these key initial primary contests.

Overall, the findings so far suggest that the contemporary end result of few Republican female U.S. representatives (Elder 2008) has been initiated through a process of GOP women being less likely to enter open seat primaries in core Republican districts where the probability of ultimate success is greatest. They have not taken advantage of the greater opportunities within the Republican Party during this period. They may have been less likely to run perhaps because patriarchal conservative leaders discouraged them from running or at least were not encouraging, they were less likely

TABLE 3.5. Mean Number of Opponents, Open Seat Primary Candidates by Party and Sex

	Mean Number of Opponents	Standard Error
Total Female Candidates	4.08	.202
Total Male Candidates	4.37	.081
Democratic Female Candidates	4.10	.312
Democratic Male Candidates	4.26	.152
Republican Female Candidates	4.06	.215
Republican Male Candidates	4.45	.083

Source: Data compiled by the author.

to have the credentials to run having less local office-holding experience, or from a belief that they cannot win. These factors most likely interact, resulting in their greater invisibility in the most winnable situations for their party. These factors deserve much more detailed study. Republicans in 2010 touted their efforts to recruit and support female candidates (Politico 2010; Rosin 2011). Scholars should analyze conservative women's groups' recruitment and training of women to run and investigate the effect of Sarah Palin's efforts to increase the pool of Republican female candidates in these core Republican districts as we continue to investigate this political puzzle.

Women's Presence and Primary Competition

The lack of female candidates in districts with potentially the most promising outcomes continues to be a major factor in the slow incremental increase in the numerical representation of women in the U.S. Congress beyond the drag incumbency has created. At the same time, we do find evidence of women seeking election in more promising circumstances and not being concentrated in sacrificial lamb situations in open seat districts that are hopeless for their party. The analysis by district competitiveness in table 3.5 illustrates this point. The finding that Democratic women have been contestants in nearly three-quarters of the open seat primaries in safe Democratic districts and that they predominantly account for the increases women have made in their numbers as U.S. representatives illustrate the significance of this strategic presence. These data add to the more general evidence of a fairly level playing field on the campaign trail for women and men, but getting on the trail is still a gendered process or at least one in which women have not been as likely to engage, especially Republican women.

I have shown the number of women running in both parties by district competitiveness. Lawless and Pearson have suggested that the major gender problem in primary elections has been that women face more competition, that is, when they enter a race they are more likely "to attract a crowd" than if a race were a male-only affair, as discussed earlier in this chapter, and that is a problem. The number of individuals attracted to an open seat primary is related to the probability of ultimate victory for one's party as previously noted in this chapter. Thus, if women act strategically then they would be more likely to enter multicandidate races leading to a positive relationship between their presence and the size of the candidate pool, rather than female candidates being perceived as more vulnerable and thus drawing a crowd once they have entered the contest. They may be just one of a host of candidates taking advantage of an opportune situation. In addition, if a woman is the only female candidate facing a pool of male contenders that may be a plus for her and something that she highlights to make her candidacy stand out and attract support.[7]

Do female candidates face greater competition than male candidates? To test this hypothesis, I use a different calculation than that of Lawless and Pearson. Rather than comparing the number of candidates in races with and without a female contender, I calculate the number of candidates the average female contender faced compared with the number of candidates the average male candidate faced and the distributions around these averages. Such an analysis does not just add a woman (or women) to the mix and see what happens in terms of number of candidates but rather the analysis proceeds outward from the individual candidate with a gender focus. This analytical approach examines the mean number of opponents and the standard deviations around the means for each sex to test the competitiveness hypothesis. Histograms are also presented to compare the distribution of competitors that male and female candidates have faced.

This analytic procedure shows little difference overall and within partisan groups regarding the competitive situation male and female open seat primary candidates have experienced. Table 3.5 shows that overall and within the parties male and female candidates had an average of over four opponents. The average was slightly higher for the male candidates. Their standard deviations were slightly tighter, most likely resulting from their much large number of cases. A *t*-test of statistical significance showed support for the null hypothesis of no gender difference in levels of competition using the size of the opponent pool as its measure. The graphs presented in figures 3.5 and 3.6 also illustrate a fairly similar distribution pattern between the sexes in the number of opponents they faced in open seat primary contests. Examined from this perspective the greater difficulty hypothesis would not be supported. On average, female candidates in open seat primaries did not have greater competition than male candidates. They were also often advantaged in being the lone female candidate facing a number of male contenders who might have a harder time distinguishing themselves.

One other feature of the entrance process should also be considered in focusing on gender and competition in future research and that centers on the timing of formal entrance into such campaigns. Consider the following situation from the 2012 election. On August 16, 2011, Bernalillo County commissioner Michelle Lujan Grisham announced her candidacy

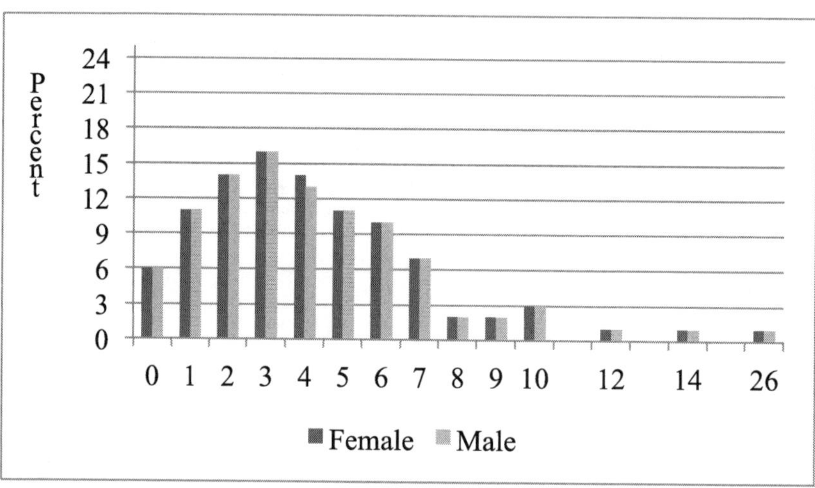

Fig. 3.5. Number of Opponents, Open Seat Primaries by Sex, 1994–2010. (Data compiled by the author.)

for the open 1st district congressional seat. She was the third Democrat to announce for the seat. Two male contenders had already announced their candidacies. She did not attract them into the contest. Did the race become more difficult for these male contenders because of her entrance subsequent to their announcement? Her entrance created more competition but not more difficulty for her. It would seem that timing would have to be factored into any assessment of a gendered focus on campaign difficulty based on candidate pools.

The Lone Female Entrant and Multiple Female Candidacies

When there has been a female presence in these primary elections, it has tended to be a sole woman competing for the nomination. Few open seat primaries have had more than one female candidate, especially on the GOP side. Only nine of the 103 Republican dominated districts had more than one female candidate in the Republican primary; 18 of the 53 Democratic dominated districts had more than one female candidate in their primaries. Thus, from a gender perspective, if a woman ran in these contests, for the most part she would have had the novelty of being the only member of her sex, and the extent to which sex mattered to voters she may been advantaged if some voters used female sex as an affirmative cue in making their decisions.

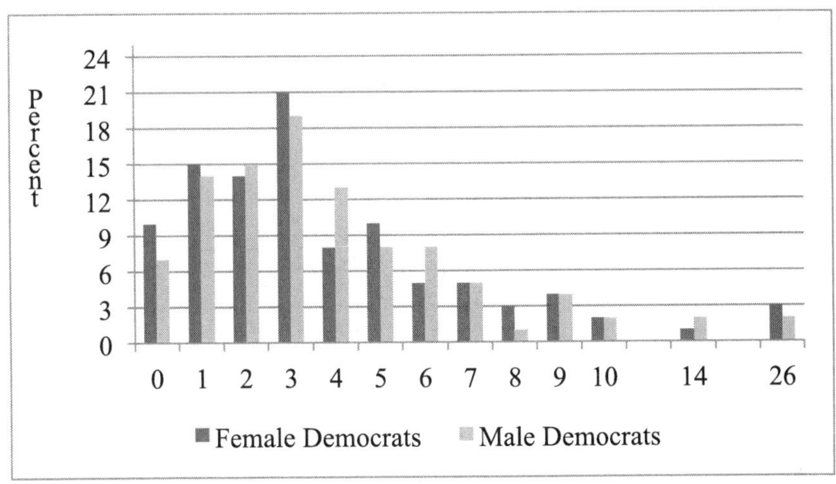

Fig. 3.6a. Number of Opponents, Open Seat Primaries, Democrats, 1994–2010. (Data compiled by the author.)

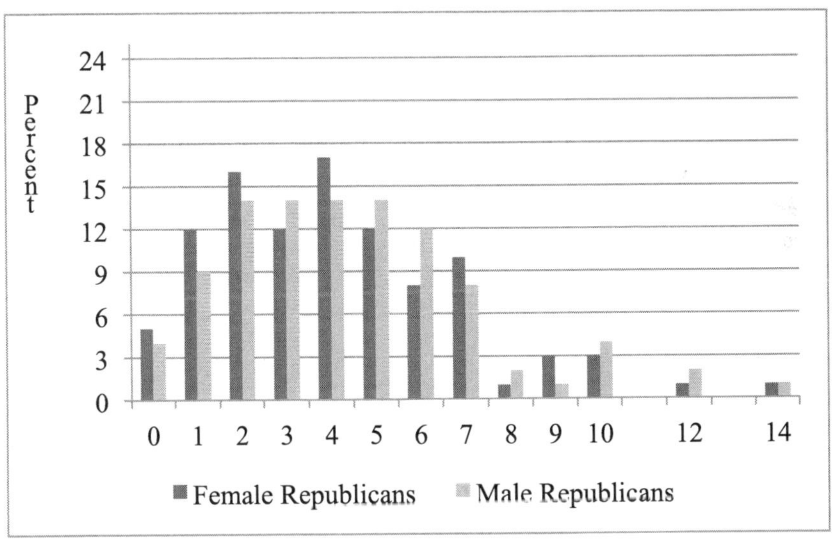

Fig. 3.6b. Number of Opponents, Open Seat Primaries, Republicans, 1994–2010. (Data compiled by the author.)

Two contests, however, stand out, with six and five female contenders each, during these nine election cycles. Both were Democratic Party affairs in Democratic dominated districts. The first case occurred in Maryland's 7th district in 1996. This primary contest combined a special election and an open seat primary into one event. Six women were contenders in the Democratic primary but they were competing against 21 men! This primary was probably one of the all-time highest collection of contenders. The race included one state senator, four state representatives, the minister of Baltimore's 10,000-member Bethel African Methodist Episcopal Church, a hospital chaplain, a social activist, a teacher, and an architect, among others. State Representative Elijah Cummings, 45 years old, won with 37.3 percent of the vote. State Senator Delores Kelley, 59 years old, came in third with 9.6 percent of the vote, the highest scoring female candidate.

The second race with five women candidates had the distinction of being nearly an all-woman event. The contest consisted of five female candidates and one male contender. This contest occurred in Georgia's 4th district in 2004 when former U.S. representative Cynthia McKinney attempted to win back the seat that she had lost in a primary two years earlier.[8] The primary race included, besides McKinney, three female state senators and the Atlanta city council president. The only nonelected official in the race was a man. Cynthia McKinney won her seat back by winning a majority of the vote in the primary, avoiding a runoff. She then safely won the general election in this Democratic dominant district.

Prior Elective Office-Holding and Women's Presence

The literature on ambition suggests that women candidates who tend to run would be more qualified than their male counterparts (see Lawless and Fox 2005; Sanbonmatsu 2005; Gertzog 2002; Anzia and Berry 2011). Thus, we would expect to find fewer "amateurs" among the viable women candidates in these open seat contests. Although some scholars have argued that women have to be "better" than their male counterparts in order to fare equally well, empirical measures of "better" have seldom been developed.[9]

I test an aspect of this assumption through a comparison of the prior office-holding experience of these male and female open seat primary candidates. Office-holding is simply measured by whether a candidate had held an elected office position prior to running for the U.S. House in these elections, following Gary Jacobson's lead (1989).[10] The percentage of previous officeholders among all candidates ranged from a low of 26 percent in 1996 to a high of 43 percent in 2006 with an overall average of 34 percent. No trend toward a greater or lesser presence of experienced candidates emerged during this time period and party differences were minimal; 35 percent of Democratic candidates and 32 percent of GOP candidates were experienced public officeholders. The majority of open seat primary candidates during this period were not experienced officeholders. Even if we exclude frivolous candidates, defined as candidates who received 5 percent or less of the vote in a primary from the pool, only 40 percent of the candidates were experienced. These findings do not necessarily represent a growing trend of more political amateurs filling the ranks of such candidacies, however; as Gaddie and Bullock noted in their study of the 1982–94 period, over one-half of all the open seat candidates also had no office-holding or policy-making experience (2000, 57).

Gender differences were present in office-holding experience. The female candidates were substantially more likely to have had prior elective office experience than the male candidates (45% to 31%).[11] Among the female Democratic open seat primary candidates, 48 percent had held elective office compared to 32 percent of their male colleagues. Within the Republican Party, 42 percent of the female candidates had prior elective office experience compared to 31 percent of their male colleagues. Men were more likely to be frivolous candidates (22% to 12%), but excluding all candidates receiving 5 percent or less of the primary vote did not affect the relationship between sex and prior office holding experience. This comparison provides support for the hypothesis that female candidates would be more qualified that other scholars have put forth, at least for candidacies in open seat primaries.

Women's Performance in Open Seat Primaries

Among the 670 open seat primary winners, 124 were women (19%). This section compares the performance of female contenders to that of male contenders. What was the success rate of both sexes and what has been the success of female candidates where the likelihood of ultimate victory for their party is greatest in the general election? Were they as competitive as male entrants in districts in which their party had a chance of victory? Previous research on the performance of male and female candidates overall in primary and general elections for the U.S. House have found gender parity in acquiring votes and winning (e.g., Burrell 1994; Fiber and Fox 2005). Thus, I hypothesize that female open seat primary candidates would perform as well as male candidates in this important subset of races.

Recall the research of Matland and King (2002) cited earlier in this chapter. They calculated the number of districts where women ran and won open seat nominations for the two major parties between 1990 and 2000. They reported "far more districts where women are running in open-seat primaries on the Democratic side than on the Republican side (by definition the opportunities are equal since an open seat is always open for both parties)." Democratic voters also showed a higher propensity to choose a female candidate than Republican voters. In 53.5 percent of the Democratic primaries in open-seat districts with a female contender, the party's voters selected a female candidate. On the GOP side, women won in just 37.5 percent of the districts in which a woman ran. They concluded that in the 1990s a significant difference had emerged in how women fared in the Democratic and Republican primaries (137). Summarizing their research, the primary process appears to have continuing partisan aspects to it with Democratic female candidates being advantaged in a series of fairly recent elections in running and winning over female Republicans.

Here, I extend Matland and King's analysis into more contemporary elections and add to their performance data by including the opportunity structure of the open seats during this time period for Democrats and for Republicans as I have done in examining women's presence as open seat primary candidates. Perhaps women disproportionately entered and won primary contests in districts where their party's ultimate chance of successfully winning in November was low, accounting for their performance advantage observed in Matland and King's study. The opportunity structure variable built into this study allows for the testing of this hypothesis.

Table 3.6 presents data on the relative performance of male and female Democratic and Republican entrants in the open seat primary elections from 1994 to 2010 in the three types of district competitiveness. The data presented include the number of candidates winning an uncontested race, the percentage of the vote obtained in contested races, and success rates. The latter two measures test the relative performance of the male and female candidates taking opportunity structure into account.[12]

A comparison of the percentage of the vote achieved shows that the female Democratic candidates tended to obtain a higher percentage of the vote across all three types of districts. The situation differs among Republicans across opportunity structures. Republican women running in safe Democratic districts obtained a lower average percentage of the vote in contested elections than their male counterparts. Both sexes running in these primaries had little chance of winning a seat in November in any event. Republican women outperformed their male counterparts in competitive districts and the two sexes performed equally well in safe districts.

Female candidates may, however, have on average achieved a higher percentage of the vote mainly because there were fewer of them to divide the vote in most of the contests in which they entered compared with male contenders, rather than their being more successful candidates in terms of winning. Thus, being a woman may have been an advantage rather than a detriment in acquiring votes. Data on success rates, *the* important factor in terms of ultimate numerical representation, shows that female open seat primary contenders also were more successful than male open seat primary contenders. A total of 34 percent of the female candidates won their primary compared with 27 percent of male candidates. Democratic women were the most successful group; 39 percent were primary victors compared with 26 percent of GOP women. Democratic men won 29 percent of their races and GOP men won 26 percent of their races.

Candidate sex may be negligible in winning but female candidates may have had to fight harder to win in more competitive races. A comparison of the percentage of the vote winners obtained to that of their closest competitor in these often multiple candidate races tests this competitive thesis. Examining contested primaries only, a comparison of average margins of

TABLE 3.6. Average Percentage of the Vote Obtained and Success Rates, Open Seat Primaries by Party Status, Party, and Sex, 1994–2010

	Democrats		Republicans	
Competition	Men	Women	Men	Women
Safe Dem Seats				
# With No Opposition	0	1	16	2
Avg. Vote Contested	15.5	21.3	30.4	22.6
Primaries	(240)	(66)	(102)	(11)
Percentage Winning	15.8	23.9	39.8	38.5
	(38/240)	(16/67)	(47/118)	(5/13)
Competitive				
# With No Opposition	28	12	27	5
Avg. Vote Contested	25.3	33.1	23.0	28.7
Primaries	(412)	(96)	(522)	(83)
Percentage Winning	31.0	41.7	28.6	28.4
	(137/442)	(45/108)	(158/553)	(25/88)
Safe Rep Seats				
# With No Opposition	39	8	3	1
Avg. Vote Contested	30.3	42.5	18.9	18.9
Primaries	(127)	(29)	(461)	(53)
Percentage Winning	45.5	59.5	19.6	20.4
	(75/165)	(21/37)	(91/464)	(11/54)

Source: Competitiveness measure based on CQ Quarterly's rankings available in *CQ Weekly Reports*, October of each election year. Data compiled by the author. Numbers in parentheses are number of candidates.

victory shows minimal difference between the sexes within both parties. Democratic female winners had a 23.7 vote margin over their nearest competitor compared with 21.2 point margin for Democratic male winners in contested races. Republican female winners also outpaced their male counterparts with an average margin of victory of 21.3 points compared to 20.1 points.[13] Across these performance indicators women who ran performed equally or better than male candidates.

District Competitiveness and Women's Success

As table 3.6 shows, 142 individuals won an uncontested open seat primary. It also shows that only one woman in each party won a primary unopposed in a district safe for her party: Republican Candice Miller in Michigan's 10th district in 2002 and Democrat Debbie Wasserman Schultz in Florida's 20th district in 2004. Term limited out of her secretary of state's position, Candice Miller considered entering the Republican primary for governor in 2002 before deciding to run for the newly created 10th district congressional seat. As with a number of the women elected to the House during this period, Congresswoman Miller had firsts in her political background. When she was elected as a Harrison Township supervisor in 1980, she was the youngest supervisor in her township's history and the first woman elected to the post. She ended up being elected to Congress in 2002 with 63 percent of the vote. Debbie Wasserman Schultz, the second uncontested female candidate in a safe seat primary, won election to the House with 70 percent of the vote in 2004. She, too, had made history in her political career. In 1992 she was the youngest woman ever elected to the Florida state legislature at the age of 26.

At the same time no male Democratic candidates got a free pass in a safe Democratic open seat primary and only four Republican males were so advantaged in safe districts for their party, which is actually a smaller percentage (1%) than the one out of 38 Republican women (2%) who had an uncontested path to her party's nomination in a safe Republican district.

Focusing on competitive and safe seats for one's party, table 3.6 shows that Democratic women had a higher success rate than Democratic men while GOP men barely outpaced their female counterparts. The biggest gap was between Democratic women and Democratic men in primary contests in competitive districts where 42 percent of the women won in the races they entered compared to 31 percent of the male candidates. Democratic women won 24 percent of their party's safe seat races that they entered compared with 16 percent of male Democratic candidates who entered these races. Republican male and female candidates did equally as well in districts their party dominated. Each group had a 30 percent success rate. Continued comparisons show open seat primary performance in recent elections is characterized by parity between the sexes or by female candidates outpacing their male counterparts.

The Impact of the South

I noted earlier that female Republican candidates were as likely to enter primaries in Republican-dominated districts in the South as they were to run in such districts outside the South. But the question still remains as to "hostility" of such southern districts toward female Republican candidates. Did female Republican candidates fare worse in the South than in other regions of the country? The answer is basically "no." Thirty-two percent of the Republican women running in the South won their primary compared with 30 percent running outside of the South. A chi-square test showed no statistically significant difference among this subgroup of candidates based on region. Democratic women running in the South, on the other hand, fared less well than their counterparts in other regions; 26 percent were victorious in the South compared to 44 percent outside of the South. Seven Republican women and 33 Republican men won their primary in safe Republican open seats in the South. Republican women running in this subset of primaries had a success rate of 28 percent compared to 17 percent for Republican male candidates.

Success and Prior Elective Office Experience

This positive gender outcome regarding woman's advancement may be the result of a gendered process in which women candidates have had to be better than men candidates to outperform their male counterparts. Thus, I take the analysis one step further, testing the relationship between prior elective office experience, one measure of the concept of better, and sex in winning recent open seat primaries employing an analysis similar to that used to investigate women's presence as candidates. How important was experience in mounting successful primary campaigns for the female candidates and how significant was it in comparison to male candidates? I hypothesize that experience was significant for both sexes but that it was more a feature for female candidates than for male candidates.

Open seats are known for drawing experienced candidates with ambition to move up the political ladder although some election years have been known for the success of amateurs, often true believers, such as the Republican first-termers whom Newt Gingrich recruited in 1994 as part of his "revolution." In other cases political amateurs have been recruited because of their special status in a particular election context such as Tammy Duckworth's recruitment in the Democratic primary in Illinois's 6th congressional district open seat in 2006. The Iraq War was of central importance in that election with increasing public disapproval of the war effort of the Bush administration. What better type of candidate for the Democratic Party to recruit than an individual with military experience in Iraq who no longer believed in this military excursion. Tammy Duckworth was a major in the Army who had lost her legs when the UH-60 Black Hawk helicopter she was copiloting was hit by a rocket propelled grenade that Iraqi insurgents had fired at it in 2004. U.S. Senator Dick Durbin, Democrat of Illinois, and U.S. Representative Rahm Emanuel, chair of Democratic Congressional Campaign Committee during that election, persuaded Duckworth to enter the Democratic primary and saw that she was heavily financed and received the necessary organizational resources to win the primary. (She actually won it over another female candidate supported by more liberal local factions of the party.)

Finally, in terms of amateurs, some individuals are recruited or supported because they are financially well off and can fund their own campaigns. Increasingly how much money an individual can raise or bring to a campaign attracts the attention of national party organizations. In 2006, for example, the Democratic Congressional Campaign Committee was just fine with letting novice candidate Dr. Steven Kagen win the Democratic primary in the 8th congressional district of Wisconsin rather than helping Nancy Nusbaum, a former county executive who had elective office experience.

Experienced candidates were more than twice as likely as inexperienced candidates to win a primary, by 42 percent to 21 percent in these election cycles as a group. Experienced candidates, although a smaller percentage of all candidates, won just over one-half of the primaries, 338 in total, and just under one-half were won by inexperienced candidates, 328 in total.

It is important to test whether having prior electoral office experience would be more important or at least more prevalent for female than male candidates based on stereotyping and the general, although unproven, perception that women need to be better than men to have equal success rates. Indeed, 60 percent of the female winners had prior elective office experience compared with 48 percent of the male winners. Forty-four percent of the experienced women won their primary; 25 percent of the female candidates without experience won theirs. Forty-two percent of the experienced men won compared with 21 percent of the inexperienced males. It may appear that experience was more important for female candidates than male candidates in winning their primary. A chi-square test of statistical significance did not find a higher correlation between prior office-holding and winning for female candidates than male candidates, however. This lack of difference probably stemmed from the fact that a greater number of female candidates had prior elective office experience.

One more question remains, requiring a return to a focus on the varied opportunity structure of open seat primaries. To complete this analysis figure 3.7 shows the percentage of winning male and female candidates of each party with prior office-holding experience within the various district competitive structures. When it comes to safe districts for their party, female winners have all had prior elective office experience. No woman who had not previously won an elective office has won a primary where she would "be on her way" to Congress as the result of a primary victory in a safe district. Male candidates without such experience have been victorious in these types of districts, particularly Democratic male candidates. In the competitive districts, Democratic female winners were 8 percent more likely to have prior office-holding experience than their male counterparts while Republican female winners were 17 percent more likely to have prior office-holding experience.

To determine the extent to which sex and experience interact to affect winning open seat primaries, a logistic regression analysis was performed for the Democratic and Republican candidates. The logistic regression equations in table 3.7 examine factors affecting whether a candidate won his or her party's primary. Winning (or losing) a primary is the dependent variable. A series of dummy variables was constructed to examine the impact of sex and experience on the probability of winning. The omitted variable for each party was inexperienced male candidates. As table 3.7 shows, compared with their inexperienced male counterparts inexperienced Democratic female candidates were more likely to win and both experienced male and female candidates were substantially more likely to win. Experience also mattered among Republican male and female candidates but the probability of inexperienced female Republicans winning was no greater or lower than their inexperienced male counterparts. Not surprisingly, it is experience which counts, more so than a candidate's sex.

Figure 3.8 shows the comparative increase in probability of winning of the experienced male and female candidates within each party over their inexperienced counterparts. The probability of winning increases substantially and

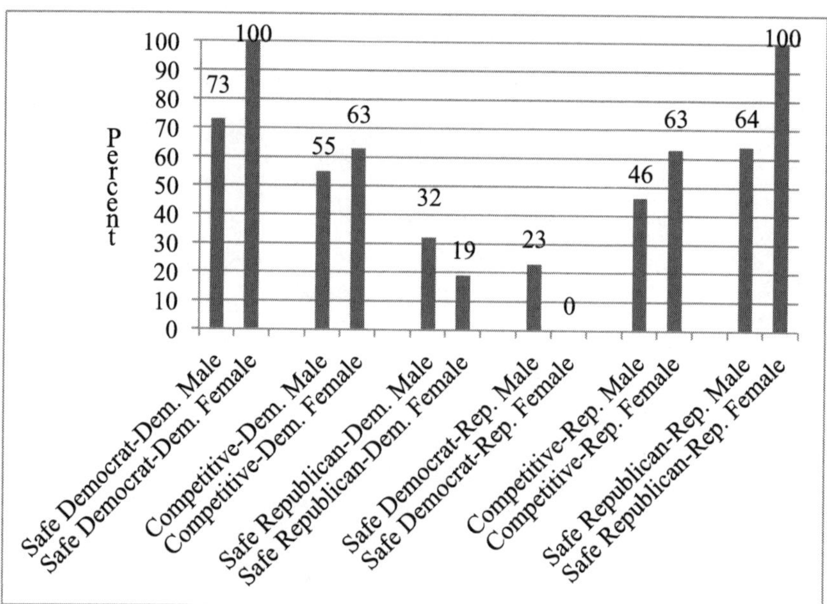

Fig. 3.7. Percentage of Open Seat Primary Winners with Prior Elective Office Experience by District Competitiveness, Party, and Sex. (Data compiled by the author.)

TABLE 3.7. The Impact of Sex and Experience on Winning Open Seat Primaries

	Democrats	Republicans
Experienced Male Candidates	1.093 (.16)**	.970 (.14)**
Women Candidates, No Experience	.484 (23)*	-.179 (.30)
Experienced Women Candidates	1.170 (.22)**	1.050 (.27)**
Constant	-1.288 (.10)***	-1.430 (.09)*
χ^2	60.03***	56.86***
Pseudo R^2	.05	.04
Percentage Correctly Predicted	68.1	74.64
N	1,050	1,280

*$p < .05$, **$p < .01$, ***$p < .001$

to approximately the same extent among both male and female experienced candidates within both parties over their inexperienced colleagues.

What these final sets of data suggest is that female candidates do not necessarily have to be "better" if we measure better by having held elective office prior to running in an open seat primary in order to win. Women *are* more likely to enter such races if they have such a credential than men. It is more a matter of perception. Women may be more likely to think that

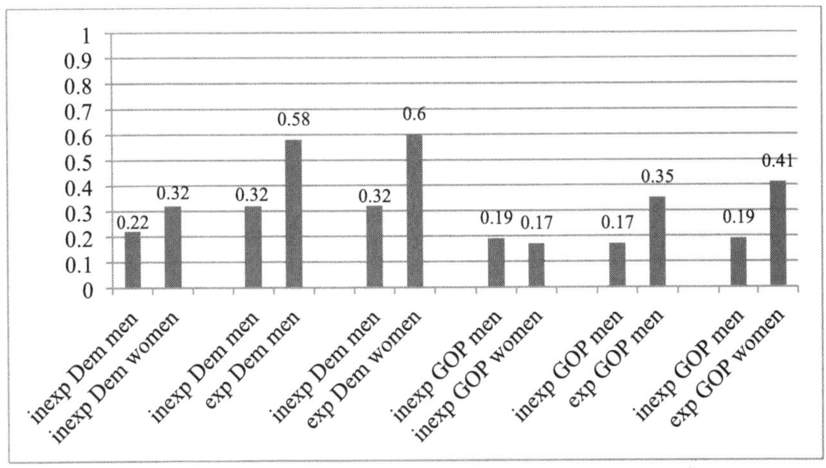

Fig. 3.8. Predicted Probability of Winning an Open Seat Primary. (Data compiled by the author. Logistic regression with control variables held at their mode.)

they have to have this experience and rely on it more than male candidates but they may not have to have it to overcome perceptions of vulnerability. The emphasis on perception would follow from Lawless and Fox's studies of sex and ambition (2005, 2010).

Conclusion

The goals of this study as outlined in chapter 1 have been to extend and update the findings about women's candidacies in earlier decades, to delve into more nuanced hypotheses about female candidates' campaign experiences that have received attention in recent research, to use these findings to assess the gendered nature of contemporary elections, and to suggest further areas for research. This chapter has contributed to these goals through a focus on women's presence and performance in primary elections for seats in the U.S. House. Surprisingly few scholars have centered their research on women's entrance patterns in congressional elections and examined in any depth what has been occurring at the primary election stage of the process.

Several main conclusions emerge from this examination of the primary election process in the contemporary era. Focusing first on the numbers of women running one might have expected a trend of increased participation over the course of these elections. We would expect such a trend due to the growth in organizations devoted to recruiting, training, and supporting women candidates. There has also been a trend toward more women possessing the resources and credentials to be perceived as viable candidates and having the ambition to be a political leader. In addition, gender bias on the part of the public has declined as the survey results presented in chapter 1 have shown. But such a trend only very loosely characterizes the numerical presence of women in congressional campaigns from 1994 through 2010. The incremental trend in women's candidacies is better understood by taking into account the political environment and the opportunity structure of each of the election cycles. Women's presence has increased marginally as their incumbency status has increased incrementally. Beyond incumbency, partisan opportunities have conditioned the number of women entering primary contests for a seat in the U.S. House of Representatives across these elections. But still women are not taking advantage of political opportunities to the same extent as men.

It is the absence of women candidates that stands out as the significant gender feature of primary elections in the contemporary era, which is not a dramatically new finding. More distinctive is my conclusion that those women who have run have not necessarily had a more difficult time as candidates. Most often when a woman has entered an open seat primary, the most likely contests for ultimate victory for nonincumbents, she has usually been the only candidate of her sex in the race; she is more likely to win than her male opponents, and have equally as large margins of victory. Victorious female open seat primary candidates are not more likely to win primaries in districts ultimately unwinnable for their party in the general elections.

The importance of the analyses of this chapter lies in its in-depth longitudinal investigation of primary contests crucial in the legislative recruitment process, rather than in grouping all types of primaries together in an analysis of the difficulty of this stage of the process for women compared to men. An additional significant aspect of the research design used here is the consideration of the partisan nature of the districts having open seat primary elections in the contemporary era; not all open seats are equally opportune situations for would-be members of the U.S. House. I have investigated two aspects of the primary process for women candidates: presence and performance, and within both the effect of prior office-holding experience.

In terms of women actually running in these open seat primaries, two findings reinforce what we have learned from other studies that have focused on other facets of women's campaign experiences. First, women have tended not to run; the majority of these primary elections had no female contenders. When they have run, Democratic women have made a more expansive effort than Republican women, with the 2010 election being an exception. Even though more of the open seats were favorable to the GOP than to the Democratic Party during this time period, Republican female partisans have not taken advantage of positive opportunities for newcomers, contributing to the growing partisan gap in female representation in the U.S. House. However, the South did not stand out as a negative factor in their presence or performance as has been suggested in other studies.

On a second dimension, however, women who did run exhibited a strategic nature to their candidacies. Democratic female candidates increased their presence substantially as districts became more favorable to their party in the general election. Republican women were slightly less strategic, running in competitive districts to a slightly greater degree than in districts safe for their party but substantially more so than in districts rated as safe for the Democratic Party. This strategic nature has meant that women candidates had few free rides in their primaries; rather, they tended to face multiple opponents but not to a greater extent than male candidates. Those multiple opponents typically were male candidates. If a woman ran, she tended to be the only female in the primary race.

The majority of open seat primary candidates during this period were not experienced officeholders but gender differences were large regarding previous office-holding experience. Female contenders were more likely in both parties to have already won an elective office. In addition, prior office-holding experience was especially important to women's success running in districts where their chances of ultimate victory were feasible. This finding provides some empirical evidence of female candidates overall being "better" than their male counterparts.

An additional important finding of this analysis centers on the victory rates of male and female primary contenders. Female candidates tended to outperform male candidates, on average receiving a higher percentage of the vote across district competitive types. They also tended to have higher success rates, winning more often than their male counterparts, and to have won with larger average margins of victory among Democrats and equal average margins of victory among Republicans.

As Richard Matland (1993) has described it, for women to get elected to parliaments "they need to pass three crucial barriers: first they need to select themselves; second they need to be selected as candidates by the parties; and third they need to be selected by the voters." In the U.S. electoral process, parties and voters come together in the primary selection stage to choose candidates for the general election stage. Much of the research on women's entrance into and progression through the legislative recruitment process in the United States has principally, although not exclusively, focused on the candidacy phase overall of this multistage process with little distinction between the primary and general election candidacy stages.

This chapter's research questions have centered on the crucial step from aspiration to candidacy, highlighting that all opportunities are not equal. Research on this stage of the process can be sharpened even further in future studies. Elements of that research should include more intensive studies of what happens when a member of Congress announces he or she will not seek reelection or when redistricting opens up new seats. Recall the entrance announcement of Gloria Negrete McLeod that introduced this chapter.

To what extent and in what ways do gendered aspects appear in the resulting political tumult as the media speculate about the advantages and disadvantages of potential contenders and party campaign officials consider who has the personal, professional, and financial resources to win while ambitious self-starters tout their distinctive credentials either as experienced officeholders or as athletes, actors, or astronauts, to borrow from David Canon's work on political ambition (1990), or who advocate transforming their business acumen into political leadership?

Why do some local leaders decide to opt in and others decide to opt out and what does that tell us about men's and women's political ambitions? Crossing that crucial threshold from aspiration to candidacy is a major step, perhaps *the* major hurdle for women, and studies of the politics of women's ambition more generally and their presence and experience in primary contests, where the chances of ultimate victory are greatest, will contribute substantially to knowledge of the recruitment process and quests for equal political leadership.

From a gendered perspective, what I have found in this investigation of the primary stage of the campaign process is that women, especially Republican women, continue to fail to take advantage of opportune situations; they lag way behind men. When they do enter, although gendered moments still get media attention along the campaign trail, systematic analysis finds few gender differences and those that are present are often to women's advantage. Finally, there is little evidence that primary campaigns are uniquely difficult for female candidates. Chapter 4 continues an analysis along the campaign trail, moving to the general election stage of the process.

FOUR

Winning in November

Men's and Women's Performance in General Elections for the U.S. House

Running for elective office is one thing, winning office is another. In contrast to the conventional wisdom ideas about women's candidacies that stimulated the research of my book *A Woman's Place Is in the House*, contemporary research now suggests that a candidate's sex has little effect on his or her chances of winning office (Palmer and Simon 2008, 129). "When women run, women win," the oft-quoted research line from Seltzer, Newman, and Leighton's *Sex as a Variable* (1997), has become the common refrain about contemporary female candidacies. *A Woman's Place* similarly concluded that "women have kept pace with their male counterparts, occasionally falling behind as a group and sometimes surpassing the men. When women have run, women have done as well as men is the description that best captures women's campaign experiences in the contemporary era" (Burrell 1994, 145). But that is not necessarily the end of the gendered story. Scholars have continued to pose gendered questions about campaign experiences asking, among other things, whether women candidates continue to face a "tougher road" (Fiber and Fox 2005), are still "outsiders" in American politics (Hoffman, Palmer, and Gaddie 2001), remain as novelties (Palmer and Simon 2008, 147), and find some districts more "friendly" toward female candidates than others (Palmer and Simon 2008).

Further, scholars have proposed that reported gender-neutral results may actually be the consequence of gendered processes in which women have had to be better than male candidates in order to achieve at the same rate, as chapter 3 explored. For example, female candidates have seemingly had to expend more resources to achieve the same rate of success as male candidates (e.g., Herrick 1996) and face a more complex electoral environment (Lawless and Pearson 2008; Palmer and Simon 2008). Gender, too, it has been suggested, matters when it comes to the retention of congressional incumbents. For example, Neil Berch has shown that at least in the 1996 and 1998 elections, women incumbents were more likely than their male colleagues to face well-funded challengers (2004). Palmer and Simon (2008), too, have suggested the road to reelection has been more complex for female incumbents with more primary opponents and facing a larger pool of oppositional party contenders in primaries. They were less likely to get a "free ride." Thus, political questions continue apace regarding men and women seeking public office in the United States at the general election stage as well as the primary stage.

This chapter begins with an analysis of women's and men's performance in general elections of the campaign process with an overview of data regarding vote totals and vote percentages. In *A Woman's Place*, the major question was posed in terms of whether the nomination of a woman candidate depressed a party's votes, enhanced its position at the polls, or made no difference in outcomes in elections from 1972 through 1992. This chapter makes gender comparisons in more recent elections. How well have women done in obtaining votes and winning within a variety of contexts? Have they kept pace with male candidates running in similar situations, outpaced them, or fallen behind? Is there any reason to suspect that female candidates would not have proceeded in tandem with their male colleagues in contemporary elections, especially as their candidacies at the national level have become more commonplace (rather than continuing to be novelties)? Or, as their presence has expanded, have they entered tougher campaigns and more difficult election terrains? By this question, I mean a greater number of more competitive contests as Democrats have developed "Red to Blue" campaigns and Republicans have sought "Young Gun" candidates to mount challenges in traditionally safe districts for the opposite party that may have affected outcomes, making for expensive and combative elections. What effect have these party organizational moves had on women's candidacies? Chapter 6 explores this latter question more fully from a party organizational perspective.

As described in chapter 2, female candidates have campaigned in a variety of election-related environmental contexts since 1992. Commentary sometimes suggested they would have a difficult time in particular election cycles such as the "war years" of 2002 and 2004, and that in other cycles media reports suggested that they would be advantaged and even perceived to be running the most competitive races as challengers, for example in 2006 and 2008 among Democratic candidates and 2010 in Republican contests. Here I assess empirically how well they have fared as open seat candidates, as incumbent challengers, and as incumbents, and as Democrats and as Republicans, when running as nominees for the U.S. House from 1994 through 2010, and take note of the environments of different campaign seasons.

Obtaining Votes

Table 4.1 compares the vote-getting ability of male and female nominees in major party contested races broken down by candidate status in each of the election cycles. The overall differences between the sexes were minimal, supporting Fox's conclusion based on data from the 2006 and 2008 elections that "there is no widespread voter bias against women candidates" (2010, 194). Indeed, the summary data presented at the end of the table show female Democratic candidates in all status categories slightly outpacing their male counterparts in the acquisition of votes. Female Republican candidates, on the other hand, slightly trailed their male counterparts.

From the perspective of individual election cycles some partisan differences were present in the relative performances of the two sexes. Democratic women in 25 of the 27 status categories obtained a higher percentage of the vote than Democratic male candidates in similar types of races. At the same time, GOP women fared worse than their male counterparts in 21 of the 27 pairings. In some situations the differences were miniscule when comparing the percentage of the vote Republican male candidates and Republican female candidates obtained. Given the small numbers of Republican women, the mean vote can be thrown off by the presence of an outlying case so the differences should not be overstated.

Since we are dealing with the entire universe of election races and not trying to generalize from a random sample to the population, tests of statistical significance are not particularly relevant, although measures of the strength of relationships remain informative. Thus, eta coefficients and the significance levels of the comparisons are included in table 4.1 as a measure of the strength of relationships. They show the relatively low to very low substantive correlation between sex and votes within the various candidate status groups across the election years with a few exceptions, such as the

TABLE 4.1. Mean Percentage of the Vote, by Sex, Party, and Candidate Status, 1994–2010

Candidate Status	Democrats		Republicans	
	Men	Women	Men	Women
1994				
Challenged Incumbents	60.1 (180)	59.5 (31) (.02)	67.6 (117)	66.9 (8) (.02)
Challengers	30.2 (98)	32.3 (27) (.13)	38.8 (187)	36.4 (25) (.07)
Open Seats	43.7 (42)	50.0 (10) (.25)	53.3 (46)	50.5 (6) (.09)
1996				
Challenged Incumbents	66.0 (133)	68.2 (27) (.09)	60.6 (192)	57.1 (12) (.08)
Challengers	36.0 (162)	38.6 (42) (.12)	29.8 (138)	32.3 (23) (.09)
Open Seats	49.0 (42)	46.8 (9) (.07)	48.0 (46)	46.0 (5) (.05)
1998				
Challenged Incumbents	67.1 (120)	68.0 (29) (.03)	62.6 (143)	59.4 (13) (.12)
Challengers	34.5 (124)	36.7 (31) (.13)	31.3 (127)	26.8 (24) (.16)
Open Seats	51.2 (24)	52.4 (11) (.05)	44.0 (30)	49.2 (5) (.14)
2000				
Challenged Incumbents	67.2 (132)	68.6 (35) (.06)	62.9 (154)	61.2 (14) (.07)
Challengers	33.0 (136)	37.4 (33) (.25)**	29.8 (146)	24.4 (22) (.18)*
Open Seats	42.3 (23)	44.6 (11) (.10)	53.5 (29)	46.0 (5) (.19)
2002				
Challenged Incumbents	66.9 (117)	66.8 (34) (.04)	66.7 (136)	62.6 (14) (.15)
Challengers	31.6 (117)	33.0 (31) (.08)	30.7 (133)	32.7 (21) (.07)
Open Seats	45.0 (37)	46.5 (9) (.06)	53.6 (37)	48.3 (9) (.19)
2004				
Challenged Incumbents	67.0 (129)	68.8 (30) (.08)	63.6 (158)	62.7 (18) (.01)
Challengers	33.6 (132)	37.4 (42) (.23)**	30.0 (138)	29.6 (24) (.02)
Open Seats	46.6 (22)	48.0 (10) (.07)	53.3 (23)	43.9 (9) (.33)

TABLE 4.1.—*Continued*

	Democrats		Republicans	
Candidate Status	Men	Women	Men	Women
2006				
Challenged Incumbents	69.4 (109)	70.0 (33) (.03)	59.5 (177)	57.0 (23) (.11)
Challengers	38.7 (163)	40.1 (40) (.07)	29.0 (127)	28.5(12) (.02)
Open Seats	53.7 (21)	53.4 (12) (.01)	43.4 (26)	43.3 (7) (.00)
2008				
Challenged Incumbents	67.1 (144)	71.7 (43) (.20)**	60.5 (140)	58.4 (17) (.06)
Challengers	37.2 (120)	40.4 (35) (.18)*	29.8 (170)	31.0 (19) (.04)
Open Seats	48.2 (26)	51.2 (10) (.12)	47.9 (34)	46.5 (2) (.03)
2010				
Challenged Incumbents	57.5 (176)	62.6 (53) (.18)**	66.0 (119)	65.2 (15) (.03)
Challengers	31.3 (107)	32.9 (27) (.09)	39.1 (199)	37.2 (30) (.05)
Open Seats	38.9 (32)	48.7 (9) (.31)*	55.2 (39)	60.1 (2) (.08)
Total				
Challenged Incumbents	64.8 (1,240)	67.0 (315) (.08)***	63.0 (1,336)	60.8 (134) (.08)**
Challengers	34.3 (1,159)	36.8 (308) (.13)***	32.6 (1,365)	31.4 (200) (.03)
Open Seats	46.1 (269)	49.2 (91) (.11)*	50.5 (310)	47.1 (50) (.09)

Source: Data compiled by the author.
*$p \leq .05$; **$p \leq .01$; ***$p \leq .001$.

comparison between Democratic male and female open seat contenders in 2010.

The data also show that in terms of acquiring votes, the "war years" of 2002 and 2004 were no different from the other election years. No evidence exists that the context of those elections hurt the women who made it to the general election stage of the campaign process, at least at the aggregate level in obtaining votes. In the Democratic-friendly years of 2006 and 2008, female Democratic candidates tended to slightly outpace their male counterparts and substantially outperformed their Republican counterparts (as did male Democrats) in attracting votes. The big difference in the Republican year of 1994 was between the parties and not between the sexes except for the 6.3 percent vote advantage the subcategory of female Democratic open seat contenders had over male Democratic open seat contenders.

These data also provide additional evidence that what gender problems remain have been centered within the Republican Party, in keeping with Palmer and Simon's (2008) and Elder's (2008) analyses. Although it might be considered a "year of Republican women" in some sense, the Republican female nominees in 2010 did not outpace their male counterparts in collecting votes, with the exception of the two female open seat nominees. In 2010, Republican challenged female incumbents and incumbent female challengers fared slightly worse than their male counterparts. However, all three status groups did outpace their female Democratic counterparts.

General Election Success Rates

With a few exceptions during this period, male and female incumbents were equally overwhelmingly successful in getting reelected and male and female challengers were equally overwhelmingly unsuccessful in winning a seat, as table 4.2 illustrates. Exceptions among incumbents involved female Democratic incumbents' lower success rate in 1994, the "year of the angry white male," when eight incumbents including six of the Democrats of the "year of the woman" class lost, and 2010, when once again a substantial subset of these female Democratic incumbents were swept away in the Republican resurgence as were Democratic male incumbents, who fared particularly badly. In 2006, the Democratic tide swept away four of the 23 Republican female incumbents. Eighteen Republican male incumbents also lost their reelection bids that year, reducing their success rate relative to other years in this time period, but because of their much greater numbers those defeats had less effect on their overall success rate. Democratic male incumbents were particularly hard hit in 2010 when only 77 percent of those running for reelection beat their Republican challenger. Male and female Republican challengers were equally successful that year. It was the best year for Republican incumbent challengers during this period.

Turning attention to the results of the open seat races, gender appears as a factor in a contradictory fashion from that found in the investigation of male and female success rates in open seat *primaries* as reported in chapter 3. Remember that in the primaries both Democratic and Republican female contenders at all competitive levels had higher victory rates than their male counterparts. At the general election stage, we find that in most of the elections during the Republican years, Republican open seat nominees did better, as might be expected, than Democratic nominees in winning their contests and the converse, not unexpectedly, occurs in Democratic resurgent years. But throughout this time period, female nominees in both parties have had lower win rates than their male counterparts. GOP female open seat nominees have almost consistently obtained smaller vote percentages and won at lower rates than their male counterparts through this time period, with the exception of the victories of both Republican female open seat nominees, Jaime Herrera in Washington state and Diane Black in Tennessee, in 2010.

A puzzle, however, emerges as we inspect the success rates of male and female open seat nominees within the Democratic Party. Whereas Democratic female open seat nominees outpaced their male counterparts in obtaining votes in six of the nine election cycles, they had a lower success rate in actually winning a seat in the House in six of the election cycles. In some elections the rate was substantially lower. Overall, 31 of the 92 Democratic female open seat nominees won, a 34 percent success rate compared with 117 of the 275 Democratic male open seat nominees, a 43 percent success rate. What accounts for this paradox of Democratic female nominees in these elections acquiring more votes but winning less often than their male colleagues? The small numbers of female open seat nominees in most of these years means that one more victory in some elections would have substantially closed the gap. Perhaps, too, a few very strong female vote-getters in safe seats might disproportionately have affected some of the vote percentage comparisons, significantly heightening the overall mean percentage of these female candidates' votes as a group but not necessarily translating into greater numbers of victories. Thus, one should be cautious in making generalizations and theorizing about the lower success of Democratic women open seat nominees. But it is a situation that deserves inspection and interpretation.

Potentially this puzzle relates to the type of districts in which male and female Democrats were nominated. The question involves both comparative presence and comparative vote-getting ability across district types based on competitiveness. All of the female candidates in open seat races safe for their party won a seat in the House during this time period, so it cannot be that that subgroup had a lower success rate than their male counterparts. No Democratic open seat candidates, male or female, won a seat in the U.S. House in a safe Republican district.

A comparison of the distribution of Democratic male and female open

TABLE 4.2. General Election Success Rate by Party, Race, and Sex, 1994–2010

Candidate Status	Democrats (# Running/# Winning)		Republicans (# Running/# Winning)	
	Men	Women	Men	Women
1994				
Unopposed Incumbents	11	3	0	2
Challenger Incumbents	155/180	23/31	117/117	8/8
	(86%)	(74%)	(100%)	(100%)
Challengers	0/95	0/27	30/187	3/25
	(0%)	(0%)	(16%)	(12%)
Open Seats	10/42	4/10	35/46	3/6
	(24%)	(40%)	(76%)	(50%)
1996				
Unopposed Incumbents	8	—	7	2
Challenger Incumbents	130/133	27/27	175/192	11/12
	(98%)	(100%)	(91%)	(92%)
Challengers	13/161	5/42	2/139	1/23
	(8%)	(12%)	(1%)	(4%)
Open Seats	21/43	3/9	27/47	2/5
	(49%)	(33%)	(57%)	(40%)
1998				
Unopposed Incumbents	34	5	53	2
Challenger Incumbents	119/120	29/29	139/144	13/13
	(99%)	(100%)	(97%)	(100%)
Challengers	5/124	0/31	1/124	0/24
	(4%)	(0%)	(1%)	(0%)
Open Seats	13/24	5/11	15/30	2/5
	(54%)	(45%)	(50%)	(40%)
2000				
Unopposed Incumbents	30	2	28	1
Challenged Incumbents	131/133	35/35	150/154	14/14
	(99%)	(100%)	(97%)	(100%)
Challengers	3/130	2/33	1/139	0/22
	(1%)	(3%)	(1%)	(0%)
Open Seats	7/23	1/11	23/29	3/5
	(30%)	(17%)	(79%)	(60%)
2002				
Unopposed Incumbents	32	4	42	2
Challenged Incumbents	119/123	33/34	140/142	14/15
	(97%)	(97%)	(99%)	(93%)
Challengers	1/114	0/31	0/127	1/21
	(1%)	(0%)	(0%)	(5%)
Open Seats	14/37	2/9	26/35	4/9
	(37%)	(22%)	(74%)	(44%)

TABLE 4.2.—*Continued*

	Democrats (# Running/# Winning)		Republicans (# Running/# Winning)	
Candidate Status	Men	Women	Men	Women
2004				
Unopposed Incumbents	21	7	32	2
Challenged Incumbents	126/131	30/30	158/160	18/18
	(96%)	(100%)	(99%)	(100%)
Challengers	1/132	1/42	3/136	0/24
	(1%)	(2%)	(2%)	(0%)
Open Seats	18/27	4/10	18/27	3/9
	(67%)	(40%)	(67%)	(33%)
2006				
Unopposed Incumbents	40	9	11	—
Challenged Incumbents	83/83	32/32	160/178	19/23
	(100%)	(100%)	(90%)	(83%)
Challengers	21/163	3/40	0/117	0/12
	(13%)	(8%)	(0%)	(0%)
Open Seats	15/21	5/12	11/26	2/7
	(71%)	(42%)	(42%)	(29%)
2008				
Unopposed Incumbents	35	7	13	—
Challenged Incumbents	140/144	42/434	127/140	15/17
	(97%)	(98%)	(91%)	(88%)
Challengers	10/120	4/35	4/170	1/19
	(8%)	(11%)	(2%)	(5%)
Open Seats	15/26	4/10	16/32	1/2
	(58%)	(40%)	(50%)	(50%)
2010				
Unopposed Incumbents	5	1	24	—
Challenged Incumbents	135/176	43/53	117/119	15/15
	(77%)	(81%)	(98%)	(100%)
Challengers	1/107	1/27	44/199	7/30
	(1%)	(4%)	(22%)	(23%)
Open Seats	4/32	2/9	33/39	2/2
	(13%)	(22%)	(85%)	(100%)
Total				
Unopposed Incumbents	216	38	242	11
Challenged Incumbents	1,162/1,240	295/316	1,274/1.336	126/134
	(94%)	(93%)	(95%)	(94%)
Challengers	53/1,106	16/308	85/1.365	13/200
	(5%)	(5%)	(6%)	(7%)
Open Seats	108/271	33/93	206/314	22/50
	(40%)	(35%)	(66%)	(44%)

Source: Data compiled by the author.

seat nominees across the categories of district competitiveness constructed in chapter 3 shows minimal differences: 19 percent of the female nominees ran in safe Democratic districts compared with 15 percent of the male nominees; 55 percent of the male nominees and 54 percent of the female nominees were in competitive districts; and 30 percent of the male nominees and 27 percent of the female nominees were running in safe Republican districts. Therefore, disparity in the types of context in which they were nominated would not seem to account for the lower success rates of the Democratic female open seat nominees.

Differences in success rates were confined to the competitive districts. Democratic male nominees were successful in 43 percent of the competitive districts compared with 34 percent of the Democratic female nominees. Their mean percentage of the vote was 47.7, while that of the female Democratic nominees in the competitive districts was 46.5, just marginally lower. In the competitive districts, eight of the 42 Democratic female nominees lost their race by a small margin, obtaining at least 47% of the vote (19%); among the 121 Democratic male nominees in competitive districts, 16 lost while obtaining at least 47% of the vote (13%). The categorization of districts as competitive covered a wide span of actual competitiveness from leaning Republican to toss-up districts to leaning Democratic districts. But the lower success rate for the Democratic women does not appear to be a result of running in more difficult competitive districts. If one compares the percentage of the vote the Republican presidential candidate received in the most immediate preceding election in these districts, we find that the mean percentage of the vote for the districts with a female Democratic nominee was 45 percent with a standard deviation of 9 points and for the male candidates it was 44 percent with a similar standard deviation also of 9 points, virtually no difference.

Thus, we have a small set of cases over nine election cycles accounting for what seems to be a substantial gender difference in success rates, 34 percent for Democratic female open seat nominees and 43 percent for Democratic male open seat nominees, suggesting greater vulnerability for female nominees.[1] Party financial support for these candidates is investigated in chapter 6 to determine its contribution to the lower success rate.

An inspection of some of the races during this time frame provides some helpful clues for understanding this discrepancy between votes obtained and wins between male and female Democratic Party open seat nominees. In 2006, as an illustration, the Democratic male and female open seat nominees were virtually tied in the average percentage of the vote they received while 71 percent of the men (15 of 21) were victorious compared with only

42 percent of the women (5 of 12 nominees). In 2008, the Democratic women open seat general election contenders slightly outpaced their male colleagues, obtaining an average of 51.2 percent of the vote compared with 48.2 percent for the men. At the same time, 58 percent of the men (15 of 26) were successful compared with 40 percent of the women (4 of 10).

A close look at all of the candidates and the percentage of the vote they obtained in these two elections provides a clue about this discrepancy. The top vote-getter in each election was an African American woman running in an overwhelming safe district—Yvette Clark in New York's 11th district (formerly Shirley Chisholm's district) in 2006 and Marcia Fudge in Ohio's 11th district in 2008. Clark obtained 89.7 percent of the vote in the general election and Fudge, who was chosen by the local Democratic organization to replace Rep. Stephanie Tubbs Jones on the ballot after Jones's unexpected death in August 2008, won with 85 percent of the vote. The highest vote-getter among the men was Albio Sires in 2006 who won the 13th district of New Jersey with 77.5 percent of the vote. Thus, the intersection of race and women winning primaries in these majority-minority districts that are distinctly uncompetitive in the general election helps to understand the higher acquisition of votes among Democratic female candidates. In these two elections, two African American men were also open seat candidates, Henry Johnson in Georgia's 4th district who beat incumbent Cynthia McKinney in the 2006 primary and went on to win in November with 75.3 percent of the vote, and Keith Ellison who won Minnesota's 5th district with 55.6 percent of the vote, becoming the first Muslim elected to the U.S. House. His religion might have kept him from achieving a higher vote total in his first election bid in the safe Minneapolis Democratic district.

Women of color have had disproportionate success in obtaining seats in the U.S. House in the contemporary period. As Elder has noted, over the past 20 years minority women have significantly increased as a share of the women in the House, almost exclusively as members of the Democratic Party. The examples of Yvette Clark and Marcia Fudge, with their extraordinary vote-getting ability in majority-minority districts, suggest the presence of such female candidates in raising the vote shares of female Democratic candidates, but their small numbers cannot overcome the losing efforts of the other female candidates. Indeed, the standard deviation of votes obtained in the 2006 general election by Democratic female open seat candidates was greater than that for their male counterparts (16 points to 11 points). In the 2008 election the difference was 14 points for the female candidates to 10 points for the male candidates. In 2010, minority women were the only Democratic female victors in open seat races. The contribution of minority female candidates in the Democratic Party Caucus in the U.S. House is substantial.

Incumbent Challengers

Turning attention to the "success" rates of incumbent challengers during this time period, male and female challengers have had similarly abysmal experiences in U.S. House races as tables 4.1 and 4.2 illustrate. In only a few election cycles have any subgroups had as much as a 10 percent election rate—male and female Republican challengers in 1994, male Democrats in 2006, female Democrats in 2008, and Republican male and female challengers in 2010. They have tended on average not to manage as much as 40 percent of the vote. Indeed, in this whole time period of nine election cycles and 4,288 general election contests for the U.S. House, only thirteen Republican women have beaten an incumbent, over half of those victories coming in 2010. In five of those 13 races, they defeated Democratic women. The only two wins, prior to 2010, over Democratic male incumbents were state representative Anne Northup's victory in 1996 over Michael Ward in Kentucky's 3rd district, a 1 point win, 50 to 49 percent, and Helen Chenowith's win in Idaho in 1994 over Larry LaRocco, beating him by 10 percentage points (55% to 45%). In 2010, six Republican female incumbent challengers defeated Democratic men and one, Kristi Noem, defeated a Democratic female incumbent, Stephanie Herseth Sandlin, in South Dakota's at-large district.

Political watchers in South Dakota were reported to have described the campaign between Noem and Herseth Sandlin as the "Battle of the Babes" (Rucker 2010). It vividly illustrates aspects of contemporary campaigns of female candidates and changes in women's candidacies and presentations. Both candidates were in their late 30s, moms with young children whom they featured in their campaign advertisements, a big change from earlier messages that female candidates tended to project. They were described as "the two youthful, attractive women"; Herseth Sandlin was described as "perky" (Rucker 2010). Noem, the challenger, was an experienced campaigner, having held state legislative office. Sarah Palin who endorsed her candidacy anointed her a "mama grizzly." Herseth Sandlin also became referred to as the "Democrats' own 'mama grizzly' straight out of the heartland." Herseth Sandlin charged Noem as being "South Dakota's Sarah Palin," while Noem lashed out at Herseth Sandlin as having voted for Nancy Pelosi to be Speaker of the House (Rucker 2010). The campaign was also characterized as a "catfight" (Hunt 2010). Both candidates raised over $2 million. In addition, the Republicans spent over $900,000 independently in support of Noem and against Herseth Sandlin while the Democrats spent approximately $500,000 in independent ads on Herseth Sandlin's behalf. Noem ended up winning 48 percent to 46 percent.

Turning to female Democratic challenger victories overall in the elections from 1994 through 2010, 14 Democratic women beat Republican male incumbents and one defeated a Republican female incumbent; in 2008 Betsy Markey defeated Marilyn Musgrave in Colorado's 4th district, only to lose her seat to a Republican male contender in 2010. The most famous, or perhaps infamous, victory of a Democratic female challenger over a male Republican incumbent occurred in 1996 when Loretta Sanchez beat Robert "B-1 bomber" Dornan in California's 46th district by a vote of 46 percent to 45 percent. Rep. Dornan, an extreme conservative member of the House, had run in the Republican primary for president that year. Loretta Sanchez had never held public office although she had been a candidate for the Anaheim City Council in 1994. After her victory Dornan filed a formal challenge to her election to the U.S. House. The House did not sustain her victory until early 1998 although she took her seat and performed as a representative in the interim period.

Loretta Sanchez's campaign violated all of the textbook recommendations on how to run a successful contemporary election and has become a distinctive case study of a different campaign approach. She "maintained a quiet, grassroots crusade that gambled on the then-unproven power of cable advertising" (Burton and Shea 2002, 89). She took advantage of the changing demographics of the district, focusing on motivating the Latino vote and Dornan's inattention to the district while undertaking a national campaign for the presidency in the Republican primary. She resisted engaging him in nasty negative exchanges until the end of the campaign season, "flying under the radar" for much of it to lull Dornan into a sense of complacency. She built "message frequency" in her campaign tactics "through grassroots tactics, cable ads, and a direct mail onslaught" (Burton and Shea 2002, 105). She was also fortunate in that Rep. Dornan had depleted his campaign war chest in his presidential quest. Although national political groups and the Democratic campaign committees initially ignored her campaign, by the fall her polls showed her within striking distance and support was forthcoming from EMILY's List and the Democratic Congressional Campaign Committee (DCCC), the center of House Democratic efforts to expand its numbers in the national legislature. (Chapter 6 provides a more detailed description of the DCCC and its Republican counterpart, the National Republican Congressional Committee [NRCC].)

Loretta Sanchez raised and spent more than Rep. Dornan, unusual for a challenger unless one is very wealthy and self-funds his or her campaign. (Sanchez did loan her campaign $120,500.) She raised $829,816 and reported spending $818,626 while Rep. Dornan raised $748,336 and spent $741,984. Interestingly, the sources of their campaign funds differed rather substantially. One might have expected, given the grassroots nature of her campaign and the late entry of national groups to her cause, that Loretta Sanchez would have raised most of her money in individual contributions whereas Rep. Dornan, with his national conservative network, would have relied to a much greater extent on PAC contributions. Both candidates received a majority of their funds from individual contributors, but for Rep. Dornan they were a much larger portion of his campaign finances—$691,915 to $446,057 for Sanchez. Sanchez raised $354,439 in PAC contributions compared with only $44,472 for Rep. Dornan.

Incumbency and Reelection: A Closer Look

Turning attention back to incumbents, women running for reelection have kept pace with their male counterparts. Both sexes have tended overwhelmingly to win reelection, Democrats and Republicans, with the two exceptions of Democratic female incumbents in 1994 and female Republican incumbents in 2006, as table 4.2 shows. Yet, other scholars have suggested these victories have not been the result of similar campaign experiences. As noted at the beginning of this chapter, Palmer and Simon's research has suggested that the "road to re-election may be more perilous for women" (2008, 127). Although male and female incumbents win reelection at equal rates, women running for reelection face a more competitive environment, they have contended. In their analysis of contests from 1956 through 2006, they concluded: "Female incumbents face more competition. They foster more competition in the opposition party's primary. They are less likely to face no competition in the general election. They are also less likely to get a 'free pass' facing no opposition in the primary and general election. In fact, female incumbents with the least electoral security, those from marginal districts, always face competition" (2008, 159). At the same time, 2 percent of male incumbents from marginal districts got a free pass over the course of this time frame, which is a rather minor difference from the experience of female incumbents. Palmer and Simon did not present trends over time in their analysis or assessment of these factors suggesting female incumbent vulnerability. Data were presented for the whole set of candidates from 1956 through 2006.

One might, however, approach a road to reelection analysis in the more contemporary years for women incumbents from a quite different theoretical perspective. Rather than "perilous," we might conceive of female incumbents as being in a "powerful" position as they contemplate reelection and as potential opponents assess challenging them, except perhaps in the two "war year" elections of 2002 and 2004. Consider what we might call the "Pelosi effect" in which women incumbents are seen as having become powerful actors in Congress. Add to that what we could call the "EMILY's List effect," which suggests that at least a subset of female incumbents (pro-choice Democrats) can call upon this group's deep financial network for monetary support and campaign workers and advisors, scaring off would-be opponents. Further, recent research has also shown that female members of Congress are better at "bringing home the pork," or obtaining earmarks for their districts (Anzia and Berry 2011), although this characteristic of female House membership has not become widely reported in the news media or "celebrated" among political pundits.

Thus, moving beyond outcome data to consider the reelection process more fully I analyze whether contemporary female incumbents have been in a more vulnerable position or a more advantageous position than male incumbents. Factors making for a more uncertain process for women incumbents seeking reelection in Palmer and Simon's analysis included the degree to which opponents in their own party's primary challenged them, they faced a major party opponent in the general election, or had a "free pass" of facing no opposition in both the primary and general elections. Chapter 3 has shown very small gender differences in facing a challenger in a primary in contemporary elections.

Examining competition at the general election stage, Palmer and Simon report, from the longer historical perspective of elections from 1956 through 2006, that 16.2 percent of male incumbents and 9.8 percent of female incumbents had no major party opponent in the general election. In the nine elections of the contemporary era, 14 percent of incumbents did not have a major party opponent in the general election. Fifteen percent of male incumbents and 10 percent of female incumbents had no major party opponent in the general election. The percentages for the two sexes were similar within both parties.[2]

Differences varied across the contexts with no trend toward equality or advantage between the sexes. In some election cycles the difference was minor and in others it was more substantial. For example, Democratic female incumbents in the Democratic resurgence elections of 2006 and 2008, even with the elements of strength that were mentioned above, were 9 percent less likely not to have an opponent in the general election than male Democratic incumbents. No Republican female incumbent was unopposed in the general election in these years. Nor were any of them in that position in the Republican resurgence of 2010. Overall, however, the differences between male and female incumbents having to face a major party opponent were not dramatic. The female incumbents were not substantially disadvantaged by having to compete to a greater extent in a more complex environment.

To this point I have presented data showing parity in election results for male and female incumbents in the contemporary era and for parity in one of the three internal components of competition along the road to reelection, the presence of a primary challenge, and near parity in the second component of no major party opponent. But who gets a "free pass," having no primary opponent and no major party general election challenger? For the Palmer and Simon historical period of 1956–2006, 6.6 percent of female incumbents had a free pass compared with 12 percent of male incumbents. Although the percentages are small for both groups with a male advantage, these data covering 40 years do not indicate whether there is a trend toward parity in getting a free pass.

Data from the elections of 1994 through 2010 show that female incumbents continue to be less likely to enjoy the luxury of getting a free pass of having no opponent through both stages of the campaign process. The percentages differ little from that of Palmer and Simon's longer time period and my inclusion of even more recent elections; 12 percent of male incumbents and 8 percent of female incumbents got "free passes" in elections from 1994 through 2010. Virtually no partisan difference existed between the sexes. Six percent of female Republican incumbents had a free pass as did 7 percent of female Democratic incumbents. Twelve percent of both Democratic and Republican male incumbents had a free pass. Substantively, these are minimal differences.

Further, as suggested in earlier analyses, the small number of Republican female incumbents means that a one or two person increase could make a substantial hike in the percentage of "free passes." Thus, I would conclude that the reelection environment in contemporary campaigns is only minimally more "perilous" for female incumbents; differences in facing primary opponents, having general election challengers, and not facing any opposition at either stage of the reelection process are minor between the sexes but for each factor female candidates are slightly more challenged than their male colleagues. They have not quite reached parity, but neither are they particularly disadvantaged.

Summary

Consider the dynamics of the competitive environment through the reelection process for incumbents within the context of ultimate equally high reelection rates for both sexes, 93 percent for female and 94 percent for male incumbents. The dynamics of the competitive electoral environment to reach that point was also one of near parity between the sexes. The analyses undertaken for this chapter show first that approximately three-quarters of both sexes have not been primaried, that is, did not face a challenge from a fellow partisan to their reelection, including 74 percent of the female incumbents and 76 percent of the male incumbents. Second, only 1 percent of each sex lost a primary bid for reelection. Moving on to the general election stage, only a small minority had the pleasure of no major party opposition in the general election; male incumbents were slightly advantaged (15%) over female incumbents in this regard (10%). Through the whole electoral process of these nine elections, a total of 12 percent of the male and 7 percent of the female incumbents got a "free pass."

Women vs. Women Races

Women vs. women contests for U.S. House seats have been an uncommon occurrence historically. Palmer and Simon report that such contests were most uncommon prior to 1972. From 1972 through 2006 the data they present indicate that there was no "slow and steady increase in these numbers. Only one percent of all general election contests during this time were contests between Republican and Democratic female candidates" (2008, 130).

In the elections from 1994 through 2010, there is a slight uptick in women vs. women general election contests to 2 percent, 90 of the 3,825 general elections (table 4.3). Thirteen, 4 percent, of the 335 general election open seats contests have been between Democratic and Republican women.

Given the much larger number of contests between an incumbent and a challenger, most women vs. women contests have involved a female challenger opposing a female incumbent (77 of the 90 contests). Since many more Democratic women have been incumbents during this time period, the number of Republican female challengers (n = 51) has been much larger than the number of Democratic women challenging Republican women incumbents (n = 28). However, if one takes into account the disproportionate opportunity structure afforded female Republicans to challenge female Democratic incumbents during this time period a different picture emerges. There were 356 Democratic female reelection attempts and only 121 Republican female reelection attempts between 1994 and 2010. The Democratic incumbents had a female opponent in 14 percent of their general election contests while female Republican incumbents had female Democratic challengers in 23 percent of their contests.

In only seven contests overall were the challengers in these contests victorious over the incumbent. Six Republican challengers were victorious and one Democrat was successful. In 2008, Democrat Betsy Markey defeated Republican Marilyn Musgrave, 56 percent to 44 percent, in Colorado's 4th district, the only contest in this time period in which a female Democrat beat a female Republican incumbent. In that favorable Democratic year, Republican Lynn Jenkins bested Democrat Nancy Boyda in Kansas's 2nd district 51 percent to 46 percent. Nancy Boyda had been one of the few challengers to upset an incumbent in 2006 in a district that substantially favored the other party. She refused help in her reelection bid from the Democratic Congressional Campaign Committee and from EMILY's List, while Lynn Jenkins had both party organizational support and the endorsement of the EMILY's List counterpart in the Republican Party, the WISH List. Boyda's independence from the national party and its presumed liberal reputation had been crucial in her upset bid in 2006, and she considered maintaining distance and a moderate voting record

TABLE 4.3. Women vs. Women General House Races, 1994–2010

Year	Democratic Incumbent	Republican Incumbent	Open Seat	Total
1994	9	3	0	12
1996	2	1	2	5
1998	8	2	2	12
2000	7	3	1	11
2002	5	3	3	11
2004	5	3	3	11
2006	2	5	1	8
2008	6	5	1	12
2010	7	3	0	9

Source: Center for American Women and Politics Fact Sheets, Rutgers University, http://www.cawp.rutgers.edu/.

essential to keeping her seat in 2008, but it was not quite enough to retain her seat.

In addition to the 2010 Noem versus Herseth Sandlin contest in South Dakota described earlier, one of the more intriguing woman vs. woman campaigns of this time period was the 2000 race in which state Representative Eleanor Jordan won the Democratic nomination to challenge Republican incumbent Anne Northup in Kentucky's 3rd district. Rep. Jordan was attempting to become the first African American elected to Congress from Kentucky. For a good portion of the campaign season the contest was considered to be highly competitive although ultimately Jordan made some mistakes that led to her losing by 9 points. Near the end of the campaign Mary Leonard of the *Boston Globe* characterized the race in the following way:

> Women candidates may well hold the keys to control of the US House, and the ferocious race here in the Bluegrass State between Anne Northup, a Republican, and Eleanor Jordan, a Democrat, is showing that this isn't your mother's election. . . . The airwaves crackle day and night with slashing ads. Millions of dollars have poured in from business, labor, environmental, and women's groups around the country. Northup, a two-term congresswoman, accuses Jordan of 'deceitful' tactics and of distorting her record. Jordan, an African-American state legislator, says Northup is using subtle racial slurs to malign her. . . . It is also a good example of a trend in this year's struggle for control of the House and Senate: Women are fierce and well-financed competitors in a large number of the country's hottest and nastiest races. (2000)

Eleanor Jordan had been a single mother in high school who had been on welfare but then obtained a college degree, ran a day care center, and became active in community and political affairs, leading to her election to the Kentucky General Assembly in 1996. The Democratic Congressional Campaign Committee endorsed her during the primary season, an unusual move for the party organization. She also had the support of EMILY's List. President Clinton campaigned for her. Both sides characterized the race as one of the nastiest in the country.

Congresswoman Northup was an example of the ability of female representatives to provide their districts with earmarks as suggested above about female representatives more generally (Anzi and Berry 2011). Having defeated a one-term Democratic incumbent in a long-time Democratic district in 1996 by just over 1,000 votes the House Republican leadership rewarded her with a seat on the powerful Appropriations Committee, and in the 2000 campaign she would take credit for bringing $450 million in aid home to Louisville, from money for bridge construction to a gorilla exhibit at the zoo (Leonard 2000). She lost her seat in the Democratic resurgence of 2006 and unsuccessfully attempted to get it back in 2008.

Summary

Although we would say that women vs. women races are not unheard of, they are more uncommon than common given the total number of elections and the total number of cases of female nominees. But we should expect them to increase as the number of women incumbents steadily climbs, and perhaps if the Republican Party acts on promises of recruiting more women and sees it to their advantage to promote women in the opportune situations of open seats, that too might stimulate a greater number of all-women general election campaigns. It is a potential worth watching.

The decline of gender distinctiveness in congressional elections is also evident in that women incumbents were not more likely to face female opponents than male incumbents. During this time period equal percentages of male and female incumbents (14%) faced a woman challenger in the general election. These findings do not refute a role model effect attached to women's victories. Certainly the steady incremental rise in the number of female U.S. representatives and their increasing prominence within the House leadership should have served as a positive factor in more women seeking seats in the House. But a stronger explanatory factor in women's presence as candidates is an increasing strategic nature to their campaigns based on their gaining of credentials in lower level office and increasing levels of ambition to be leaders, not just "sacrificial lambs." Commentary in the contemporary era has not suggested that women's candidacies were disproportionately losing efforts but rather have highlighted their experience and toughness. They have continued to keep pace with their male counterparts in acquiring votes and winning elections with the important exception of Democratic female open seat nominees in competitive districts. Female incumbent vulnerabilities have also diminished.

Special Elections

As noted earlier, the 2010 midterm election resulted in one less female representative in the U.S. House of Representatives than in the 211th

Congress, the high-water mark of female members and the first decline since the surge in 1992. However, that decline did not last long. When New York Republican Christopher Lee, married and the father of a young child, was forced to resign amid a scandal involving flirtatious e-mails and a shirtless picture he had sent to a woman he met on Craigslist, Republican Party leaders chose state Representative Jane Corwin as their nominee in the special election to fill his seat. Democrats selected Kathy Hochul, the clerk of Erie County, as their nominee. Although the district traditionally had been a safe Republican seat, Hochul defeated Corwin, 47 percent to 43 percent, in May 2011.

The campaign became a referendum on the congressional Republican plan to change Medicare under a budget proposal U.S. Representative Paul Ryan (R-WI), chair of the House Budget Committee, had put forth. Corwin had indicated her support for this plan. Hochul's ads blasted Corwin including one in which a deep-throated male voice with dramatic music in the background quoted Jane Corwin as saying "I would have voted for the 2012 House budget today." The ad went on to state it would essentially end Medicare and seniors would have to pay $6,400 more for the same coverage.[3] EMILY'S List contributed over $27,000 to Hochul's campaign. Corwin spent over $3 million, including more than $1 million of her own funds, while Hochul spent close to $2 million. These figures do not include monies that the NRCC or the DCCC spent independently or the large amounts that outside groups used to flood the airways and get out the vote. With Hochul's victory, this special election resulted in the number of women in the House returning to the previous high of 73 representatives.

Congressional elections' scholars have given little systematic attention to special elections. In the fifth edition of *Congressional Elections*, Paul Herrnson did note that special elections bring out even larger numbers of primary contenders than normal open-seat elections, especially when a longtime incumbent has vacated the seat presumably due to pent-up ambition and the opportunity to run without giving up an already held elective office (2008, 26). But Herrnson did not present any numbers or data analysis in support of his assertion.

Lee Sigelman did analyze special elections for the U.S. House of Representatives between 1954 and 1978 from the perspective of their being seen as referenda on presidential approval and products of national forces. He found that in the great majority of special elections party control of a House seat does not change hands. When party control does change hands, most often the party of the president has been the loser of the seat (1981). Gaddie, Bullock, and Buchanan in 1999 updated this line of research, investigating special elections from 1973 through 1997 by integrating constituency and candidate factors with presidential approval indicators, asking "what is so special about special elections." Their conclusion was that "special elections are subject to most of the same influences as other open-seat contests." Constituency attributes, spending, and experience were particularly strong in special elections.

Gender factors have been the focus of two other special election studies. Nixon and Darcy's stimulus for their research reported in "Special Elections and the Growth of Women's Representation in the U.S. House of Representatives" (1996) was that special elections 'provide women with an important, yet overlooked, point of congressional entry." One-third of all women who entered the House from 1979 through 1992, the time of their investigation, did so through the special election route and they entered these contests with high qualifications, producing high success rates.

On the other hand, Gaddie and Bullock's research covering essentially the same time frame (1981 through 1994) focused on the question "Is there a sexual bias?" in open seat and special elections (1997). Women, Gaddie and Bullock stressed, did not capitalize on these opportunities (similar to the findings of this study on women's emergence in open seat races). They ran in far fewer numbers than men. These authors also reported that whatever factors constrain the emergence of women as candidates in regular open seat elections apparently were at work when sudden vacancies occurred. At the same time, they concurred with Nixon and Darcy's findings that women who did run were as successful or more successful than their male counterparts, although there was "some indication that Republican women run under more restrictive conditions and performed poorly compared to both Democratic women and Republican men" (467), again a theme consistent with broader longitudinal studies.

The number of special elections varies from Congress to Congress but has tended to average about four per year over the course of these authors' election periods and in the more recent elections that this work has explored. Special elections are difficult to systemically analyze. Research on special elections is confounded by the variation across states in their nomination selection processes and the structure of these elections. Some states combine "primary" and "general" contests into one election, some states allow local party organizations to choose their nominees, some states operate under the traditional two-stage process of party primaries and then a general election, while others use a runoff system if no individual receives 50 percent of the vote in a first-stage multicandidate, multiparty contest. In some states the runoff consists of the top vote-getter in each of the major parties, and in other cases it is between the top two vote-getters regardless of party. Georgia has even held a nonpartisan special election.

This variation in the electoral structure of special elections adds complexity to any analysis of them as a distinct set of campaign events. In addition, some of the specials coincide with an open seat primary, resulting in an open seat primary election victor becoming the incumbent in the general election. A twist on this distinctive situation occurred in 2008 when incumbent Albert Wynn, who had lost the primary election to Donna Edwards, resigned before the end of his term, resulting in a special election to complete the last few months of the term with the candidates primarily being the open seat primary winners. Incumbent primary election challenger and victor Donna Edwards won the subsequent special election to become the incumbent in the November general election. In 2002, Rep. Patsy Mink succumbed to pneumonia in the fall after she had been renominated for her seat and after the deadline for substituting another candidate in her place. She was reelected posthumously, which resulted in a special election to fill the remaining month of her term in the 107th Congress (2001–02) and then another special election in January 2003 to fill her seat for the 108th Congress.

Between 1993 and 2010, a total of 62 special elections filled House seats. Fifty-six percent of these elections were to replace Democratic incumbents and 44 percent were to replace Republican incumbents. The following gender analysis includes 57 of these elections, excluding those contests that coincided with an open seat primary involving essentially the same contenders. Herrnson's contention that special elections have especially large pools of candidates is borne out in the contemporary period. As noted in chapter 3, the contest in Maryland's 7th district, with its 32 candidates (27 Democrats and 5 Republicans), held the record. (It simultaneously was an open seat primary and a special election and thus not one of the special elections included in this analysis.) Four other contests had over 20 candidates, combining both Democratic and Republican contenders.

Women were 15.8 percent of the candidates in these special elections. Their share of the pool of contenders barely exceeded that of Gaddie and Bullock's share during their time frame in which women made up 14.3 percent of candidates. A total of 449 major party candidates entered these 58 contests, 212 male Republicans, 25 female Republicans, 156 male Democrats, and 46 female Democrats. The partisan gap so prominent in other facets of the congressional campaigns of this era is also present in the special elections; women were 23 percent of the Democratic candidates but only 11 percent of the Republican candidates. From a district perspective, women ran in 37 percent of the Republican special elections beginning at the "primary" stage and in 54 percent of the Democratic special elections.

Women won 14, one-quarter, of these elections. Three Republican and 11 Democratic women were victors, including two Democratic widows and one Republican widow. A fourth widow, Maria Macias Brown, lost her attempt to succeed her husband in California's 42nd district in 2000. The female Democratic candidates had the highest success rate, with the other three subgroups trailing behind; 24 percent of the female Democrats were successful compared with 14 percent of the male Democrats, 13 percent of the female Republicans, and 12 percent of the male Republicans.

Special elections thus contributed marginally to the numerical representation of women in the U.S. House in the contemporary era, bringing in 14 new female members. They also contributed to the partisan gap regarding gender representation. However, just as Gaddie and Bullock found, "the level of female candidate emergence at the initiation of the campaign indicates that these opportunities are not capitalized on by women in large numbers." The analysis of the gender characteristics of special elections adds to the conclusion that it is presence, not performance, that matters in the incremental opportunities for women to advance their numbers in the U.S. House.

Special elections have also been held to replace female representatives who have died, been appointed to a position in the executive branch, or assumed an executive position outside the government. For example, upon assuming office President Obama appointed Rep. Hilda Solis to be secretary of labor and Rep. Ellen Tausher to be undersecretary of state for arms control and international security affairs, resulting in two special elections in 2009. This aspect of special elections also contributes to their incremental as opposed to substantial nature as a method of increasing the numerical representation of women in Congress.

Conclusion

The search for gender bias in contemporary elections for seats in the U.S. House of Representatives has found little supporting evidence based on research that has centered on the obtaining of votes, success rates, and the extent of incumbent opposition. Women acquire the same percentage of votes, win at the same rates, and pretty much face the same level of opposition when seeking reelection as do male candidates. It is the lack of presence of female candidates that is the problem and that is not a new theme in women and politics studies.

One puzzle about gender and the campaign process remains for future research. That puzzle involves the sense among scholars that in order to achieve at the same level as male candidates, female candidates need to be "better" or more qualified to overcome citizens' hesitation to vote for them, to be able to acquire campaign resources, and to overcome their own underestimation of their qualifications. Recall Lawless and Pearson's concluding comment in their 2008 article, noted in chapter 3, that "[w]omen, in other words, have to be 'better' than men in order to fare equally well." The lingering suspicion that this gender bias underlies the new conventional wisdom of parity stems primarily from experiments and survey data that have suggested voter bias against female candidates, and surveys of women in the eligibility pool who have expressed a greater sense than men in the eligibility pool that they are not qualified to run and that they would not win if they did run.

A "Jackie (and Jill) Robinson Effect" stimulated the recent work of Anzia and Berry (2011) in which they analyzed the relative success of male and female members of Congress in delivering federal monies to their districts and in sponsoring legislation. The electoral realm analogy of the "Robinson" effect centers on the perception that discriminated groups have higher performance standards in order to be allowed to play or to be hired. In the political realm a sex-based selection process for public office results in only the most qualified, politically ambitious women emerging as candidates. Anzia and Berry state that "[i]f voters are prejudiced against women, then a woman must be better than the man she runs against in order to win. Moreover, if women anticipate discrimination by voters, or simply underestimate their own qualifications, then only the most formidable women will run for office to begin with" (480). They continue to theorize that

> [i]f only higher-quality female candidates will actually run for office, then we would not necessarily expect to observe a vote or campaign funding differential between male and female candidates even if there is, in fact, discrimination by voters and donors. Yet, if the average female candidate is of higher quality than the average male candidate but receives the same amount of funding and wins the same number of votes, she is clearly not on equal footing with the man. Therefore, existing studies that simply compare women's and

> men's vote shares are not directly informative about the presence or absence of discrimination by voters. The workings of the candidate selection stage confound measurement of voter discrimination at the electoral stage. (481)

Little empirical research on actual campaigns provides confirmation or rejection of a "better" or "higher quality" hypothesis, however. Also, the most recent survey data described in chapter 1 show little indication of voter bias against women as political candidates, an important factor in the "better" theory. In chapter 3 I also showed that the electoral context of open seat primaries has not been a greater hurdle for female candidates in terms of their competitive nature. How then does a researcher operationalize the abstract concept of better and empirically test hypotheses about candidate quality and outcomes from a gendered perspective?

The measure of candidate quality that scholars have primarily used has been prior elective office-holding experience. Chapter 3 showed that female candidates in open seat primaries are more likely to have had elective office experience in the contemporary era as opposed to the past. Chapter 7 will show that among the individuals elected to Congress in the contemporary era, a greater percentage of the female representatives had elected office experience. Thus, overall female candidates as a group have been more experienced, which is a transformation from findings of studies of female candidates in earlier eras (Herrick 1995).

But it is a separate research step to determine a differential impact of that qualification on the vote-getting ability of female candidates. If, indeed, female candidates were more qualified than male candidates and no bias were present, then they should have been outperforming their male counterparts, but this appears not to be the case to any great extent. However, given the partisan structure of congressional districts, a ceiling might exist for any set of candidates to win at higher rates or obtain a greater percentage of the votes no matter how outstanding their qualifications might be. Stellar female Democrats would not be particularly more likely to win in safe Republican districts although they might attract more votes than lackluster candidates or simple "sacrificial lambs" of their party. But then their party's congressional campaign committee is hardly likely to invest in their race nor are they likely to get the endorsement of EMILY's List. The same is true among the Republicans.

The place to test the "better" hypothesis in future studies should be in districts rated as competitive. Researchers also should keep in mind that a quality candidate can make a district competitive. Robin Toner, for example, commented in a New York Times piece in 2006 titled "Women Wage Key Campaigns for Democrats" that "Democratic women are running major campaigns in nearly half of the two dozen most competitive House races where their party hopes to pick up enough Republican seats to regain control of the House." Not all of these races were against incumbents but a number were. At the end of that campaign season, too, Allison Stevens (2006b), writing in Womensenews, called readers' attention to "Female Dark Horses Surg[ing] to Election's Finish Line." She reported that "overlooked by political odds makers for most of the 2006 election cycle, a number of obscure female congressional candidates are surging in their final sprints to the Nov. 7 finish line and improving the odds that women will make significant gains in the House of Representatives on election day."

These observations were anecdotal in nature and not systematically suggestive of greater candidate quality but they are worth noting as stimuli for further research. Rebekah Herrick (1995) has encouraged researchers to compare female candidates with their opponents and not with all other candidates to assess gender bias in elections. Aggregate comparisons, she has asserted, may overstate the competitiveness of women (30). In 1992, female candidates in open seat general election contests for the U.S. House had more resources than male candidates overall but fewer resources than their opponents. At the same time, they received "as many, if not more votes, than their better-funded, more experienced opponents" in that distinctive election year for female candidates (1995, 35), a finding that complicates the idea of needing to be better to perform at an equal level.

As the financial dynamics of these campaigns are explored in chapter 5, Herrick's insightful approach will be taken into account. The fund-raising prowess of male and female candidates in the contemporary era and whether the financing of men's and women's campaigns has a differential impact on their performance is the focus of this next chapter. Female congressional candidates gaining of parity with male candidates in the financing of their campaigns was a key finding of the study of gender in elections of the feminist era. Ideas about fund-raising disparities and female candidates facing greater difficulty acquiring funds for their campaigns still permeates the political atmosphere of elections. In addition, money and its acquisition have become ever more central in congressional campaigns, stimulating continued research on the relation between gender and the financial resource aspect of these campaigns.

FIVE

Financing Men's and Women's Campaigns for the U.S. House

In 1998, state Representative Jan Schakowsky of Illinois entered the Democratic primary for the open seat in the state's 9th congressional district. Knowing it would be a very expensive primary she devised a clever strategy to enhance and distinguish her fund-raising effort. She called as many of the female lawyers in Chicago as she could to solicit funds. She left the following message:

> This is state Representative Jan Schakowsky. I'm calling successful women like you because I'm sure you agree that Illinois should have at least one woman in our congressional delegation. I need your help. Please call me.

Schakowsky raised $1,448,368 in the primary, $1,214,630 of it in individual contributions, with women contributing 57 percent of her campaign funds (Stevens 2002). She won the primary with 45 percent of the vote over two other opponents. The 9th district was a safe Democratic district. Thus, having won the primary she was "on her way" to Congress. She won the general election with 75 percent of the vote.

In the 2010 election cycle Republican Rep. Michele Bachmann of Minnesota was the top fund-raiser in U.S. House contests. She raised over $13.5 million, $13 million of it in individual contributions. In addition she had a leadership political action committee, MichelePAC, which spent approximately $1 million on others' campaigns. Her opponent, Tarryl Clark, raised $4.7 million, 91 percent in individual contributions in a losing effort. The most expensive U.S. House race in 2008 was New York's 20th district in which over $12 million was spent in great part because the Republican challenger, Sandy Treadwell, contributed nearly $6 million of his own money to his $7 million campaign. At the same time, first-term incumbent Kirsten Gillibrand raised $4.6 million. In contrast to Treadwell's largely self-funded campaign, Rep. Gillibrand reported raising nearly $1.2 million in political action committee (PAC) contributions and over $3.2 million in individual contributions. These examples illustrate not only diverse fund-raising mechanisms but the fund-raising prowess of female congressional candidates in contemporary times. Conventional wisdom had suggested otherwise in earlier decades. Perceptions still exist regarding fund-raising being particularly problematic for female candidates but empirical evidence suggests otherwise.

A desire to test the conventional wisdom that women lacked the skills, the assertiveness, and the connections to raise the kinds of money needed to be viable candidates that dominated election commentary was the main incentive for my initial research on gender and congressional elections (see Burrell, 1985). My central research question was whether the experiences of women who had entered contests for election to the U.S. House actually conformed to this belief. In particular, were they deficient fund-raisers compared to male candidates? The examination of the amounts of money raised and spent and the sources of campaign contributions from a gender perspective in congressional campaigns had not been the subject of research.

Prior to 1972, scholars had no way of conducting such research. But then, as a result of the Federal Election Campaign Act of 1971 and subsequent amendments, candidates who raised at least $5,000 for a federal election campaign had to report contributions to their campaigns to the newly established Federal Elections Commission (FEC). The commission has made these financial reports public and consequently has provided scholars with a rich source of data to study a centrally important aspect of democratic politics, the role of money in federal elections. Among other research questions, scholars could now test conventional wisdom ideas regarding the financing of men's and women's campaigns.

Comparing a number of dimensions of the financial aspects of male and female campaigns for a seat in the U.S. House from 1972 through 1992, I concluded my search for evidence in support of long-standing convention wisdom that the inability to raise campaign funds has been a major factor in the dearth of women in the national legislature in the following passage:

> But on each of the elements of fund-raising—total amounts raised and spent, PAC contributions, large donations, and the acquisition of early money—women candidates have competed equally with male candidates or in recent elections surpassed them. The conventional wisdom does not need to be explained. Whether we look at totals, sources, or timing, women candidates in similar situations as male candidates generally do as well and sometimes even better in financing their campaigns for national office. Further, a significant phenomenon of contemporary elections has been the involvement of women's PACs that have been able to supplement or compensate for other financial sources in women's campaigns for national office. (1994, 128)

Other scholars have built on these findings, both supporting them and adding nuanced research contributing to a greater understanding of a complex financial process and its gender implications. Some have suggested that the seeming absence of a male fund-raising advantage masks underlying gendered processes. As Milyo and Schosberg have pointed out, "Equivalent campaign spending may not produce equivalent results" (2000, 42). (See also Berch 2004 and Herrick 1996.) Candidates may also be taking diverse paths to achieve an equal outcome. Further, a number of works have presented figures that have updated the basic comparative picture of the fund-raising efforts of male and female nominees (see Burrell 2005, 2008; Fiber and Fox 2005).

Even though examples of female candidates as successful fund-raisers have been abundantly presented in recent elections, news media commentary continues to note the difficulty of raising money as a factor keeping women from advancing their numbers in the U.S. Congress (although as cited throughout this work, other media stories have emphasized women's skills at financing their campaign), and those who seek to promote women's candidacies still cite fund-raising as a problem, such as the Women's Campaign Fund (WCF) in its "Vote with Your Purse" effort. Based on research analyzing men and women as donors to political campaigns WCF concluded in 2009 that "[w]omen candidates struggle to match the fund-raising totals of their male counterparts" because women were not donating to campaigns to the same extent as men and they were not giving to female candidates (Women's Campaign Forum 2009).

From an academic perspective hesitancy about fund-raising equity has also been noted. For example, Kira Sanbonmatsu in her 2005 work on women candidacies for seats in state legislatures concluded that she

> did not anticipate the extent to which interview subjects would identify campaign finance as a factor that disproportionately discourages women from running for office. Many interview subjects argued that fundraising no longer constitutes the barrier for women candidates that it once was; others argued that fund-raising is difficult for men and women alike. However, many other respondents identified fund-raising as a major obstacle—if not the major obstacle—to women's candidacies. Interview subjects believe that cultural norms make it more difficult for women to raise money for themselves rather than for a cause. In addition, because men and women candidates come from different networks and occupations, those interviewed perceived men as having much better access to donor networks and interest groups. (200)

Note, too, Sue Thomas's introduction in the second edition of *Women and Elective Office: Past, Present and Future* in which she states that "the existence and success of EMILY's List and WISH List has, to a great extent, trained our gaze away from evidence that women still have a harder time raising money from traditional sources and raising large sums" (2005, 10).

But, perceptions aside, empirical evidence of the money raised and spent has clearly shown that women can compete dollar for dollar with male candidates when it comes to running for national office. For all of the "power" reasons cited in chapter 4, we should not have any particular grounds for expecting that since 1992 women candidates would have backtracked in their fund-raising prowess relative to men. But the contemporary world of campaign finance remains to be described and analyzed from a systematic gender perspective to provide continued evidence for the equality thesis.

Certainly the fund-raising skills of Jan Schakowsky, Michele Bachmann, and Kirsten Gillibrand illustrate the capability of women candidates to adequately finance their campaigns. Further, female members of Congress have moved into campaign leadership positions in their parties, created their own leadership PACs, and established special financial campaigns for women candidates. Chapter 6 explores these domains of activity in depth.

In good measure, Nancy Pelosi won her initial leadership position within the Democratic Party Caucus in the U.S. House in 2002 and her subsequent historic election to the speakership in 2007 because of her formidable success in raising money and distributing it among her Democratic colleagues, acquiring supporters in the process (see, for example, McCormick and Sandalow 2006). Women's organizations led by EMILY'S List also have acquired many dollars for women candidates.

The main hypothesis of this chapter is that the financial aspects of men's and women's campaigns for a U.S. House seat and retention of seats is no longer a gender issue and that to the extent to which sex is related to various financial aspects of congressional campaigns female candidates are advantaged. For example, Crespin and Deitz have studied the creative use of bundling and donor networks, which has advantaged female candidates, particularly female Democratic candidates (2010).

In the 2009–10 election cycle the Federal Election Commission reported that Democratic and Republican U.S. House candidates raised a total of more than $1.1 billion. Democratic candidates raised an average of $790,000 and a total of nearly $510 million while Republican candidates raised an average of approximately $500,000 and a total of $588 million. These figures give us a general picture of what a prospective candidate needs to consider when contemplating mounting a viable campaign for a U.S. House seat. Successful candidates in open seat races raised over $1.4 million on average in that election cycle and, as the figures cited earlier suggest, highly competitive campaigns can require millions more dollars.

Party organizations now spend millions in additional independent expenditures to promote their most competitive candidates and mount negative advertising campaigns against their opponents. Further, candidates in open seat primaries in districts favorable to their party need to worry about amassing an early campaign finance war chest to appear viable and to scare off challengers. Indeed, the initial impetus for EMILY's List, the "grand dame" of women's PACs, was that female candidates needed access to early money to overcome negative stereotypes about their fund-raising abilities; thus, its acronym, EMILY, stands for "early money is like yeast, it makes the dough rise."

Male and Female Nominees and Campaign Receipts

An analysis of the fund-raising dynamics of men's and women's campaigns for the U.S. House since 1992 needs to take into account all of these complexities and factors. That is the goal of this chapter for the contemporary election period. The chapter begins with a presentation of a number of figures showing the comparative amounts of money male and female major party nominees in contested races raised to finance their campaigns in the contemporary era.

As in the case of defining candidates' status, I have had to construct a decision rule regarding candidates' receipts. Only candidates with a major party opponent in the general election are included in this analysis. Unopposed incumbents are excluded. How much money candidates raised and spent and the sources of funds raised—individual contributions, PAC contributions, and candidate self-financing—is determined from FEC financing reports. Candidates who raise $5,000 or more must file quarterly reports with the FEC. But some candidates, even general election nominees, do not raise that minimal sum of money requiring that they file with the FEC, so they do not become part of its reports. However, to systematically analyze the financing of congressional candidates' campaigns this group of contenders needs to be included in the database. All of these candidates, sometimes as many as 40 general election candidates in an election cycle, have been added to the financial databases used in this study and are included in the analyses of this chapter as well as in the primary and general elections' chapters.

The decision rule that must be made is the construction of an estimate of the amount these low funded candidates raised under $5,000. If their receipts are considered as missing data then average amounts raised and spent will be overestimated and relationships may be underestimated. An arbitrary amount has to be assigned to each of these candidates. One would expect that they would have spent something even if it is a token sum. I have chosen to set their receipts at $2,500, the midpoint between no dollars and the $5,000 triggering amount for official reporting requirements. This figure is small enough that it would only minimally affect average amounts raised but allows for the inclusion of all major party nominees and assumes that they raised and spent some amount of money.

Figure 5.1 displays the average amount raised by male and female nominees in races with a major party opponent in each of the nine election cycles of this analysis. Mean campaign receipts are adjusted for inflation using 1994 as the base year. Two features of figure 5.1 stand out. First, the money raised in congressional campaigns has increased across the elections even controlling for inflation. Second, for most of the election cycles, the average amounts male and female nominees raised were nearly equal without even taking into account candidate status or party affiliation. Only in 2006 was the difference statistically significant, with female major party nominees in contested races being advantaged in the amount of money they had raised to finance their campaigns. Female nominees as a group outpaced their male counterparts on average in all election cycles since 2000. The sexes were virtually equal in the 1994 election cycle and

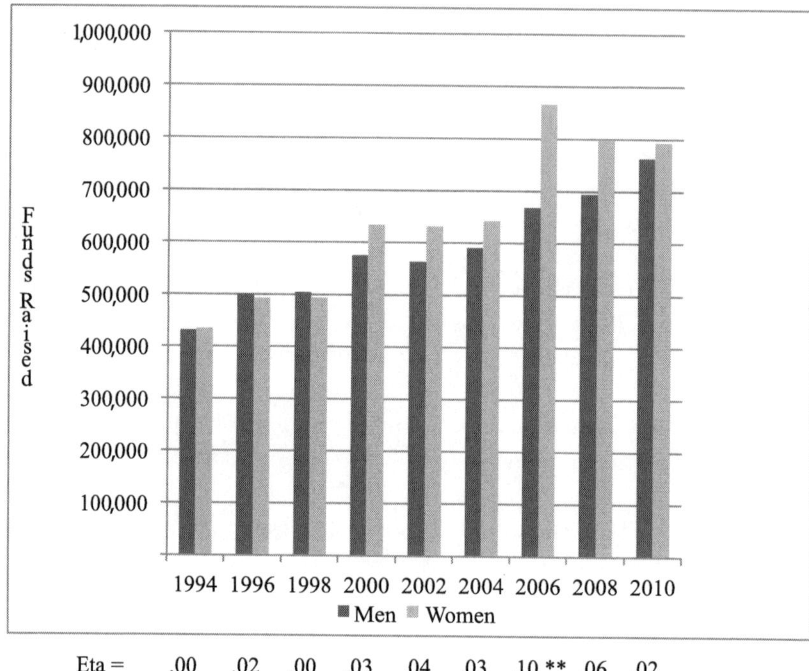

Eta = .00 .02 .00 .03 .04 .03 .10 ** .06 .02

Fig. 5.1. Average Receipts by Sex, Major Party Nominees, 1994–2010. (** $p \leq .01$.) Candidates with major party opponents only. (Data compiled by the author.)

the male nominees marginally raised more money on average in 1996 and 1998. The eta correlations presented with the figures illustrate a primarily weak relationship between sex and campaign receipts across the years.

The data in figure 5.1 only introduce an analysis of the role of sex in the financing of contemporary campaigns for a seat in the U.S. House. They suggest that candidate sex has not been a major factor when it comes to the financing of congressional campaigns, but these overall comparisons may hide underlying gender experiences. The first most important factor to notice is that male candidates as a group should have been expected to have acquired more campaign funds on average solely due to generic incumbency advantage. But finding that on average male candidates did not have higher receipts, and in the years when they did their advantage was small, actually suggests a greater financial prowess on the part of female candidates since they tended to equal or outpace male nominees in contested races even with the male candidates disproportionately being incumbents. In assessing relative fund-raising one also needs to take into account the fact that the Republican Party has been financially advantaged during this time period and female candidates have disproportionately been Democrats.

Thus, the second step in the financial analysis of men's and women's campaigns is to construct a more detailed investigation of sex and money in congressional campaigns through a comparison of amounts raised within subgroups of candidates. I compare relationships within the two parties and further divide the data to compare receipts of male and female candidates within candidate status groups, as incumbents, as challengers, and as open seat contenders. Figures 5.2a through 5.4b present the results of these comparisons across the nine election cycles of this study. An overall perusal of the bar graphs in figures 5.2a through 5.4b shows a lack of a consistent pattern of differences between the sexes across candidate status groups within the parties over the election cycles examined here.

Gender and Incumbency Fund-raising

Among incumbents, for example, male Democrats in contested races tended to raise more money than female Democratic incumbents, but Republican female incumbents tended to raise more than Republican male incumbents scanning the data across election years. Fund-raising efforts on the part of incumbents have been shown to be related to the level of competition. Thus, it may be that female Democrats tend to represent safer Democratic districts than their male counterparts and have weaker challengers. Thus, they have less incentive to acquire a large war chest. On the other hand, female Republicans may represent less safe Republican districts and therefore have stronger competition on average, requiring more effort to acquire funds. Indeed, the women friendly district analysis of Palmer and Simon certainly suggests that this indeed has been the case in this political landscape. The vote percentages presented in chapter 4 also provide support for this hypothesis. Female Republicans tend to face greater competition and therefore expend greater effort raising money to finance their campaigns. Fund-raising differences based on sex among incumbents, however, were statistically weak overall, suggesting the marginal nature of gender in affecting fund-raising differences.

Gender and Challenger Fund-raising

Among challengers, Democratic female contenders across the elections on average raised more than Democratic male challengers while a sex advantage among Republicans varied across the elections. As figures 5.3a and

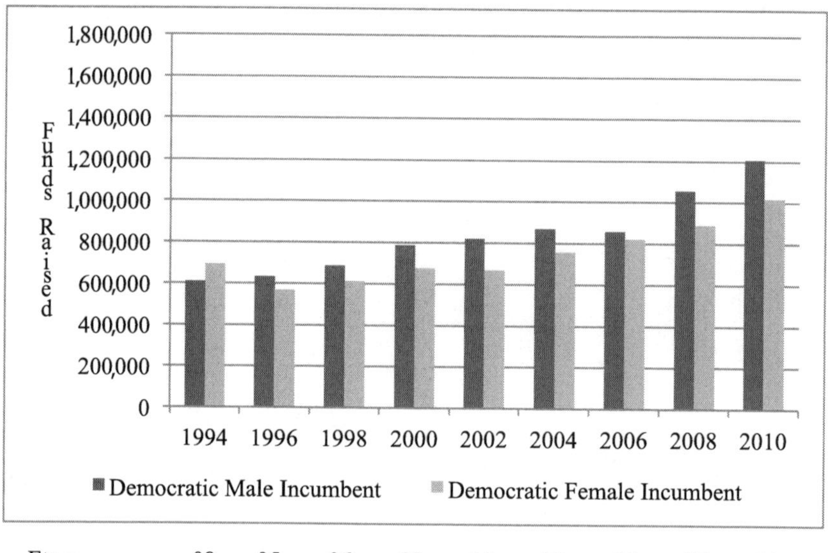

Eta = .08 .05 .06 .09 .11 .08 .04 .12 .10

Fig. 5.2a. Average Campaign Receipts, Democratic Male and Female Incumbents. (Data compiled by the author from Federal Election Commission information; www.fec.gov.)

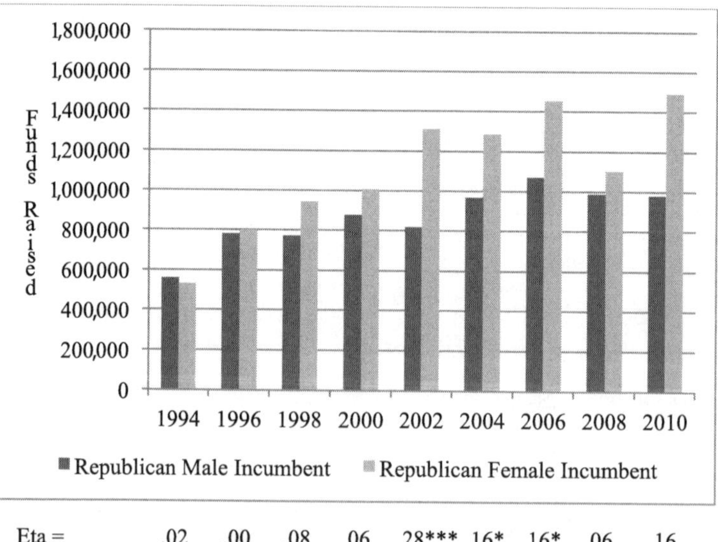

Eta = .02 .00 .08 .06 .28*** .16* .16* .06 .16

Fig. 5.2b. Average Campaign Receipts, Republican Male and Female Incumbents. (* $p \leq .05$; ** $p \leq .01$; *** $p \leq .001$.) (Data compiled by the author from Federal Election Commission information; www.fec.gov.)

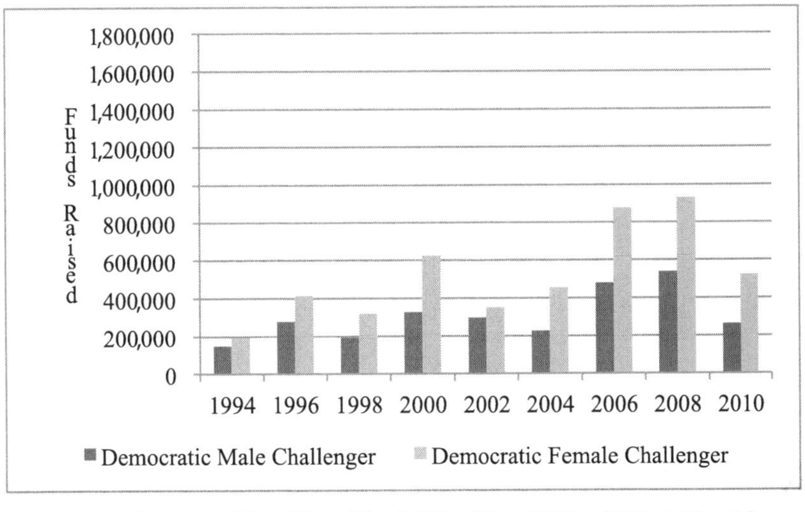

Eta = .08 .13 .15 .20** .02 .20** .19** .18* .14

Fig. 5.3a. Average Campaign Receipts, Democratic Male and Female Challengers. (* $p \leq .05$; ** $p \leq .01$; *** $p \leq .001$.) (Data compiled by the author from Federal Election Commission information; www.fec.gov.)

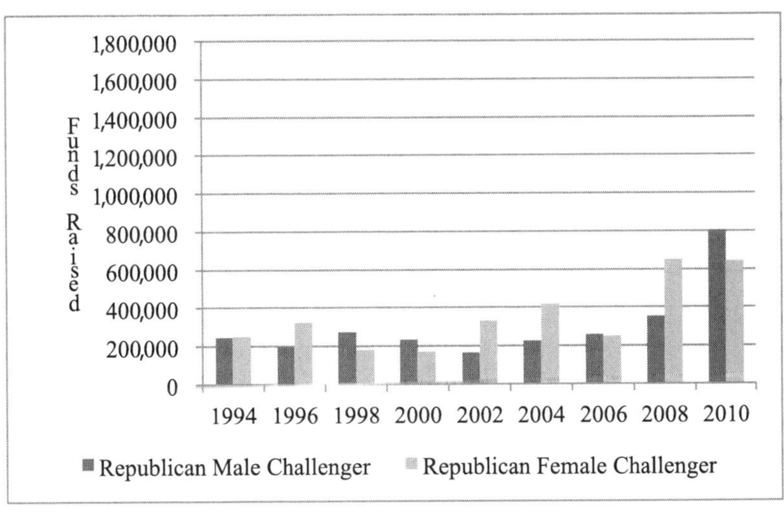

Eta = .00 .15 .08 .06 .14 .14 .00 .10 .05

Fig. 5.3b. Average Campaign Receipts, Republican Male and Female Challengers. (Data compiled by the author from Federal Election Commission information; www.fec.gov.)

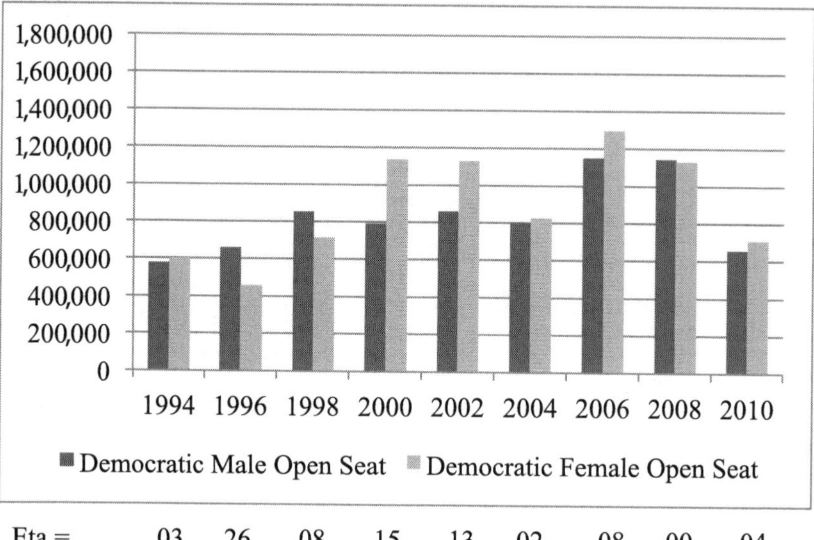

Eta = .03 .26 .08 .15 .13 .02 .08 .00 .04

Fig. 5.4a. Average Campaign Receipts, Democratic Male and Female Open Seat Candidates. (Data compiled by the author from Federal Election Commission information; www.fec.gov.)

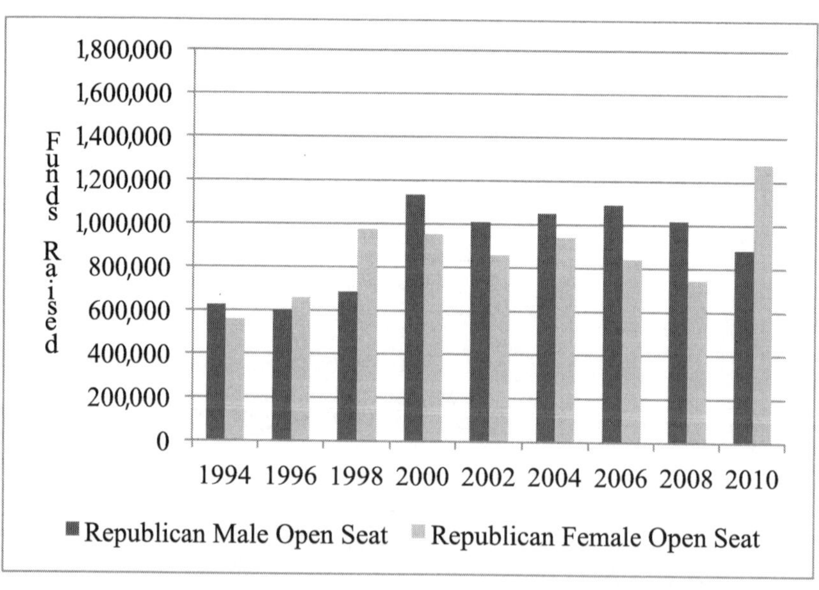

Eta = .04 .05 .19 .10 .09 .07 .09 .10 .17

Fig. 5.4b. Average Campaign Receipts, Republican Male and Female Open Seat Candidates. (Data compiled by the author from Federal Election Commission information; www.fec.gov.)

5.3b demonstrate, challengers are at a substantial disadvantage when it comes to acquiring financial resources to mount viable campaigns for a seat in the national legislature. For the most part they do not come anywhere near raising $1 million to underwrite their campaigns.

Differences between the sexes within both parties vary across the years but female challengers have tended to fund-raise more than their male counterparts, anemic as almost all of the efforts have been. Democratic female challengers particularly in 2006 and 2008 outpaced their male counterparts, raising on average nearly $1 million in each election. Their competitiveness was cited in earlier chapters, yet they were not notably successful. The 2010 election, the election in which Republicans regained control of the U.S. House, was a bad fund-raising year for both male and female Democratic challengers.

In four of the nine election cycles Republican female challengers also raised more money on average than Republican male challengers. The large difference in 2008 between male and female Republican challengers is primarily accounted for by the outlying case of Dr. Deborah Honeycutt in Georgia's 13th district. She raised a phenomenal $5.2 million. However, she had little to show for this effort, getting only 31 percent of the vote in a safe Democratic district. She also was the subject of a good deal of criticism because most of her money went to a Washington-based direct mail business. Few funds seem to have been spent getting her name and message out to the voters. If she is excluded from the analysis, female Republican challengers still did better than male Republican challengers but the gap shrinks greatly to a difference of just over $50,000 ($403,970 to $345,097).

Gender and Open Seat Fund-raising

Candidates in open seat races tended to acquire the highest amounts of money compared to incumbents but not in every election cycle. From a comparative gender perspective, figures 5.4a and 5.4b show a mixed picture over time. Within both parties in some election cycles female candidates were the leaders and in others male candidates led and they were not necessarily the same cycles for both parties. We do need to keep in mind the small numbers of candidates especially on the female side who are included in some of the election cycles. For example, in 2010 female Republican open seat nominees far outpaced any other open seat candidate group. Yet there were only two of them, both of whom won.

Moving to a systematic assessment of the role of sex in acquiring funds for one's campaign over the course of these elections, taking partisanship

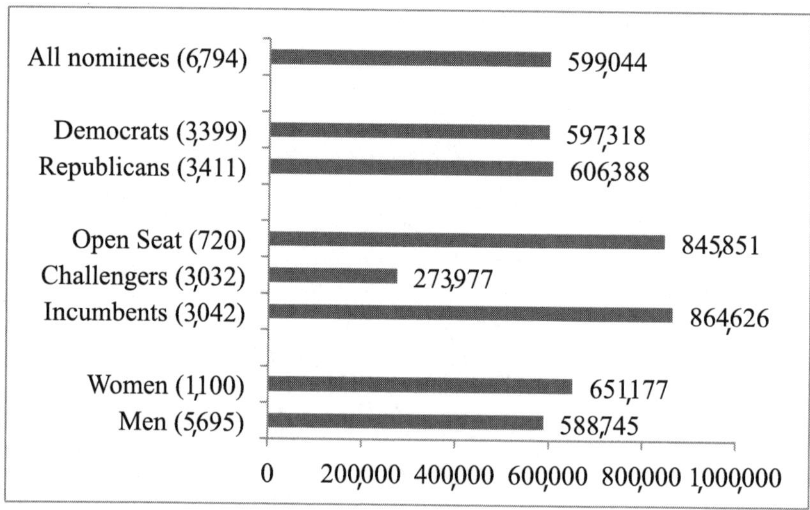

Fig. 5.5. Mean Receipts, All Nominees in Contested Races, 1994–2010. (Data compiled by the author from Federal Election Commission information; www.fec.gov.)

and candidate status into account from a statistical perspective, I pooled information across all of the election cycles. Figure 5.5 displays the average total receipts for a number of groupings as a baseline before proceeding to the next stage of estimating the effect of sex once other important structural factors are taken into account. The average amount nominees in contested races raised across the nine election cycles, controlling for inflation, was nearly $600,000 per candidate. Republicans raised on average slightly more than Democratic candidates; incumbents acquired the highest sums, closely followed by open seat nominees. Incumbent challengers lagged far behind. One should keep in mind that other studies have shown that incumbent fund-raising increases as the quality of the challenger increases. Finally, women have greater average receipts than male candidates as figure 5.1 also illustrated.

Table 5.1 presents the results of a multiple regression analysis incorporating all of these factors to explain variation in campaign receipts. The goal is to determine the impact of being a female candidate once these other factors are controlled. Receipts are the dependent variable, weighted for the impact of inflation. The independent variables are sex, party, district competitiveness, and a set of dummy variables for candidate status, with opposition party nominees as the excluded variable. District competitiveness in this analysis is based on presidential vote in the district. To construct a district competitiveness measure, the percentage of the vote for the Republican presidential candidate in the most recent election was first entered. Then its distance from 50 percent is calculated to assign a neutral competitiveness rating to each district. The larger the resulting number, the less competitive the district. (A score of 50 percent represented an equally competitive district between the Democratic and Republican candidates.) The sign of the coefficient is flipped in the table so that the positive relation between the competitiveness of the district and campaign dollars is shown.

All of these variables—party, candidate status, competitiveness, and sex—are statistically related to the amount of money nominees acquired to fund their campaigns, as table 5.1 shows. Incumbency has the biggest impact and controlling for the other variables, Republicans were advantaged. Most important for the purposes of this research is that controlling for candidate status and party, female candidates were significantly more likely to raise more money than their male counterparts to finance their campaigns. Gender mattered to the advantage of female candidates to the sum of more than $100,000 on average.

Summary

The answer to questions about whether the contemporary fund-raising character of women's campaigns for Congress has depressed, enhanced, or had little effect on candidates' financial resources is that when it comes to financing their campaigns male and female candidates are equally adept

TABLE 5.1. Effect of Party, Candidate Status, and Sex on Fund-raising, Major Party Nominees in Contested Races

Variable	*b*	Beta	Significance
Party	–$35.6 (13.9)	–.027	.010
Incumbent	$593.8 (14.6)	.453	.000
Open Seat	$541.9 (23.6)	.256	.000
Sex	$103.2 (18.9)	.058	.000
Competitiveness	$14.1 (.78)	–.193	.000
Constant	$441.6 (15.5)		.000
Adjusted R^2 = .24			
N = 6,795			

Source: Data compiled by the author from Federal Election Commission information; www.fec.gov.

Note: Party was coded 0 = Republican, 1 = Democrat; Sex was coded 0 = male, 1 = female. Coefficients in 1,000s of dollars; *b* = unstandardized coefficient; Beta = standardized coefficient.

at raising money to fund them, and more often than not when a subgroup has been advantaged in an election cycle it has been female candidates. Figures 5.1 through 5.5 make a total of 65 comparisons between the sexes. In 38 of these comparisons, average amounts raised were higher for the female candidates. In 23 of the comparisons male candidates had higher average amounts and in three comparisons average amounts were virtually the same between the sexes. In many cases involving an advantage for one group the advantage was marginal. The small number of female nominees in some categories also minimizes any sense of a general gender advantage.

Financial Structure of the Campaigns

Candidates acquire financial resources for their campaigns from a number of sources. They can self-fund their campaigns with an unlimited amount of their own money. They can solicit contributions from individuals, as Jan Schakowsky's effort described in this chapter's introduction illustrates, and they can seek funds from political action committees. Federal law limits the amount individuals and PACs can contribute directly to a candidate. In addition, party organizations can contribute a small amount in direct contributions (limited by law), provide more in coordinated funds, and spend unlimited amounts in independent expenditures on a candidate's campaign. The latter source of support will be explored in chapter 6. In addition, campaigns may vary by how much they attain in total, by how they are funded, by the size of donations, and by the timing of donations, all of which can affect the viability of their campaigns and their ability to acquire votes.

From a gender perspective, research has examined whether the end result of female candidates' equal or greater campaign war chests is a consequence of similar or different fund-raising paths. Earlier studies have shown that female candidates have not necessarily relied on many small contributions to keep pace with male candidates who successfully solicited contributions in larger dollar amounts (Burrell 1985; Crespin and Deitz 2010). Furthermore, male and female candidates have been shown to gain equal contributions on average from PACs and from direct contributions by party organizations (Burrell 1994).

Types of Funding Sources

The FEC requires that federal candidates' quarterly financial reports be broken down by direct PAC contributions, candidate contributions of

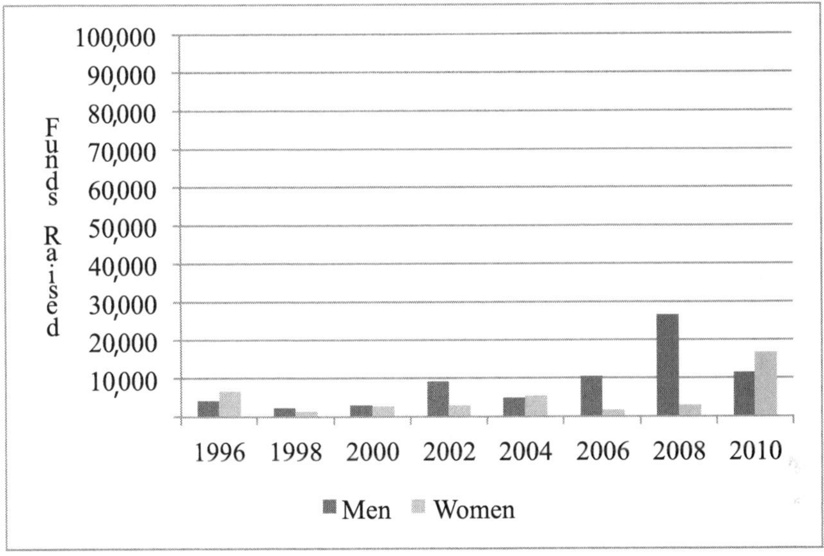

Fig. 5.6. Mean Candidate Contributions, 1996–2010, Major Party Nominees, Contested Races. (Data compiled by the author from Federal Election Commission information; www.fec.gov.)

their own money, and individual contributions. Individual contributions of donations over $200 must be itemized. Candidates have to report these receipts in addition to the amount they have spent each quarter of the election cycle. Figures 5.6 to 5.8 display the comparative amounts both sexes have raised from each of these three sources, their own money, PACs, and individual contributions, and what percent each source makes up of their total receipts over the course of these nine election cycles. (Candidate contribution figures are not available for 1994).

Figure 5.6 shows the average amounts candidates contributed to their campaigns from their own funds in the elections from 1996 through 2010. It suggests that that source of financing is a minimal aspect of campaign financial resources across these elections. Using the median instead of the mean to characterize candidate contributions of their own finances to control for outliers, over half of the major party nominees reported contributing nothing in the way of their own money to their campaigns. A few outliers in the opposite direction also exist. The substantially higher average amount that male candidates contributed to their campaigns in the 2008 election is a prime example of the outlier effect. Sandy Treadwell's nearly $6 million donation to his campaign in his unsuccessful bid to unseat Kirsten Gillibrand cited in the introduction to this chapter is one of those

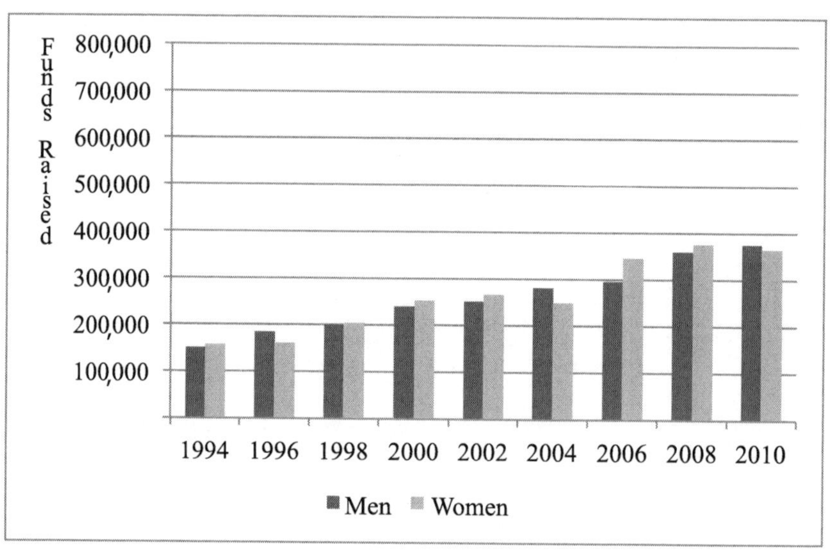

Fig. 5.7. Mean PAC Receipts, 1994–2010, Major Party Nominees, Contested Races. (Data compiled by the author from Federal Election Commission information; www.fec.gov.)

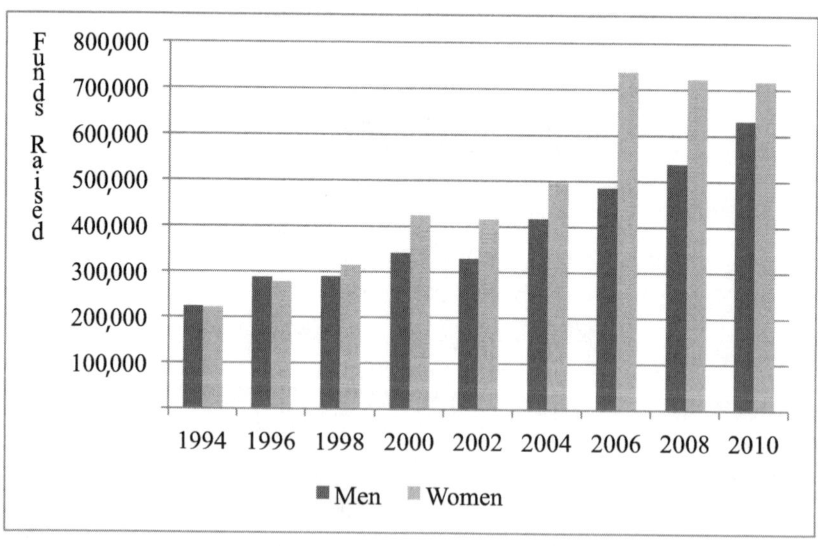

Eta = .00 .01 .02 .07 .08* .11**.16*** .11** .04

Fig. 5.8. Mean Individual Contributions, 1994–2010, Major Party Nominees, Contested Races. (* $p \leq .05$; ** $p \leq .01$; *** $p \leq .001$.) (Data compiled by the author from Federal Election Commission information; www.fec.gov.)

outliers. In addition, Jared Polis contributed over $5 million to his campaign in the 2008 open seat primary in Colorado's 2nd district. Removing those two outliers from the analysis, the average amount of self-funding of the male and female candidates in 2008 is much more in line with that of the other election cycles. Male nominees' average dropped to $7,800. Less than 1 percent (50 of 6,796 major party nominees in contested elections) contributed $100,000 or more to their campaigns. Nine female candidates and 41 male candidates self-funded their campaigns at this level. Finding financially flush candidates may be a priority from a party organizational perspective but from the perspective of candidates contributing their own money is not a widespread phenomenon.

Few gender differences appear in the average amount of PAC and individual contributions male and female nominees in major party contested elections acquired over the course of these nine elections (see also Crespin and Deitz 2010). Generally male and female major party nominees acquired PAC support in equal amounts on average. From 1998 on female nominees as a group raised more in individual donations than male nominees. In some election cycles the average differences were substantial.

Figure 5.9 combines data on the sources of campaign resources for the whole election period and presents the average amounts male and female candidates raised from each category. Inflation is built into these analyses. The data displayed in figure 5.9 continue the theme of equality regarding funding sources of the campaigns of male and female nominees in contemporary elections. The average amount they raised from PACs and contributed themselves to their campaigns is virtually equal between the sexes while female nominees raised more on average from individual contributions. An examination of the distribution of sources for campaigns as a whole also highlights the similar character of male and female nominees' fund-raising. For both sexes 3 percent of their receipts came from their own contributions, 32 percent and 33 percent came from PACs, respectively, for female and male nominees and 65 percent and 64 percent came from individual contributions, respectively, for female and male nominees.

Summary

Female nominees have definitely not been laggards and often have been leaders in acquiring funds for their campaigns in the contemporary era. Even though self-funding has been a criterion emphasized in party recruitment efforts in recent elections, candidate contributions to their campaigns has been a small factor in these elections for both male and female candi-

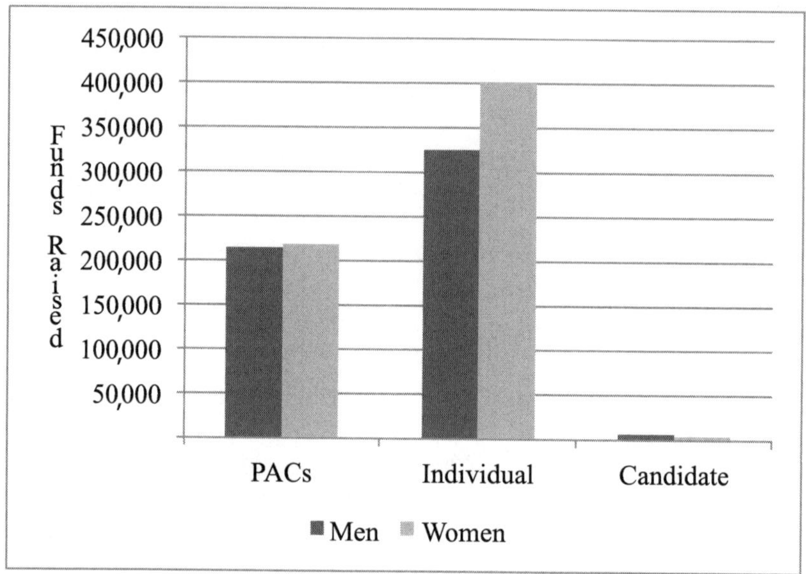

Fig. 5.9. Mean Contributions by Type of Contribution, 1994–2010, Major Party Nominees, Contested Races. The 1994 election is excluded from the Candidate Contribution mean. (Data compiled by the author from Federal Election Commission information; www.fec.gov.)

dates. Female candidates have kept pace with male candidates in acquiring funds from PACs and in the most recent elections have had more individual contributions. The next section delves more deeply into questions about the structure of those individual contributions.

The Structure of Individual Contributions

The extent to which candidates have access to large donors and the degree to which they are dependent on many small donations is potentially a gender factor in congressional campaigns even if female nominees surpass male nominees in attracting individual contributions. Dabelko and Herrnson (1997), for example, report that while female nonincumbent candidates raised more than men in individual contributions in the 1992 election, one-fourth of their total receipts came in the form of individual contributions of less than $200 compared with one-fifth for their male counterparts.

These authors provided a positive interpretation of this finding, surmising that women may rely on a broader base of financial supporters, even though the differences they reported were not substantial. Female candidates may also have been forced to expend time and energy on raising funds from smaller donors due to less access to large contributors or discrimination on the part of "heavy hitters" who make smaller donations to female candidates than male candidates. One could hypothesize, however, that such discrimination has faded with the growth of strategic, assertive, and successful female contenders.

My analysis of campaign financial structures in 1980 and 1982 showed that in neither year were female candidates especially disadvantaged in the number or amount of large contributions they received. In that study, contributions of $500 or more were classified as large (1985, 262). An extension of that analysis through the 1990 election found that the gender gap in large contributions varied from election to election (Burrell 1994, 116). Male candidates in four elections from 1980 through 1990 surpassed female candidates, while women did better in 1988 and the sexes were equal in 1982 in acquiring large individual contributions.

For the elections from 1994 through 2006 the FEC has provided finance data at four levels of individual contribution categories: total individual contributions, contributions between $200 and $499, between $500 and $749, and $750 or greater. (Unfortunately for research purposes, it discontinued such reporting after 2006.) It also has provided the total number of contributions a candidate has acquired in each category for those elections. These data allow for a more detailed analysis of the internal financial structure of men's and women's campaigns and their donor bases to address more detailed questions about gender factors in congressional campaign finance. There is reason to suggest that male candidates finance their campaigns from a greater set of large donors and reason to speculate that female candidates have come to equal or exceed their male counterparts in the quest for large donors, taking party and candidate status into account. But I hypothesize no gender differences in the structure of contribution pools of the campaigns of men and women in contemporary elections.

Individual contributions are the primary funding source in congressional campaigns as figure 5.9 has shown. Contemporary congressional nominees in major party contested races in the seven elections between 1994 and 2006 raised on average an inflation adjusted $313,178 in reported individual contributions with a standard deviation of $376,678. The large standard deviation suggests great variation in amounts raised from individual contributors. Eight percent of the nominees did not report raising any money in individual contributions. The first row of table 5.2 lays out the structure of individual contributions for all of the major party nominees in these election cycles, providing information on the average amounts raised in each category of giving, the average number of contribution in each category, and the percentage of all individual contributions each category consists. The figures show the diversity of individual giving.

Overall and within both parties, female candidates raised more money on average within all of the large donor categories and they acquired a greater average number of contributions in each of the categories (table 5.2). In addition, female incumbents and challengers raised more in the largest category of individual contributions and virtually tied men among the open seat contenders. In this central aspect of campaign resources, gender made a difference and that difference was to female candidates' advantage. Male candidates did raise a slightly higher percentage of their funds in contributions of $750 or more than female candidates and female nominees raised a slightly higher percentage of their funds in contributions of less than $200 both overall and within the two parties. But the female

TABLE 5.2. Structure of Individual Contributions, 1994–2006, Major Party Nominees in Contested Races

	Individual Contributions											
	< $200		$200–499			$500–749			$750+			
Candidates	$	%	#	$	%	#	$	%	#	$	%	Total
All (5,257)	8.78	28	176	3.88	12	113	5.16	17	135	13.56	43	31.35
Men (4,419)	8.16	27	169	3.71	13	111	5.07	15	133	13.34	40	30.29
Women (838)	12.00	32	212	4.64	12	126	5.61	17	147	14.73	44	37.01
Democrats	8.06	28	170	3.78	13	109	4.92	17	123	12.34	42	29.09
Men (2,080)	6.89	25	156	3.49	13	104	4.75	18	120	11.98	44	27.11
Women (539)	12.55	34	222	4.87	13	125	5.57	15	136	13.74	37	36.70
Republicans	9.50	29	182	3.94	12	118	5.39	16	147	14.78	46	32.61
Men (2,339)	9.29	28	180	3.90	12	117	5.36	16	144	14.55	44	33.11
Women (299)	11.08	30	196	2.42	11	127	5.67	15	167	16.58	44	37.55
Incumbents	11.43	26	238	5.21	12	162	7.37	17	197	19.62	45	43.63
Men (2,040)	11.02	26	236	5.15	12	162	7.38	17	195	19.48	45	43.04
Women (324)	13.99	30	252	5.57	12	164	7.32	15	207	20.45	43	47.33
Challengers	5.24	34	89	1.98	13	51	2.31	15	56	57.11	38	15.34
Men (1,930)	4.59	33	80	1.78	13	46	2.12	16	51	52.00	38	13.70
Women (396)	8.42	37	135	2.93	13	72	3.22	14	80	81.99	36	22.76
Open Seats	12.25	26	273	5.93	13	167	7.62	16	202	20.56	44	46.37
Men (448)	10.54	23	249	5.42	12	158	7.28	16	200	20.46	49	43.71
Women (118)	18.75	33	363	7.84	14	202	8.93	16	206	20.93	37	56.46

Source: Data compiled by the author from Federal Election Commission information; www.fec.gov.
Note: Dollar figures are divided by 10,000.

candidates still raised more on average in total amounts from the higher dollar donors. These findings are all the more remarkable because they are present without a control for incumbency. Their greater incumbency status should have led the male nominees to have acquired more contributions from larger donors than the female nominees as a group but that was not the case. The other rows in table 5.2 show the results of analysis of sex differences by candidate status. In ten of the 12 donor categories, women raised more on average. Thus, we can conclude that female nominees in contemporary congressional elections are not only as competitive, if not more competitive, than male nominees, they also achieve their advantage from a broader base of financial supporters at all levels of giving. Contributing to this edge has been the rise of female donor networks, as Crespin and Deitz have shown (2010).

Table 5.3 presents the results of a systematic multiple regression of the financial structure of the nominees' campaigns to more precisely determine the impact of sex on contributions for each of the donor levels once other political factors are taken into account. The dependent variables are the inflation-controlled amount raised in each donor dollar category. The independent variables are sex (0 = male, 1 = female), party (0 = Republican, 1 = Democrat), a set of dummy variables indicating candidate status with

TABLE 5.3. Individual Contributions by Level, 1994–2006

	<$200		$200–$499		$500–$749		$750+	
	b	Beta	*b*	Beta	*b*	Beta	*b*	Beta
Sex	46,928	.11	11,809	.10	9,463	.06	27,473	.05
	(5,686)**		(1,581)***		(1,972)**		(7,078)**	
Party	–17,563	–.06	–2,161	.02	–4,773	–.04	–24,596	–.06
	(4,146)**		(1,153)		(1,438)*		(5,161)**	
Incumbent	62,886	.20	32,649	.36	50,752	.43	139,249	.35
	(4,358)**		(1,211)***		(1,152)***		(5,425)**	
Open Seat	65,282	.13	38,028	.26	51,326	.27	143,030	.22
	(6,999)**		(1946)***		(1,842)**		(8,714)**	
Competitiveness	2,030	.12	754	.15	988	.15	–2,970	.13
	(233)**		(65)**		(81)**		(290)**	
Constant	124,537		39,669		45,180		127,859	
	(6,939)**		(1,929)**		(2,406)**		(8,638)**	
N	5,257		5,257		5,257		5,257	
Adj. R^2	.07		.175		.21		.14	

Source: Data compiled by the author from Federal Election Commission information; www.fec.gov.

Note: In the table, the competitiveness relationship is flipped for readability purposes. A positive relationship indicates greater competitiveness. Sex: male = 0, female = 1; party: Republican = 0, Democrat = 1.

$^{*}p < .05$, $^{**}p < .000$.

challengers being the excluded category, and a district competitive variable as constructed earlier.

All of the independent variables had a statistically significant relationship with the amount of independent contributions that candidates in contested general election races raised. Not unexpectedly, an examination of the standardized coefficients shows that incumbency has the biggest impact across all contribution levels. Open seat contenders have the highest levels of receipts at each contribution level once other factors are controlled in the unstandardized coefficient analysis. The more competitive the districts are, the larger are the amounts raised at all levels, also not unexpectedly. Republicans have tended to do better than Democrats but the differences are not as significant as the other factors. Finally, controlling for other factors female nominees have done consistently better at all four of the donor levels. For example, women had over a $27,000 advantage from donors making contributions of $750 or more.

Female Open Seat Nominees and Their Opponents

These analyses comparing women as a group to men as a group in various candidacy and party statuses, while substantively of central importance, may be an incomplete assessment of their relative fund-raising. Among the few contemporary studies that have examined the relationship between sex and campaign receipts Rebekah Herrick (1996) and Pamela Fiber and Richard Fox (2005) have importantly suggested that what matters is not so much the comparison of female candidates as a group with male candidates as a group but female candidates compared to their individual male opponents. Herrick, for example, determined that female candidates had to raise more money than their male opponents to win at the same rate (1996). Inspecting open seat campaigns in 1992, she found that women fared less well when compared to their opponents than when all female candidates were compared to all male candidates (Herrick 1995) in their total receipts. They still were not disadvantaged at the ballot box, however. Her study is an important contribution to research on gender effects in congressional elections, although its analysis of only one election year and one subgroup of candidates limits its generalizability.

Fiber and Fox's longitudinal study also shows that in open seat elections from 1980 to 2000 men running against women raised substantially more money than their female opponents (1995). Male open seat candidates in this time period raised roughly $100,000 more than their female opponents (but they still did not win more votes). Herrick's and Fiber and Fox's studies have generated more in-depth knowledge of the financial aspects of our campaigns of interest.

Two additional related political questions need to be addressed in reflecting on these studies that are particularly significant for this study of the nine most recent elections. If one extends the Fiber and Fox analysis into the 21st century, when female candidates' financial prowess and sources of funding have expanded even further, these female deficits versus their opponents may have vanished. Second, although it perhaps can be teased out in these earlier two studies, the apparent female disadvantage when compared with her individual male opponent may be the result of a partisan factor rather than a gender factor. The majority of female open seat general election candidates have been Democrats over the course of these nine elections (81 to 41 nominees). Republican nominees in contested races have tended to raise more money than Democratic nominees.

Thus, an individual level contest analysis of female open seat nominees versus their male opponents should take party into account and not only make an overall comparative assessment of amounts raised between male candidates and their female opponents. One needs to assess how well female Democrats have fared against their male Republican opponents compared with how well Democratic male candidates do against their Republican opponents and also the converse party and sex comparisons (Republican female and male candidates against their Democratic opponents). In other words, we need to control for party.

Table 5.4 presents data on the average amount female open seat nominees spent, controlling for inflation, as a group and then breaks the amounts down by party and shows the figures for male Democrats and Republicans running as a group and for subgroups having female opponents. Two open seat elections were uncontested (Georgia Republican Thomas Price in 2004 and Florida Democrat Frederica Wilson in 2010) and 11 of the 324 contests were female versus female events. Republican male candidates raised $103,187 more than their male Democratic opponents but only $62,000 more than their female Democratic opponents, the opposite of what we would have expected based on the earlier analyses. And while on average they outspent their female Democratic opponents, in one-half of these 68 contests the Democratic female contenders actually outspent their Republican male opponents. Democratic male open seat nominees' deficit against male opponents reversed to a $280,000 advantage against their female Republican opponents, clearly a substantial advantage. Across these 28 cases Republican female nominees actually outspent 13 of their Democratic male opponents.

Among the 15 Democratic male nominees who outspent their female opponents were two outliers, James Humphreys and Phillip Maloof, both of whom primarily self-funded their campaigns. Humphreys spent $7 million of his own money and Maloof contributed $8 million of his own wealth to his campaign. Both were defeated by their female Republican opponents, Shelley Moore Capito in West Virginia in 2000 and Heather Wilson in New Mexico in 1998, respectively. Excluding those two cases, the Democratic male open seat nominees spending reverts to a deficit of $78,000 versus their Republican female opponents. Thus, the proposition that men raise and spend substantially more money than women in male-female races has little support in contemporary elections based on this analysis of these contemporary open seat general election contests including a breakdown by party. In the next section I make one final foray into an investigation of a financial aspect of open seat candidacies, those crucial races for increasing the numerical presence of women in the national legislature, the raising of early money.

A Note on Early Money and Open Seats

At least anecdotally early money has increasingly become an important part of national campaigns. Campaigns to fill coffers at the close of a reporting period are big news stories and much discussed among pundits looking for signs of viability. To add to the overall picture regarding financial resources I present findings on early money and open seat primary elections in four of the election cycles in which data are available to address questions about the relationship between gender and the timing of fund-raising efforts. To mount a credible campaign requires not only raising a substantial amount of money but also to show financial prowess at key points in the election

TABLE 5.4. Open Seat Nominees' Spending, 1994–2010

	Women Candidates	Men Candidates	Men Running against Women
Total Spending	$934,486 (122)	$825,960 (526)	$1,050,675 (96)
Democrats	$884,546 (81)	$799,954 (243)	$1,356,890 (28)
Republicans	$1,033,148 (41)	$848,376 (283)	$924,587 (68)

Source: Data compiled by the author from Federal Election Commission information; www.fec.gov.

season. Entrants into open seat primaries and those who would challenge vulnerable incumbents need to report substantial amounts of money raised in the early FEC reporting periods to discourage would-be competitors, show viability, and attract PAC and party organizational support.

For candidates seeking open seat primary nominations in districts favorable to or competitive for their party, showing that they are aggressive fund-raisers early in the process is one of the most important campaign steps to create an aura of success and invincibility. Traditional stereotypes and continuing perspectives have suggested that women's greater difficulty in raising money to support their campaign has been a major factor in keeping them from undertaking more efforts to win a seat in the national legislature and in their being perceived as more vulnerable than male contenders. Indeed, as is well known, the initial stimulus for the formation of EMILY's List was to overcome these perceptions by helping women amass a large early war chest.

A Woman's Place Is in the House and subsequent studies (Burrell 2008b) have shown that contrary to conventional wisdom women entering open seat primaries were competing on a level playing field with their male opponents or were outpacing them in acquiring early money. Especially with the growth of EMILY's List and for a time its Republican counterpart, the WISH List, at least viable pro-choice women candidates should have continued in the most contemporary election cycles to have mounted financially well-funded campaigns early in the process or at least not to have suffered from a deficiency of campaign receipts relative to male contenders.

As noted earlier, the FEC requires candidates for federal office who have raised $5,000 or more in campaign contributions to file reports on a quarterly basis. Those reports not only provide us with information for "early money" analyses but they have come to serve as fund-raising motivators for interest groups to demonstrate a supported candidate's financial muscle. Unfortunately, while the quarterly reports are made public by the FEC during an election cycle, with each new reporting period the amounts raised and spent are aggregated across the whole cycle to date. Thus, for analysis purposes the quarterly reports have to be downloaded when they are made public and before they are folded into the next reporting period or become part of the total fund-raising efforts of candidates for the whole election cycle. I have been able to capture these data only for four of the election cycles in this time period, for 1994 (because of earlier research) and for the three most recent cycles, 2006 through 2010.

Data on the amounts of money reported at the end of June of each of these election years are presented in this analysis. I use June data rather than March data or even earlier reported data because of the dynamics of seats becoming open. By June most incumbents who do not plan to seek reelection have announced their intention to step down, although not all. Some announce retirement plans at the end of the previous election, giving potential successors sufficient time to mount their campaigns and raise money, while other incumbents do not make a public decision to retire until close to the filing deadline for seeking reelection. Those deadlines vary across the states relative to primary dates. Some states, such as Illinois and Texas, have held their primaries in the spring of the election year, while a number of other states have not held their primaries until September, such as New York and Massachusetts.

Figure 5.10 compares the median and mean reported amounts of male and female open seat primary campaign receipts by the June reporting period in these four election periods. Both median and mean amounts are presented to illustrate whether a few outlier candidates contributing significant amounts of their own money and whether the substantial number of candidates not having raised any money affect comparisons based on means. As figure 5.10 clearly shows, on both of the indicators—means and medians—female open seat primary contenders have outpaced their male counterparts in raising early money. In some comparisons, the differences are large while in others the male and female candidates are nearly equal. Only in 2010 did the female candidates lag behind male candidates. Initially, not being able to raise early money does not appear to be a factor disadvantaging female candidates.

Describing average differences between open seat male and female primary candidates in their early financial efforts only begins an analysis of the relationship between sex and this important aspect of candidate viability. More sophisticated investigation of the political puzzles surrounding early money as it relates to gender issues as well as election issues more generally should be undertaken in future research. Such analyses would require the tracking of retirement announcements and capturing fund-raising efforts early on and at various stages of the primary process. In addition, if the research effort is on gender aspects of the campaign process, then incorporating the entrance of women's PACs and networks into campaigns would be important to the research design.

Hannagan, Pimlott, and Littvray's study on the relationship between an EMILY's List endorsement and electoral success is an excellent effort in this direction (2010). The authors use a propensity scoring method to

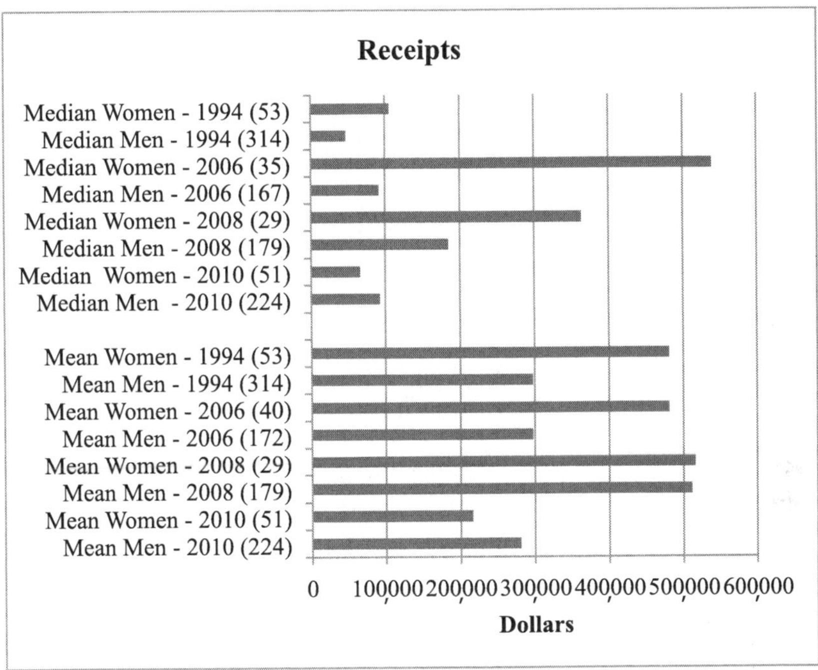

Fig. 5.10. Early Money—Average June Receipts, Open Seat Candidates by Sex; 1994, 2006–10. (Data compiled by the author from Federal Election Commission information; www.fec.gov.)

divide the characteristics of female Democratic candidates' campaigns into quartiles as to the likelihood of an EMILY's List endorsement given its strategic decision-making process regarding entering a race. Using experimental methodology, they examine the impact of an endorsement within each of the quartiles. The impact varies across the comparison groups. In the unlikely case of an EMILY's List endorsement of a candidate who has little money and organization in place, obtaining an endorsement almost quadruples the likelihood of success. Among other things, in their call for further research these authors highlight "the need to include a variable capturing the timing associated with any EList endorsement" (507). Crespin and Deitz's research (2010), which shows the significant effect of women's donor networks on the fund-raising of female candidates between 1998 and 2002, especially for Democratic female candidates, also has advanced our knowledge in this domain although their work has not centered on timing of donations.

Sex, Money, and Votes

This chapter has shown that female congressional candidates compete on a fairly level playing field with male candidates in contemporary elections when it comes to building campaign war chests. They also are just as good or better in some cases at obtaining voter support and winning elections with some blips here and there. But whether spending is translated into votes in a similar fashion for male and female candidates is a crucial question regarding outcomes and whether men and women compete equally in acquiring votes. An investigation of the effect of campaign spending on votes between the two sexes in general elections between 1974 and 1980 showed that female challengers gained proportionately more votes for their dollars than male challengers (Burrell 1985). But the analysis of that study was hardly definitive and much may have changed in thirty years.

Scholars have generated numerous hypotheses about various possible gender dynamics in contemporary congressional elections and investigated trends in those dynamics as cited throughout this work. Yet few scholars have investigated more nuanced gender aspects of the relationship between campaign fund-raising and vote shares and winning. An analysis of campaign finance resource data was not included in Palmer and Simon's extensive longitudinal research. Herrick's research has considered the important question of whether male and female candidates need similar levels of resources to get votes (1996). Taking into account campaign spending, party strength, party identification, and previous experience, she examined the campaigns of male and female nonincumbent candidates from 1988 through 1992. Contrary to my earlier findings, for these election cycles male challengers received more value from money and party strength than did female challengers. Gender differences in the value of resources, however, were much smaller in open seat races (76). (See also Milyo and Schosberg's study [2000] of sex and incumbency in the 1984–92 elections.) It is curious that the availability of FEC financial records have not stimulated more research about their gendered consequences in election outcomes. I end this investigation of campaign financial resources then with a return to the question I asked in 1985: Does money buy the same in votes for both sexes (263) or, in the words of Rebekah Herrick, "is there a gender gap in the value of resources" in obtaining votes (1996, 69)?

Table 5.5 displays the results of multivariate analyses examining the impact of campaign spending on votes for incumbents, challengers, and open seat contenders in contested races for the nine elections of this study. The dependent variable is the percentage of the vote a candidate obtained in the November election. Independent variables include inflation-controlled expenditures, sex, party, and competitiveness measured by the most recent Republican vote for president in the district. To test for the effect of gender on the value of candidate spending I have included an interaction variable by multiplying sex by spending.

Democrats were disadvantaged in obtaining votes across the candidate status categories as would be expected given Republican dominance in seven of the nine elections. Their disadvantage was greatest in open seat contests. Female candidates were advantaged across the status groups as the earlier bivariate relationships also showed. The amount spent was negatively related to the vote share incumbents obtained, which would be expected given the research that has shown that they spend in response to the strength of the challenge they face (see, for example, Jacobson 1990). Spending has a positive impact for challengers and open seat candidates. Campaign spending helps male more than female candidates in all three status categories, as Herrick found for earlier election periods, but the effect is minimal and it is not statistically significant in two of the three categories. For every $100,000 a male candidate spends, he receives 0.1 percent more votes than does a female candidate spending $100,000. Thus, the gender value of financial resources is quite insignificant.

TABLE 5.5. Effect of Campaign Spending on Vote Share, 1994–2010

	Incumbents		Challengers		Open Seats	
Variables	*b*	Beta	*b*	Beta	*b*	Beta
Party	−1.55***	−.08	−1.74***	−.09	−3.03***	−.12
	(.366)		(.330)		(.913)	
Party Strength	−.22***	−.31	.251***	.35	.012	.01
	(.014)		(.012)		(.038)	
Sex	1.17*	.04	.511	.02	1.42	.04
	(.709)		(.435)		(1.75)	
Spending	−.007***	−.37	.012***	.53	.005***	.26
	(.000)		(.000)		(.001)	
Sex × Spending	−.001*	−.04	−.001	−.017	−.001	−.05
	(.000)		(.001)		(.002)	
Constant	79.4***		20.65***		45.75***	
	(.756)		(.486)		(1.93)	
Adjusted R^2	.26		.40		.07	
Number of Cases	3,026		3,032		720	

Note: The number of challengers is greater than the number of incumbents because there were six cases of incumbents being independents.

*$p \leq .05$; **$p \leq .01$; ***$p \leq .001$.

Men and Women as Donors to Political Campaigns

The regression analysis of factors affecting campaign receipts showed that gender mattered in that female candidates more often raised more money to fund their campaigns than male candidates, controlling for party and candidate status. Data on the internal structure of campaign financial resources suggested that gender was a factor in raising funds to a modest extent, again to the advantage of female candidates. If, in conclusion, attention is turned from elites seeking office to the general public as donors in election campaigns research has shown that gender matters substantially and in this case women lag far behind men. For example, in their survey of large donors to congressional candidates in 1996, Francia et al. found that contributors to U.S. House and Senate campaigns are "overwhelmingly middle-aged white men" (2003, 27).

Trying to get women to open their checkbooks for female candidates in 1992, former Texas governor Ann Richards challenged women at a campaign rally to consider that "for just one good pair of Ferragamo shoes you can write Barbara [Boxer] and Dianne [Feinstein] a check. Then pass up an Ellen Tracy jacket and give some more. Then an Anne Klein pair of pants . . ." (Ayres 1992). This chapter's introductory anecdote highlighted Jan Schakowsky's targeting of women as donors. Getting women to open their pocketbooks, their checkbooks, and now make online donations using their credit cards has been a major target of women's PACs and cheerleaders for female candidates, as Gov. Richards's words illustrate. From their analysis of contributors in 1996, Francia et al. concluded that "those women who give are more likely than men to be occasional donors, and they give smaller amounts to fewer candidates" (2003, 29).

Things seem not to have changed. Since 1990 the Center for Responsive Politics has tracked the demographics of individuals giving $200 or more to federal campaigns based on Federal Election Commission reports. On Women's Equality Day, August 26, 2011, the Center issued a statement "that women have a long way to go until they see equality as political donors. At the federal level, men consistently give more than two-thirds of all donations reported in an itemized fashion to the Federal Election Commission—when measured by number of donors and amount of money contributed" (Beckel 2011).

General survey data have shown that women have been less likely to engage in the political process by contributing money to candidates and party organizations. One of the consistent findings regarding political participation has been that while women tend to vote at higher rates than men, they lag behind men in political financial giving. According to Burns, Schlozman, and Verba's participation study (2001), men give money while women give time to political campaigns. On an individual level women have less money than men and less control over the money in their households (Ford 2006). At the same time, women control 51 percent of the nation's personal wealth (Women's Campaign Forum 2007).

Few male or female Americans, usually less than 10 percent, report making financial contributions to political candidates in election years. In the 2000 American National Election study, 9 percent of men and 5 percent of women said they had made a financial donation to a political candidate; however, in the 2008 ANES study, an equal percentage of male and female respondents reported giving money to a candidate. The Center for Responsive Politics' "The Big Picture" reports, available on its Opensecrets.org website, provide demographic information on contributors to federal candidates over time including a comparison of men's and women's donations of $200 or more. Only a tiny fraction, less than 1 percent, of the adult male and female population gives contributions large enough to be itemized and used in research analyses. In 2010, for example, only 0.35 percent of the adult population donated $200 or more to congressional candidates, 0.18 percent of adult females and 0.46 percent of adult males. Men were 70 percent of the donors and gave 74 percent of contributions of $200 or more. Figure 5.11 shows the comparison of the total dollar amounts men and women have contributed in each of these election cycles between 1994 through 2010. The figure shows both trends in the growth of dollars donated and the persistent advantage of male givers over female donors. The margin of difference remains fairly consistent.

The Women's Campaign Forum's 2007 "Vote with Your Purse" study and follow-up studies after the 2008 and 2010 elections have provided a more detailed account of the financial giving of men and women in which it argues that women could even "change the world for the price of a pair of shoes" (4). The WCF's "Vote with Your Purse" studies are examples of how women's political groups are expanding the ways in which they impact the political process in favor of women's candidacies. The Forum wanted to find out why women were not giving more, how could they be stimulated to be more active donors, and how that might affect the financial resources of women candidates. Their studies have included analyses of FEC data in conjunction with the Center for Responsive Politics. In addition, in the 2006 election it also undertook a survey of 300 men and 300 women and focus groups in three cities to gain a better understanding of the problem.

In the 2006 election "Vote with Your Purse" reported that women

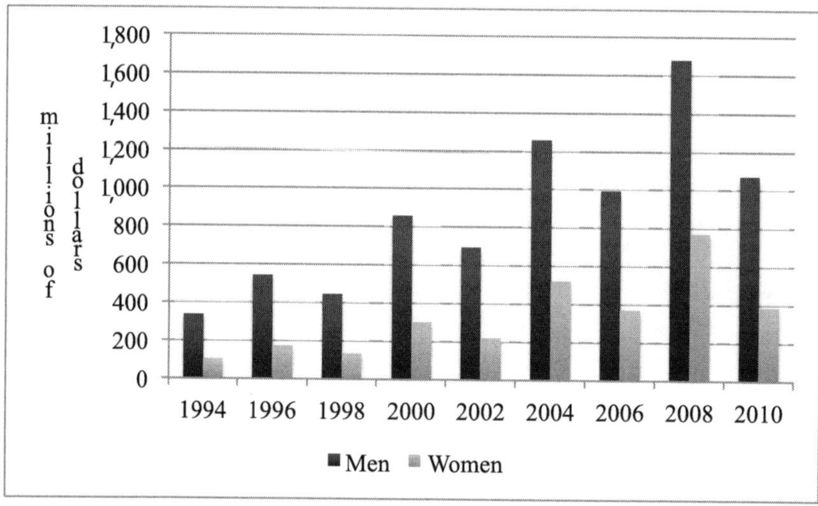

Fig. 5.11. Total Amount of Contributions of $200 or More to Federal Candidates by Sex. (Data compiled by the author from Federal Election Commission information; www.fec.gov.)

represented only 27 percent of individual direct money contributions to candidates, party committees, and political action committees at the federal election level. They gave just 28 percent of single or combined contributions of $1,000 or more, and of the 778 U.S. House races the FEC tracked, only 27 candidates raised the majority of their individual funds from women. When women did give, they prioritized female candidates. Women gave 30 percent of their dollars to female candidates; men gave female candidates just 17 percent.

A consistent gender gap in giving to candidates of the two major parties has also existed in these nine election cycles, with women giving a larger percentage of their itemized donations to Democrats. The gap in 2010 was 10 percent; female donors contributing $200 or more gave 48 percent of their donations to Democratic candidates compared to 36 percent of the male donors. They gave 39 percent of their donations to Republican candidates while men gave 43 percent of their donations to Republicans. The rest of their donations went to PACs rather than candidates. This finding should not be surprising given the contemporary gender gap in voting in presidential and congressional elections, and the preponderance of women's donor networks promoting Democratic female candidates. The 2010 election, however, seemed to energize conservative women, led by Sarah

Palin. But whether they sought to influence that election and continue to financially participate through "opening their purses" to a greater extent than in the past is another ripe question for more research.

The "Vote with Your Purse" report following the 2010 election, which was issued in April 2012, shows that women's giving as a percentage of total giving of campaign contributions of $200 or more to federal candidates fell to 26 percent from 31 percent in 2008. Their individual contributions to candidates, their contributions to party committees, and to PACs all declined. Only four out of 2,215 candidates relied on women for more than half of the individual contributions to their campaigns. A disjunction between the giving of women as donors and the fund-raising of women as candidates continues to characterize our national elections.

Tracking and analyzing female donors and their contributions to candidates of both parties in the election cycles of the second decade of the 21st century should be a focus of future women and politics research concerned with political leadership in the United States. This chapter also suggested that timing decisions regarding donations is another area of potential research to even more deeply assess gendered aspects of the campaign finance world.

Chapter 6 extends the analysis of the financial structures of these campaigns through an examination of party organizational support and the impact of women's PACs and female donor networks. It also describes the movement of women into party campaign leadership positions, illustrating the contemporary fund-raising prowess of women engaged in the political process. It provides evidence of the further demise of the folktale of women being deficient financiers of their campaigns.

This chapter has also shown that not much evidence exists suggesting that women need more funding to do as well as men. I have searched through many of the facets of campaign financing that have been suggested as possible hurdles for female candidates and ways in which they may have been handicapped and found few disadvantages. If anything, female candidates have been advantaged, at least marginally. Yet the idea of a financial disadvantage and greater fund-raising hurdles for female candidates persists.

SIX

Political Parties, Women's Organizations, and the Election of Women to Congress

The focus of previous chapters has been on individual candidates, their strategic entrance into congressional elections, their accumulation of financial resources, and their vote-getting ability. Investigating the performance of male and female candidates to investigate gender factors in congressional campaigns has been at the center of this inquiry, with considerations of partisanship and candidate status framing the analyses. These individual efforts, however, are embedded in a complex and robust electoral organizational world that consists of three primary elements. First, these organizational factors include national party organizations and subgroups within them charged with enhancing women's candidacies. Second, they include female representatives taking on leadership roles within these organizations and individually establishing leadership PACs. Third, they involve women's PACs, women's issue PACs, and donor networks, all of which have become prominent actors in congressional elections as a distinctive force on women's candidacies and election in the contemporary era. This chapter investigates these aspects of contemporary congressional elections to enhance our understanding of women's political leadership quests.

Political party organizations have reemerged and been revitalized as important resources in the candidate-centered world of contemporary politics. Party scholars Gary Jacobson and Paul Herrnson have spotlighted this resurgence. Jacobson describes "the flowering of national party activity" (2009, 82) and Herrnson has concluded from extensive analysis and observation that "[t]he national parties responded to these needs, not by doing away with the candidate-centered election system but by assuming a more important role in it" (2008, 88).

Additionally, women's campaign organizations have come to play key roles in the campaigns of female candidates both within the party organizational umbrella and as separate distinct organizations. In the age of the gender gap in partisanship and voting behavior, it would be to the parties' advantage to create incentives for their female activists to run for elective office and provide them with organizational support. Female members of Congress have also taken on assertive roles as financial leaders within their party's campaigns.

One of the major trends identified in elections since the 1992 "year of the woman" election has been a growing partisan gap in the presence of Democratic and Republican female candidates for elective office and in the their numbers among the membership of the U.S. Congress, as shown in figure 1.1 in this book's introduction and discussed throughout this work. As primary candidates, general election nominees, and as winners, since 1990 the proportion of female Democrats has climbed while the proportion of Republican female candidates has leveled off or declined (Palmer and Simon 2008). The slowed progress of women's congressional representation has principally been a function of a lag in Republican women's candidacies until 2010 (Elder 2008).

Laurel Elder has shown that three factors account for the partisan gap among women in Congress. The congressional pipeline has "become more effective at advancing Democratic women than Republican women"; a regional realignment of the parties in the House and Senate, with Republicans making gains in the South, the region most inhospitable to women, while losing ground in other regions; and "the disproportionate success rates of women of color in obtaining seats in Congress combined with their almost exclusive Democratic partisanship" have contributed to the party gap.

Data in this study show that lack of a presence by Republican women in the vitally important open seat primaries is the biggest partisan and gender gap aspect of contemporary congressional campaigns. When they have run, their experience has not been very different from their Democratic female counterparts or their fellow male partisans, although they occasionally have been hardest hit by unfavorable electoral contexts.

One might expect that the success of its female delegation would be positively correlated with the overall success of a party. The greater the number of total winners in the party, the larger the number of female winners, and female members' reelection rate would be positively related to the party's total reelection rate. However, Palmer and Simon (2008) have shown that the parties have differed in the relationship of the success of their female candidates and success of the party overall. Examining trends from 1956 through 2006, they found that the worse Democrats did overall the better their female candidates did whereas party success more generally for Republicans has had a positive impact on their female candidates. The correlation between the proportion of Democrats in the House and women as a proportion of House Democrats was –.76 over these fifty years. They surmised that "when Democrats fare poorly in the electoral arena, male Democrats absorb the bulk of the electoral losses" (2008, 169). For the Republicans the expected positive correlation was found. The correlation between the proportion of Republicans in the House and women as a proportion of the Republican Conference was .58. The presence of Republican females depended on the overall success of Republicans at the polls, they concluded. The implication Palmer and Simon assert is that "when Democrats suffer at the polls, incumbent males are the 'first to go.' When Republicans suffer, the relationship is reversed, with incumbent women being the most likely electoral casualties."

The 1994 election, however, in which the Republicans took over control of the House after decades of Democratic dominance, had little effect on the proportion of women in either party's caucus. Democratic female members' losses paralleled male losses and female Republicans gained at the same rate as the party overall. Their proportions of their party's membership in the U.S. House remained unchanged. Following their large loss in the 1994 election, Democrats barely altered their share of the House membership between the 1996 election and the 2004 election. At the same time, female Democrats marginally improved their proportion of that party's membership, climbing from 15 percent to 21 percent. Both men and women advanced in the Democratic resurgent elections of 2006 and 2008, producing no gains in the female proportion of its caucus. Male Democrats were harder hit than female Democrats in 2010, resulting in their female proportion increasing to 24 percent of the membership. Remember also that four women of color had newly won Democratic seats in that election. During the same interval, Republican female representatives' share of their party's House membership was essentially static in these most recent congresses. Even in 2010, with the large Republican gains, female Republican membership neither gained nor declined proportionately. It was 10 percent prior to the 2010 election and 10 percent at the inauguration of the

112th Congress. These figures and trends provide a context for exploring organizational cultures and actions fostering female candidacies and elections in the contemporary era.

Organizational Promotion of Women Candidates

Since the early 1970s the women's movement in the United States has increasingly centered on electoral and partisan politics to promote its goals of equality. An extensive network of organizations and political action committees has developed with the common purpose of electing more women to public office. The largest and most successful of these organizations, EMILY's List, has been noted throughout this work. These groups have pressured the political parties to advance women as candidates, formed groups within the parties to recruit women, provided resources for their campaigns, and worked independently to elect women.

The first such organization, the National Women's Political Caucus, was formed in 1971 to "help elect women and also men who declare themselves ready to fight for the needs and rights of women and all underrepresented groups." Its statement of purpose pledged to oppose sexism, racism, institutional violence, and poverty through the election and appointment of women to political office; to reform political party structures to give women an equal voice in decision making and the selection of candidates; to support women's issues and feminist candidates across party lines; and to work in coalition with other oppressed groups. Although it is a bipartisan organization it has more effect on the Democratic Party.

The Democratic Party's distinct culture made it the site of early action regarding the promotion of women candidates (Freeman 1987). Feminists, as an accepted organized group within the party, gained leadership attention and obtained a sympathetic ear within the party's liberal wing. As early as 1974, the Democratic Party sponsored a "Campaign Conference for Democratic Women" aimed at electing more women to political office (Scott 1974). The 1,200 women who attended the workshop passed resolutions urging their party to do more for potential female candidates. Most of the few female members of the U.S. House of Representatives in the 1970s were Democrats, including a number who won their seats not because they were championed within their local party organizations but because they challenged local party structures and beat them.

The Republican Party did not begin to hold similar conferences until nearly a decade later. This later Republican start does not mean that their party has been less receptive to female candidacies, however. Indeed, feminist leaders Eleanor Smeal, former chair of the National Organization for Women (NOW), and former congresswoman Bella Abzug have argued just the opposite (Freeman 1989; Abzug 1984). Republican women have tended to credit men with bringing them into the organization during the feminist era (Romney and Harrison 1988). But as we know from the analyses in the preceding chapters, the Republican Party has become a trouble spot in the quest to increase the numbers of women in elective office and attain a "critical mass" and more in the national legislature in more recent years.

Wanting to appear supportive of women in the face of an emerging gender gap among voters in the 1980s, Republican leaders in particular publicly acknowledged the importance of public support for women's candidacies. Republican Senatorial Campaign Committee (RSCC) chair Senator Richard Lugar issued a press statement in 1983 declaring that "a concerted drive by the Republican Party to stamp itself as the party of the woman elected official would serve our nation as well as it serves our own political interests. The full political participation of women is a moral imperative for our society and intelligent political goal for the Republican Party." He pledged to "commit the RSCC to the maximum legal funding and support for any Republican woman who is nominated next year, regardless of how Democratic the state or apparently formidable the Democratic candidate. I am prepared to consider direct assistance to women candidates even prior to their nomination, a sharp departure from our usual policy" (Lugar 1983).

The Democrats in 1984 included a section "Political Empowerment for Minorities and Women" in their party platform, the major document each party produces outlining its principles and policy positions. The section stated, "We will recruit women and minorities to run for Governorships and all state and local offices. The Democratic Party (through its campaign committees) will commit to spending maximum resources to elect women and minority candidates and offer these candidates in-kind services, including political organizing and strategic advice. And the bulk of all voter registration funds will be spent on targeted efforts to register minorities and women."

In 1988, both national party platforms included statements recommending support for women's candidacies. The Democrats endorsed "full and equal access of women and minorities to elective office and party endorsement," while the Republicans called for "strong support for the efforts of women in seeking an equal role in government and [commitment] to the vigorous recruitment, training and campaign support for women candidates at all levels." However, these pledges did not include any action plans for implementation. Prior to 1990, party organizational calls for increasing the number of women candidates were only rhetorical, as there were few substantive actions to ensure that women were nominated in favorable electoral circumstances.

Then, for a variety of reasons, 1992 developed as the "year of the woman" in American politics as cited in chapter 1. With the end of the Cold War, attention was increasingly turning away from foreign policy and defense and toward domestic issues in which women were perceived to have expertise. The confirmation hearings for Clarence Thomas's nomination to the U.S. Supreme Court shined a spotlight on the absence of women in the Senate and upset women who thought that Anita Hill's charges of sexual harassment against Thomas were trivialized. The reapportionment and redistricting process also resulted in more open seats than usual, creating new electoral opportunities.

All of these forces stimulated the parties to direct an even greater share of their recruitment activity toward women than in previous years. The leadership of both parties' congressional campaign committees made special efforts to seek out qualified female House candidates. The Democratic Senatorial Campaign Committee (DSCC) formed a women's council that raised approximately $1.5 million for Democratic women running for the Senate. These affirmative steps did not, however, spur the parties to clear the field of primary competition for women or discourage anyone, male or female, from running against women (Biersack and Herrnson 1994).

Republican women, too, have initiated specific efforts to recruit and train women as political and public leaders. These endeavors have included the work of the National Federation of Republican Women and the Republican National Committee's Excellence in Public Service Series. The Federation has provided training for potential Republican women candidates. As early as 1976, it published a booklet, *Consider Yourself for Public Office: Guidelines for Women Candidates*. The Excellence in Public Service Series is a political leadership development program Republican women's groups offer in 12 states; most of the programs are named for prominent Republicans. The Lugar Series in Indiana, which was initiated in 1989, was the first such program. Typically, the yearlong series of programs, with eight monthly sessions and a three-day leadership seminar in Washington, DC, is offered to selected women willing to make a commitment to play an active role in the political arena. Classes are designed to encourage, prepare, and inspire women leaders to seek new levels of involvement in government and politics.

Women have also increasingly become prominent actors within the party organizations. A woman first managed a presidential campaign in 1988, when Susan Estrich ran Democrat Michael Dukakis's campaign. In 2000, Donna Brazile became the first African American woman to manage a presidential campaign when she assumed the helm of Democratic Vice President Al Gore's presidential quest. In 2004 Mary Beth Cahill was campaign manager of the John Kerry quest for the presidency. In the 2004 Republican campaign, former White House assistant Karen Hughes, while not a campaign manager, was a key advisor in the Bush reelection effort, the same position she held in the 2000 election. Hillary Clinton's campaign for the presidency in 2008 was managed by women, first Patti Solis Doyle and then Maggie Williams. Neither Barack Obama nor John McCain in 2008 had a woman as a campaign manager. Indeed, the Obama campaign was criticized during the primaries for being a "boy's club" (Brown 2008). John McCain, after being accused of having a campaign heavily dominated by male advisors, brought a number of high-profile women from the world of business to the forefront of his organization.

Congressional Campaign Committees and Women's Candidacies

The parties' congressional campaign committees have developed into significant organizations in the contemporary campaign era. They recruit candidates in opportune races for the party to enhance its congressional numbers either by taking on vulnerable incumbents of the opposite party or winning open seats. They provide candidates with assistance in managing their campaigns and raising money and connect them with technical experts. They also shore up their own vulnerable incumbents. These organizations have become major sources of campaign money, services, and advice for congressional candidates (Herrnson 2008). Especially since the passage of the McCain-Feingold Bipartisan Campaign Reform Act in 2002, their independent expenditures on behalf of candidates in the final days of the election have become a crucial campaign resource. For example, in 2008 the Democratic Senatorial Campaign Committee spent $7 million on behalf of Kay Hagan's senatorial campaign in North Carolina.

To assess gender parity issues surrounding congressional party campaign organizations requires an investigation of their recruitment of female candidates and, importantly, their equitable financial assistance to their campaigns and a chronicling of female members' involvement and leadership in these groups. Important questions center on the role women legislators play in these organizations and whether the party leaders have seen women as viable candidates to the same degree as potential male candidates and have assisted them in winning to the same extent. When it comes to pouring money into races in the final weeks of the election, are the same amounts of cash spent on advertising for their female candidates and against their opponents as for their would-be male members? If the parties act rationally, they would certainly be doing so.

These congressional organizations are the Democratic Congressional Campaign Committee and the National Republican Congressional Committee in the U.S. House, and the Democratic Senatorial Campaign Committee and the National Republican Senatorial Committee in the U.S. Senate. By federal law, the congressional groups may directly contribute only $5,000 for a primary race and $5,000 for the general election to any one candidate's campaign. Beyond these funds, these organizations can spend larger but limited amounts in coordinated activities, such as financing a public opinion poll for several candidates. But they can spend unlimited amounts in independent expenditures, such as buying TV ads sponsored by the party committee and shown "independently" of candidates' campaigns in their districts. Independent expenditures took on a new prominence after the passage of the McCain-Feingold Bipartisan Campaign Reform Act, signed into law in 2002, which banned soft money, or unregulated money used in support of party activities.

The use of primary elections to nominate party candidates for public office has weakened the control of party organizations over candidate selection. But the parties have initiated aggressive recruitment endeavors to encourage those they believe will be the most viable candidates to run in competitive districts and provide resources and expert advice to general election candidates.

In 2004, the DCCC inaugurated the Red to Blue program in which it would mount major efforts to recruit and support strong Democratic candidates in normally Republican districts. In a 2006 press release Rep. Rahm Emanuel, that election cycle's DCCC chair, described it as "an exclusive program that will reward the candidates and campaigns that are most skilled, not only at raising money on their own, but at getting their message across to the voters they hope to represent (Democratic Congressional Campaign Committee 2006). It has now evolved into a three-tiered program with Emerging Races, Majority Makers, and Red to Blue races. Candidates move through these stages as their campaigns evolve. The DCCC's campaign apparatus works with and observes a campaign's development to determine if at some point in the process it merits Red to Blue status and the independent infusion of advertising resources.

The Republicans followed suit in 2008, establishing a Young Guns program, and have also expanded it into a three-level fund-raising and infrastructure program for open-seat and challenger candidates. Candidates move from On-the-Radar status to Contender status and then on to being a Young Gun. The party organizations have also initiated other targeted efforts to shore up vulnerable incumbents. The Republican incumbent protection program is titled the Patriot program and the Democratic effort is their Frontline program.

Democratic Congresswomen and Campaign Committees

In recent election cycles female members have advanced into leadership positions within these congressional campaign committees. On the Democratic side they have established subgroups to promote the candidacies of women. In 1994, for example, a group of Democratic congresswomen traveled across the country to boost each others' candidacies, most of whom were first-termers from swing districts facing tough reelection contests. The road show consisted of attending fund-raising events in which they spoke of the difference women make in Congress. The road show featured an amusing video, "Women in Congress: Making a Difference," a seven-minute, 45-second trip from the day that women got the vote through the first woman in Congress, the Equal Rights Amendment, Geraldine Ferraro, and Anita Hill to the "year of the woman" in 1992 (Byrne 1994).

In the 107th Congress (2001–02), Rep. Nita Lowey of New York became chair of the DCCC and Senator Patty Murray of Washington chaired the DSCC. (She returned as its chair in the 112th Congress.) In 1999, Rep. Lowey had founded Women Lead, a fund-raising subsidiary of the DCCC to target female donors and contributors to female candidates. When Lowey became chair of the DCCC, she appointed Representative Jan Schakowsky to head Women Lead. In the 2001–02 election cycle, that committee raised approximately $25 million for women candidates. Lowey had admired Schakowsky's fund-raising prowess in her initial run for an open House seat in 1997 as described in chapter 5. Rep. Schakowsky continues to raise money for Democratic female House candidates, most prominently through her annual "Ultimate Women's Power" Lunch held in a Chicago hotel each spring with an all-star line-up of speakers. Speaker Pelosi was the featured speaker in 2008 and Valerie Jarrett, senior advisor to the president for intergovernmental affairs in the Obama administration, headlined the 2009 event. In 2012 the scheduled keynote speakers were Lilly Ledbetter, after whom the Lilly Ledbetter Fair Pay Act is named, and

Senator Amy Klobuchar, Democratic U.S. senator from Minnesota. Occasionally Hollywood stars have headlined the program. The Women Lead program continues. In the 112th Congress Reps. Karen Bass (D-CA) and Jackie Speier (D-CA) cochaired the program.

Prior to being appointed to chair the DSCC, Senator Murray had launched a similar program in 1999 called Women on the Road to the Senate, which helped elect four women senators in 2000. In 2002, the program was renamed the Women's Senate Network and Senator Debbie Stabenow of Michigan became its head. In the 2004 election it raised $1.3 million on top of some $2 million collected through various events early in that election cycle. Fund-raising activities included $1,000-per-person issue conferences on topics such as terrorism, national security, and the economy that showcased Senators Hillary Rodham Clinton, Dianne Feinstein, and other "prominent senators who happen to be women." Stabenow noted that it irked her that her female colleagues were so rarely interviewed on such topics (Stolberg 2004). In 2004, an event in California raised $200,000 for Senator Barbara Boxer's campaign for reelection.

I have previously told the story of Democrat Debbie Wassermann Schultz who was elected to Congress from Florida's 20th district in 2004 (Burrell 2006). The typical relationship in open seat contests is for the candidate to make the case that he or she should be a recipient of financial and other resource support from his or her congressional campaign committee. But in a unique twist, candidate Wasserman Schultz donated $100,000 to the Democratic Congressional Campaign Committee. DCCC spokesperson Greg Speed said it was the first ever six-digit donation to that organization from a Democratic nonincumbent. Schultz, endorsed by U.S. House minority leader Nancy Pelosi in March, faced no opposition in the Democratic primary (as noted in chap. 4) to succeed Congressman Peter Deutsch, for whom she had worked as a legislative aide when he had been a state representative (Harrell 2004). The 20th congressional district is a staunchly Democratic area, and Wasserman Schultz was considered the overwhelming favorite to win in November against Republican Margaret Hostetter. Raising over $1.5 million for her campaign, Wasserman Schultz won election to Congress with 70 percent of the vote. She certainly characterizes the contemporary female candidate sophisticated in electoral prowess, strategically oriented, and formidable as a political actor. According to a report in *The Hill*, a Capitol Hill newsletter, she was putting herself in a position to obtain a seat on the Commerce and Energy Committee once she had been elected to the House. House leadership determines committee assignments that provide members with influence within the body and with assets that bring benefits to their constituents. She ended up being appointed to the Financial Services Committee.

In the 2006 election cycle first-termer Wasserman Schultz of Florida was put in charge of the DCCC's Frontline campaign, which assisted its ten most vulnerable incumbents. In 2008 Rep. Schultz was appointed cochair of the Red to Blue program along with Reps. Bruce Braley and Artur Davis. In the 111th Congress she was named a vice-chair of the DCCC. Rep. Chris Van Hollen, who had chaired the committee in the 110th Congress, chose to continue his leadership of the DCCC for 2009–10 Congress. Although one of three contenders to chair the DCCC in the 112th Congress, Wasserman Schultz was not selected. However, President Obama nominated her in 2011 to be Democratic National Committee (DNC) chair and the DNC elected her to that position. She became the second woman to ever serve as its head. In the 112th Congress, Pennsylvania Rep. Allyson Schwartz chaired the DCCC's Recruitment and Candidate Services Program and Maryland Rep. Donna Edwards chaired its Red to Blue program.

Given the leadership Democratic female members have shown in fundraising, their independence in organizing on behalf of women candidates, and their involvement in the party's campaign committees, contemporary hypotheses about Democratic Party support for its male and female candidates start from the null hypothesis of no gender difference in financial assistance and campaign promotion rather than the much older "sacrificial lamb" hypothesis. That hypothesis, however, will be tested below after reviewing the situation in the Republican Party.

Republican Congresswomen and Campaign Committees

Through the 108th Congress (2003–04), no woman had chaired a corresponding Republican campaign committee, although Representative Anne Northup of Kentucky had headed up recruitment for the NRCC. However, for the 109th Congress (2005–06), Republicans elected Senator Elizabeth Dole of North Carolina to head the National Republican Senatorial Committee. She won the position by defeating Senator Norman Coleman of Minnesota by one vote in the Senate Republican Conference. Dole had campaigned for the presidency in the early stages of the 2000 election before winning her Senate seat in 2002. She had also served in two cabinet positions in earlier Republican presidential administrations. Described as "about as close to a rock star as the Republican Senate has," she was considered to be a celebrity within the party (Dettmer 2004). She helped raise over $16 million for the NRSC in the 2004 election cycle (D. Dolan 2004). In addition, "Dole's supporters argued that she would help Republicans win over female and minority voters by putting a 'different face on the party'" (Frommer 2004).

Dole's leadership of the NRSC proved otherwise. The NRSC fell $30 million behind the DSCC in the 2006 election cycle. Some of the losing Republican Senate candidates blamed Sen. Dole and her committee for not backing them intensively enough and making bad decisions regarding advertising in support of their campaigns and against their opponents. The Associated Press reported that "President Bush's low approval ratings, the unpopular war on Iraq, voter concern about corruption and Democratic fund-raising all figured in the GOP loss of Senate control in last month's elections. But among Republicans, long-hidden tensions are spilling into view, with numerous critics venting their anger at the GOP Senate campaign committee headed by North Carolina Sen. Elizabeth Dole" (Espo 2006). The Republican National Committee set up outside checks on the NRSC (Frontrunner 2006). Given both GOP Senate and House losses and President Bush's low approval ratings the NRSC should not take total blame for GOP loss of control of the Senate, however.

In 2007, NRCC chair Tom Cole charged Representative Candice Miller of Michigan to lead an effort to recruit women as candidates for the House (Blake 2007; also see Elder 2008). No media reports followed this announcement about subsequent recruitment activities nor did the NRCC issue any follow-up press releases about action in this area. Further, the miniscule number of Republican women mounting candidacies for House seats in the 2008 election, especially in the 26 House districts Republican incumbents vacated, suggests this effort was anemic at best.

Looking toward the 2010 election the Republicans at least publicly addressed the problem once more. The Republican National Committee announced that its "Women's Coalition is making an early push to identify women for 2010 as part of its 50-state plan." Rep. Cathy McMorris Rodgers reported that she was "bringing in groups of women from different regions of the country for tours of Capitol Hill in the hopes of getting some to run" (Lovley 2009). At the end of the election, as described in chapter 2, McMorris Rodgers issued a press release lauding 2010 as the "year of Republican women." The story of their recruitment efforts remains to be told along with assessment of Sarah Palin's endorsements of "mama grizzly" campaigns.

Leadership PACs

Congressional members' donations to other candidates have grown since the Republican revolution in 1994 as narrow legislative majorities have prompted extensive efforts on the part of both parties to maintain and regain control of the House and Senate (Jacobson 2009, 80). A major characteristic of this effort has been the development of members' own PACs to raise funds and distribute them to electorally threatened colleagues and viable challengers. Female members have not been shy about engaging in this activity, led by Speaker and Minority Leader Nancy Pelosi with her PAC to the Future. As Peters and Rosenthal note, Nancy Pelosi as a House member "had been the leading fundraiser for House Democrats for years" (2008).

Opensecrets.org lists 346 members of the U.S. Senate and House having leadership PACs in the 2010 election cycle and distributing a total of $38,817,585 in PAC contributions. Fifteen of the 17 female senators (88%) had a PAC as did 38 of the 74 female U.S. representatives (51%). At the same time 63 percent of the male U.S. representatives had a PAC and 82 percent of the male senators. The Republican House leaders, Eric Cantor and John Boehner, led the way, contributing $1,715, 346 and $1,314,050, respectively. The Democratic leaders, Steny Hoyer, James Clyburn, and Nancy Pelosi, contributed $1,206,000, $1,119,500 and $825,500,.respectively. Keep in mind that they also head up fund-raising events across the country for their members and would-be members, vastly expanding their financial significance. Table 6.1 shows the breakdown of "rank and file" leadership PAC contributions by house and party. Examining these members' PACs, the male members in both chambers outpaced their female counterparts on average in the amount they contributed to other candidates from their PAC. GOP legislators principally account for the male advantage. Seniority and committee leadership positions also account for the male advantage. Future research might informatively investigate the impact that female leadership PAC giving has had on the campaigns of female candidates.

Party Financial Support for Women Candidates

The key financial contributions of the congressional party organizations in recent elections on behalf of their candidates have been their independent expenditure efforts, which are unlimited by federal law. The key to financial gender parity from a party organizational perspective is the amounts of independent expenditures these committees pour into the campaigns of male and female candidates in the final weeks of the campaign season. In 2012, the NRCC appointed the first woman to run its independent expenditure unit, Joanna Burgos, and the DSCC appointed its first female independent expenditure director, Martha McKenna. Burgos was promoted from within the Republican Party organization, having worked her way up the ranks. Prior to this appointment, McKenna had a long career working for female candidates and as a staffer for EMILY's List. Her career links the movement of women into party leadership with a commitment to the promotion of female candidates. This linkage is an important aspect of contemporary organizational politics and individual candidacy politics for female contenders.

The allocation of independent dollars is a dynamic decision-making process for the party organizations. Candidates and their campaigns have to prove they have the ability to win to earn the expenditure of independent party money on their behalf during the final election push. Proving competitiveness is key for campaigns to win party organization expenditures on their behalf and against their opponent. From a gender perspective questions center on the comparative funds these organizations have expended on their competitive male and female candidates and incumbents in difficult reelection situations.

Further questions center on the naming of female candidates as

TABLE 6.1. Contributions Made by Leadership PACs, 2010

Chamber Number	Average Total Contribution
Senate	
Total Male PACs—68	$167,284 ($103,963)
Total Female PACs—15	$138,708 ($57,173)
Republican Men—33	$184,376 ($111,000)
Republican Women—3	$149,465 ($48,933)
Democratic Men—35	$151,168 ($95,663)
Democratic Women—12	$136,018 ($60,708)
House	
Total Men—221[a]	$77,243 ($125,038)
Total Women—37[a]	$58,001 ($103,588)
Republican Men—115	$91,069 ($140,707)
Republican Women—9	$43,608 ($44,516)
Democratic Men—106	$62,243 ($104,048)
Democratic Women—28	$62,627 ($116,742)

Source: www.opensecrets.org.
Note: Figures in parentheses are standard deviations.
[a]Excludes the five House leaders.

Young Guns within the Republican Party and as Red to Blue candidates within the Democratic Party. Is there any evidence of gender bias in obtaining these designations? Being included in these programs is highly related to having independent expenditures invested in one's campaign. Earlier in this work I have noted some media commentary suggesting dissatisfaction with the Republicans' Young Gun program having a male bias. But it is difficult to sort out where a bias occurs within the dynamic nature of the election process. There first have to be female candidates in competitive races so recruitment to and self-starting of campaigns has to be investigated. The campaign prowess of individual contenders who have announced a candidacy needs to be weighed in the process as well as an assessment of opportune situations for a party's pickup of seats. Thus, many variables must be factored into a thorough investigation of gender regarding party organizational support.

In its 2004 inaugural year the DCCC named 24 candidates to it Red to Blue program. Eight of these candidates were women. The number of candidates winning Red to Blue status expanded to 56 in 2006 and then 63 in 2008. In 2010, on the defensive and devoted to maintaining incumbents in office, only 29 candidates obtained Red to Blue status. The NRCC designated 18 candidates as Young Guns in 2008, the inaugural year of that program Two of the 18 were women. That number expanded to 54 in 2010 including four women.

Since the Bipartisan Campaign Finance Reform Act of 2002, independent expenditures are where the action has been regarding party organizational financial support of their candidates. Because of reporting requirements, these expenditures are available for scholarly analysis. Because the Act banned soft money—money not subject to federal regulation—the amounts party organizations spend independently on behalf of their candidates come from hard money, which must be reported. The parties report the money separately as funds expended on behalf of a candidate and funds expended in opposition to a candidate. Thus, for the last four election cycles of this study comparisons can be made between the Democratic and Republican campaign committees' independent expenditures in support of the candidacies of their male and female nominees.

To provide a context for the financial resources the party organizations devoted to these efforts, figure 6.1 presents the total amounts of money the DCCC and the NRCC reported spending in each of these four election cycles, which includes direct contributions to campaigns (limited to a maximum of $5,000 in a contested primary and $5,000 in the general election) and the total amount of independent expenditures reported that

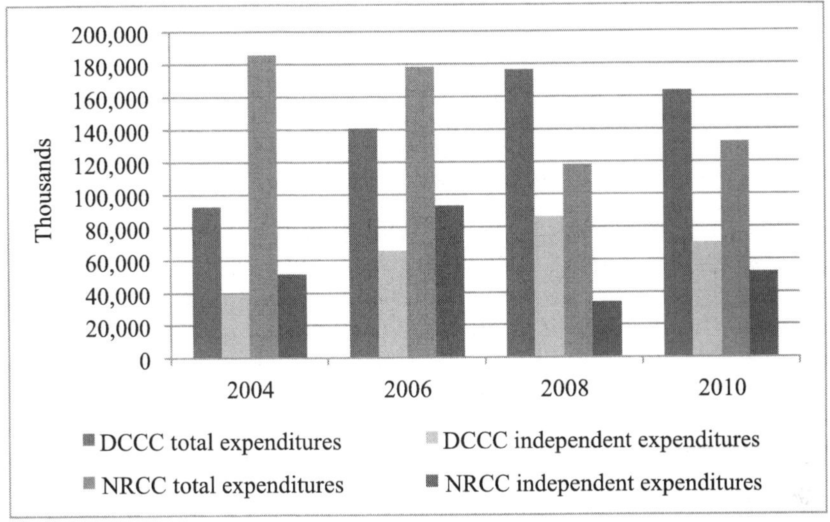

Fig. 6.1. Total Expenditures and Total Independent Expenditures, DCCC and NRCC, 2004–10. (Data from Opensecrets.org.)

were spent for and against candidates. The NRCC outpaced the DCCC in the first two election cycles in total expenditures and then the DCCC dominated in the latter two election cycles. As figure 6.1 shows, the party organizations have spent between $100 million and $200 million in each of these election cycles. They also reported substantial independent expenditure amounts into the competitive races of each election cycle. The largest independent expenditure on the Democratic side was $3.6 million spent on the 2004 South Dakota special and general elections won by Democrat Stephanie Herseth. On the Republican side the largest expenditure was nearly $4.7 million spent against Democratic challenger Lois Murphy in Pennsylvania's 6th district in 2006.

The FEC provides the total amount of independent expenditures including coordinated expenses and communication costs. These figures are used to investigate the comparative support the party organizations have given their male and female nominees in these four elections. The FEC lists the amounts expended for a candidate and against a candidate's opponent separately but they are combined here for analysis purposes. Independent expenditures of $100,000 or more have been included in this analysis in order to limit the analysis to meaningful party organizational investment. A number of reasons exist that suggest a lack of any bias against the female nominees in these four election cycles. With the closeness of the division between the two parties in these congresses, getting or maintaining the majority in the U.S. House is the *only* goal of these committees. The parties calculate the chances of winning a district and the most important factor seems to be how well a candidate is doing managing his or her campaign and showing positive numbers in opinion polls regardless of his or her sex. Additionally, why would the parties want to answer media criticism and women's organizations' admonishment that they were being sexist in their actions? Why would they engage in such behavior when they have set up subgroups to promote the candidacies of women? Further, women have become key actors within the congressional campaign committees as described earlier. They would be unlikely to give their party's female contenders less consideration. Thus, the hypothesis would be that no differences exist in the independent expenditures of the parties on behalf of their male and female nominees after taking competitive factors into account, although some female candidates not favored might complain of sexist treatment.

The NRCC made independent expenditures of $100,000 or more to 184 candidates in contested elections of these four election cycles and the DCCC made such expenditures to 204 such candidates. Female candidates in both parties were slightly overrepresented among the recipients of these funds relative to their presence among contested general election candidates. Republican women were 12 percent of the contested candidates but 17 percent of the campaigns having party independent funds expended on their campaigns; the Democratic percentages were 23 percent of candidates but 25 percent of the campaigns advantaged by this largesse.

Table 6.2 shows the mean and median amounts over $100,000 independently expended on the parties' male and female candidates over the course of these four elections. It presents a mixed picture regarding the relationship between candidate sex and financial investment. Female Democratic candidates were advantaged on average using the mean but not if medians are compared. The reverse relationship is found for the Republican candidates.

TABLE 6.2. Mean and Median DCCC and NRCC Independent Expenditures over $100,000 by Sex, 2004–2010

	Mean (s.e.)	Median	*N*
Democratic Male Candidates	$1,114,483 (55,849)	$1,121,069	153
Democratic Female Candidates	$1,148,788 (109,769)	$981,226	51
Republican Male Candidates	$1,074,648 (78,038)	$762,752	152
Republican Female Candidates	$1,039,051 (144,622)	$896,756	32

Source: Data compiled by the author from Federal Election Commission; www.fec.gov.

For a more detailed analysis of the relationship between candidate sex and party independent expenditures, the independent expended amounts over $100,000 (in $10,000s) were regressed on sex, district competitiveness based on presidential votes, and candidate status for each party. Candidate status is a set of dummy variables with incumbents as the excluded category. Table 6.3 shows the results.

This set of factors explains only a small amount of the variation in party independent expenditures as reflected in the adjusted R^2s. We need to keep in mind that the expenditure amounts have been restricted to amounts over $100,000, limiting variation but allowing for a focus on substantively meaningful dollars used to affect the election outcome. The parties first and foremost made sure that their challenged incumbents were helped, represented by the coefficients for the constant term. Open seat contenders were next in line for party investment in their campaigns, especially among the Democrats. Competitiveness acted in the expected way. The more competitive a district the more money the party organizations poured into a race. Sex had little impact on expenditures once these other factors were controlled. Female candidates were slightly underfunded within both parties but the relationship was not statistically meaningful. Thus, little empirical evidence exists of a party organizational bias against female candidates for the U.S. House.

Women's PACs and Women's Candidacies

As noted earlier, the emergence of women's groups promoting female candidates has been a notable feature of contemporary politics. They have been integral in prodding the parties to advance women's candidacies and have also taken matters into their own hands—recruiting, training, and

TABLE 6.3. Factors Affecting Party Independent and Coordinated Expenditures, 2004–10

	Democrats		Republicans	
	b	Beta	*b*	Beta
Challenger	24.70 (11.48)*	.17	–49.50 (15.41)**	.04
Open Seat	46.53 (12.24)***	.19	10.72 (17.43	.03
Sex	–8.07 (11.36)	–.05	–8.88 (17.94)	–.04
Competitiveness	2.95 (1.00)**	.20	2.80 (1.32)*	.15
Constant	109.93 (10.74)***		141.96 (13.67)***	
Adjusted R^2	.09		.09	
N	204		184	

Source: Data compiled by the author from Federal Election Commission; www.fec.gov.

providing resource bases for women candidates. The formation of women's political action committees, which are established to provide financial contributions to political candidates, has been especially significant. Women's PACs that raise money primarily or exclusively for female candidates stand "at the nexus of political change and politics as usual: bringing women into positions of power by mastering the political money game" (Day and Hadley 2005).

In addition to setting up PACs that allow them to contribute a set amount of money to federal candidates, some of these organizations have formed donor networks, encouraged women to run, trained them in campaign tactics and strategy, raised vital early money to start their campaigns, and provided a network of supportive organizations that could sustain a campaign during the final weeks of the election (Nelson 1994; Rozell 2000). Donor networks engage in bundling donations to political candidates. EMILY's List created the idea of bundling and made it into a political art. Bundling involves an organization collecting checks from individuals made out to a specific candidate the group has endorsed and bundling them together to give to the candidate in one package (or perhaps several packages over the course of a campaign). The organization gets credit from the candidate for this infusion of cash to her campaign but since the checks are written directly to the candidate's campaign and are from individual donors, not the PAC, they do not violate FEC rules on the amount a PAC can contribute directly to a campaign.

Over the course of contemporary elections, women's campaign organizations have formed at the local, state, and national level. Some have been short-lived while others have developed into sustained, viable groups. They have been both partisan and bipartisan in nature and have adopted diverse philosophies on how best to advance the numerical representation of women in public office.

EMILY's List, the WISH List, the National Women's Political Caucus (NWPC), and the Women's Campaign Fund have been the most prominent national women's groups recruiting, training, and providing resources to women candidates in the contemporary era although the latter two have a longer political history. The NWPC is the oldest of the four groups, while the Women's Campaign Fund, founded in 1974, was the first to establish a PAC to provide resources for women candidates. These two groups are bipartisan, supporting both Democratic and Republican candidates who are pro-choice. The vast majority of their money has gone to Democratic candidates, however, since they tend to be more supportive of reproductive rights than female Republican candidates. The leading role the NWPC

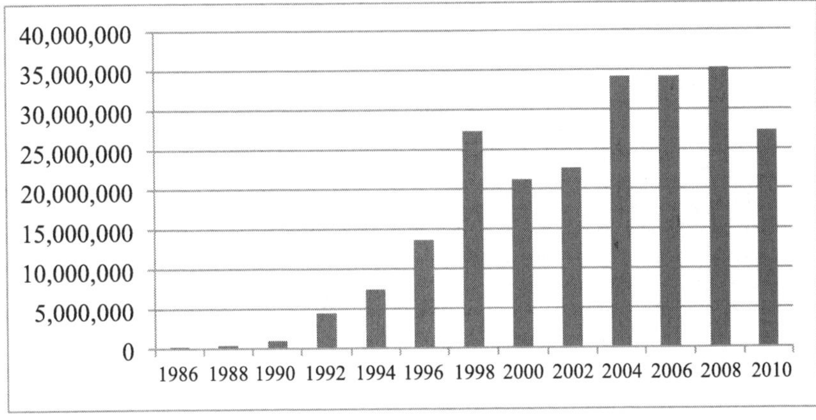

Fig. 6.2. EMILY'S List Receipts, 1986–2010. (Data from www.emilyslist.org.)

played in earlier years in recruiting and providing resources for women candidates has faded in recent election cycles as the two intraparty groups, EMILY's List and the WISH List, became key players. EMILY's List was established in 1985 and the WISH List was founded in 1992.

As suggested earlier, EMILY's List is a distinctive group. Jamie Pimlott describes it as having developed into a "multipronged influence organization that simultaneously functions as a PAC, an interest group, a campaign organization and a party adjunct" (2010, 148). In recent elections EMILY's List has been a leader among all political action committees, not just women's PACs, in the amount of financial resources it has accumulated and contributed to campaigns. The Center for Responsive Politics with its Opensecrets.org website counts EMILY's List as one of its "heavy hitter" groups. Figure 6.2 shows the growth in the amount of money EMILY's List has raised over the past two decades. Indeed, Democratic Party efforts to recruit women candidates have become virtually indistinguishable from the candidate recruitment strategies of EMILY's List, according to Rosalyn Cooperman's research (2001).

As with any highly successful and dominant political group, EMILY's List has acquired its critics and commentators have come to question its continued success. In an extensive 2008 article Bara Vaida and Jennifer Skalka of the *National Journal* asked "Can EMILY's List Get Its Mojo Back?" What seemed to be the problem? In part it stemmed from EMILY's List's lackluster success rate in 2006 when only eight of the 31 (26%) House and Senate challengers it endorsed won in a big Democratic year.

A challenge for a group like EMILY's List with its focus on abortion rights is to reach the next generation of voters not as engaged with this issue and to generate new Internet fund-raising techniques. EMILY's List achieved a somewhat better success rate in 2008 in the candidates it backed. Twelve of the 26 House candidates it endorsed won for a 46 percent success rate and the two Senate and two gubernatorial candidates it endorsed were victorious. In 2010, a bad year for Democrats, 34 percent of EMILY's List's U.S. House endorsed candidates won (10 of 29 candidates). Two of the four U.S. Senate endorsed candidates, both incumbents, won—Patty Murray and Barbara Boxer. Both candidates had strong challengers. In assessing EMILY's List's success and impact we have to keep in mind that it is very much a risk taker, entering the most competitive, high-stakes races.

The WISH List was created as a Republican counterpart to EMILY's List, supporting pro-choice Republican female candidates with a similar organizational strategy in 1992. Although it enjoyed some prominence for a number of election cycles the inability to recruit viable pro-choice female Republican candidates led to its marginalization. In 2010 it ceased to exist as an independent organization and merged with Republicans for Choice. The National Organization for Women, the principal feminist organization of the women's rights movement, also established a PAC (NOW-PAC) in the 1980s to support feminist candidates, both men and women. At the national level, it engages primarily in presidential elections. In 2004, it contributed financial support to former U.S. senator Carol Moseley Braun in her race for the Democratic Party nomination for president. Most of NOW's PAC contributions for U.S. Senate and House races come through its state chapters. NOW, along with the Feminist Majority, has adopted a strategy of encouraging large numbers of women to run for political office in major party primaries regardless of the likelihood of their winning a nomination and actually getting elected. This strategy contrasts with that of EMILY's List and the WISH List, which adopted a more strategic philosophy regarding their financial aid, endorsing only "viable" candidates who show evidence of a well-organized campaign with a good chance of winning in competitive races.

Sometimes the Susan B. Anthony List, a pro-life women's PAC, is also included in these listings of national women's PACs. However, the goal of the Susan B. Anthony List is to increase the *percentage* of pro-life women in Congress and high public office. Thus, as their website describes their goals, the List "recruits and endorses pro-life women candidates, our primary focus, endorses pro-life men challenging pro-abortion incumbent women, endorses pro-life male incumbents challenged by pro-abortion women candidates, and endorses pro-life male candidates challenging pro-abortion women candidates in open seats." This emphasis on defeating pro-choice women candidates, not just electing pro-life women candidates, makes the Susan B. Anthony List an anomaly in the women's PAC community.

In 2008, the Susan B Anthony PAC contributed $85,000 to 19 Republican House candidates including 14 women candidates. Marilyn Musgrave and Melissa Hart, seeking reelection, received over $20,000 each. In Arizona's 1st congressional district, it endorsed and supported Republican nominee Sydney Hay in an open seat against Democrat Anne Kirkpatrick who had EMILY's List endorsement and financial support. An interesting side note is that the Republican establishment worked hard to recruit another candidate than Hay to run in this district while at the same time the DCCC endorsed Kirkpatrick during the primary. The DCCC endorsement was an unusual but not unheard of action for a party organization that publicly tends to refrain from primary endorsement in multicandidate races while maneuvering behind the scenes for the candidate who they believe has the best chance of winning the general election, usually the candidate with his or her own deep financial pockets to help finance their campaign. (That was not the case in the Kirkpatrick endorsement.)

In 2010, the Susan B, Anthony List made PAC contributions to 38 U.S. House candidates, 26 women and 12 men. Keep in mind that all of the male candidates endorsed were running against pro-choice women. It also endorsed five male U.S. Senate candidates running against pro-choice female candidates as well as six female Senate candidates, one of whom was successful, Kelly Ayotte in New Hampshire. It also reported nearly $178,000 in independent expenditures. I find it problematic to classify the Susan B. Anthony List as a "women's PAC," given its specific aim to defeat a specific group of female candidates and incumbents. But it does have a female orientation and has disproportionately funded female candidates.

Throughout this time period, female Democrats have disproportionately profited from women's PACs and donor network aid. It is possible that the elections of the second decade of the 21st century might experience a more even and challenging nature to women's groups' advocacy across the parties. To an extent the 2010 election saw the emergence of conservative PACs, which may come to represent a financial counterbalance to the liberal hegemony of women's PACs of the contemporary era. Maggie's List was organized during that election and She-PAC was formed in early 2012. Their emergence deserves attention as possible counterweights in 2012 and beyond, in addition to Sarah Palin's SarahPAC. Maggie's List describes itself as a "group of women with a fiscally conservative economic vision." It is named after former U.S. senator Margaret Chase Smith (R-ME). In the 2010 election, it donated $12,700 to 15 U.S. House candidates and four U.S. Senate candidates as a traditional PAC. It had not yet become a major player.

She-PAC was organized to function as both a traditional political action committee that contributes directly to campaigns and as a super PAC, working as an outside group that can spend unlimited amounts of money in elections working independently of specific candidates' campaigns. "She" is an acronym for "Support, Honor and Elect." Its goal was to raise $25 million in the 2012 election. She-PAC founders are Suzanne Terrell, who ran against Louisiana senator Mary Landrieu in 2002, and Teri Christoph, creator of Smart Girl Politics. The stimulus for the formation of this group, according to Terrell, was "a dearth of organizations on the conservative side that are dedicated to raising up women in the political process. There's a lack of a structure that women can depend on to help them to get to where they can be effective" (Khan 2012). Neither group ultimately had much impact in the 2012 election. As a super-PAC, She-PAC reported only $403 in independent expenditures and raised a total of $155,000.

Sarah Palin's SarahPAC was mentioned above. I have also highlighted her "mama grizzly" campaign. SarahPAC is not particularly a women's PAC, however. "Common sense conservative" female candidates have been the beneficiaries of her PAC money and especially have benefitted from her anointing them with her support, bringing media attention to their campaigns. SarahPAC donated $452,000 to federal candidates in 2010, $342.000 to U.S. House candidates (13 female and 61 male candidates) and $110,000 to Senate candidates (five female and 16 male candidates). Thus, the majority of her PAC donations went to male candidates. But female candidates were disproportionately recipients. Women were 12 percent of all Republican U.S. House contenders in 2010 but were 18 percent of the recipients of SarahPAC donations, indicating a slight favoritism toward female candidates on the part of her PAC.

Women's Issues PACs

The Center for Responsive Politics Opensecrets.org website, in addition to the financial data on groups already noted here, provides data on PAC contributions by interest group sectors and within sectors by issue emphasis for the election cycles from 1998 through 2010. One subcategory is "women's issues" PACs. Table 6.4 lists these PACs and the number of election cycles in which they were active. The women's issue PACs primarily consist of the national groups described earlier in this chapter. It appears that criteria for a PAC to be placed in this category are based more on support for women candidates than on women's issues.

As table 6.4 shows, in the most recent seven election cycles 24 "women's issues" groups have filed with the FEC as having donated to the campaigns of federal candidates. The four groups highlighted earlier in this chapter as having dominated the national scene and having been particularly concerned with the recruitment, training, and financial support of national candidates are included in the "women's issues" category as having provided financial assistance in all seven of the election cycles for which information is available. Some of the additional groups listed are regional in nature such as the Women in Leadership PAC, which is based in Los Angeles and has contributed to female congressional candidates in Southern California.

The total amount contributed in these direct funds has been substantial, especially considering the relatively small number of candidates in each

TABLE 6.4. Women's Issues PACs, 1998–2010

Women's Political Committee—7
EMILY's List—7
Women's Campaign Fund—7
National Organization for Women—7
Wish List—7
Minnesota Women's Campaign Fund—7
Women in Leadership—7
National Women's Political Caucus—7
Women Under Forty PAC—6
Women's Action for New Directions—6
National Assn. of Women Business Owners—4
Feminist Majority Foundation—5
Women for: —4
Value in Electing Women PAC—3
Alabama Solution—3
Gorton Legacy Group—2
Value in Electing Women PAC—2
We Lead Women Engaged in Leadership Education and Leadership Action—3
Ms. President PAC—1
Santa Barbara Women's PAC—2
Women's Voter Project—1
Humane Washington—1
Missouri Women's Action Fund—1
Maggie's List—1
Women Count PAC—1

Source: Data compiled by the author from Opensecrets information; www.opensecrets.org.
Note: The numbers are the number of election cycles in which a PAC made a contribution.

election cycle who have benefitted from this largesse. As table 6.5 indicates, female Democratic candidates have especially profited from women's issue groups' financial aid. Male candidates might have been included in the donations of women's issue groups, but as their titles suggests they are primarily interested in electing women to national office.

The amount of money donated to federal candidates includes U. S Senate candidates as well as U.S. House contenders. In addition, some of these groups have contributed to male candidates, so the figures presented here provide only a superficial picture of the financial impact of women's issues' PACs on the campaigns of women running for seats in the U.S. House but they are an important part of the gendered aspects of contemporary campaigns. Also, one needs to keep in mind in assessing the impact of women's PACs on these elections that these figures only include direct donations, which federal law limits to $10,000 per election (including $5,000 for a primary and $5,000 for the general election). Thus, bundled money and person power contributed to a campaign are not included.

The importance of such resources is illustrated in the 2004 election campaign of Allyson Schwartz in Pennsylvania's 13th congressional district. EMILY's List's involvement in her primary campaign for the open seat was considerable. EMILY's List members' donations helped Schwartz lead all primary candidates in fund-raising by October 2003, a year before the general election. EMILY's List reported providing over $175,000 in expenditures on her behalf in the primary as well as sending its "Women Vote" grassroots turnout operation into her district. Note, too, the independent expenditures the Susan B. Anthony List reported in the 2010 election for a more robust assessment of their impact.

TABLE 6.5. Contributions of Women's Issues PACs to Federal Campaigns, 1998–2010

Election Cycle	Total # of Women Candidates Supported	Total Amount	Amount to Democrats	Amount to Republicans
1998	14	$801,531	$548,794	$243,287
2000	14	$818,271	$608,743	$204,278
2002	17	$753,496	$504,416	$249,056
2004	18	$637,252	$436,199	$201,053
2006	18	$740,192	$666,427	$68,765
2008	13	$721,501	$650,896	$70,605
2010	16	$726,512	$587,983	$138,529

Source: Data compiled by the author from Opensecrets information; www.opensecrets.org.

Conclusion

Vibrant women's campaign organizations, movement of female members of the national legislature into partisan campaign leadership positions, and the growth of individual female representatives' efforts to recruit, train, and fund female candidates characterize the contemporary era. Their formidable actions have even led to male opponent complaints. For example, in 2004 U.S. Representative Peter Deutsch and former president of the University of South Florida Betty Castor were vying for the Democratic Party nomination for the U.S. Senate in Florida. Deutsch, trailing in the polls but having raised $4.2 million, accused EMILY's List of trying to buy the Senate seat for Castor. EMILY's List contributors had donated more than $1 million to her campaign, and the organization was spending $800,000 on televised advertising praising her health care agenda. In a televised debate, Deutsch complained that although all three candidates had the same pro-choice views, the men in the race had a problem. "No matter what we do, unless we go through a sex-change operation, we're not getting EMILY's List's endorsement," Deutsch quipped. A Deutsch supporter filed a complaint with the Federal Election Commission, claiming the political organization and Castor were coordinating campaign strategy in violation of FEC rules. Betty Castor won the primary but lost the general election. Another example occurred in 2006, when the third-place finisher in the Democratic primary in Ohio's 13th congressional district, Tom Sawyer, filed a complaint with the Federal Election Commission claiming that winner Betty Sutton's campaign "illegally coordinated with abortion rights political action committee EMILY's List." Sawyer wrote, "I believe she is violating election laws and being illegally assisted by the very special interests she claims to oppose" (Frontrunner 2006). Neither challenge ever resulted in a finding for the complainants. Claiming women's election teams act as bullies certainly is a new political phenomenon.

Congressional party organizations now operate under the premise that their female candidates are among their most competitive contenders and pour millions of dollars in independent expenditures into their campaigns on a basis comparable to that of their male nominees. An analysis of their comparative independent expenditures suggests little discrimination exists against female nominees in recent elections. We are far from electoral periods in which only widows and sacrificial candidacies primarily described party organizational election promotion of women for national office. Democratic female candidates have especially benefitted from party organizational and women's groups activities in current electoral cycles. Republican women, while having access to training and some recruitment activities on the part of their national party organizations and women's groups, have been much less advantaged, particularly if they were pro-choice (a minority position within the activist base of the Republican Party). We may be seeing change on that score as GOP female U.S. House members ramp up their recruitment efforts and more conservative groups join them in funding female candidates' campaigns. The policy and propaganda battle in the 112th Congress and the 2012 presidential election between the two parties, highlighted as the "war on women," might contribute to a heightened and more substantial effort on the part of the Republican Party to recruit and support female candidates. Chapters 7 and 8 move the study of the process of electing women to national political leadership positions to the ultimate stage, focusing on the winners and the meaning of these electoral victories for diversity and representation in public office.

SEVEN

The Victors

The Men and Women Elected to the U.S. House

In *A Woman's Place Is in the House* I suggested that "who leads and how they get there are among the most significant political questions we ask. The backgrounds of political candidates are theoretically important because they appear to be related to success in the political sphere, illustrate the degree of openness in the political system, and affect interests and behaviors in public office, although these latter empirical relationships are complex" (1994, 58). This chapter centers on the descriptive representational nature of the U.S. House. It examines the characteristics and career paths of the men and women who initially won seats in the U.S. House during the contemporary era from among all the election and reelection attempts.

As a prologue to this investigation, however, I first provide information on the career progression of the distinctive female class of '92. The 1992 "year of the woman" election resulted in the number of female U.S. representatives nearly doubling, from 29 to 47. In that election, a record 24 nonincumbent women won a seat in the 103rd Congress. In 2011 at the beginning of the 112th Congress, 18 years and nine congresses later, how many of these newcomers to the institution in that historical election were still members, gaining seniority and perhaps leadership positions? How many had sought higher office, resigned, or retired, moving on to do other things, and how many had been defeated when seeking reelection? What was their political leadership profile at the beginning of the second decade of the 21st century? Such an accounting provides an intriguing descriptive base from which to launch an investigation of the characteristics of the women elected after that momentous election and the diversity that they may have brought to that institution.

In the 1992 election, 21 Democratic and 3 Republican women were newly elected. Of these 24 members, seven, all Democrats, were still U.S. representatives in the 112th Congress, one-third of the original number. All of the three female Republican winners in 1992 had retired after having served various numbers of terms. Six of the Democrats served only one term, being defeated for reelection in the Republican takeover in 1994. Two had moved up to the Senate. Maria Cantwell, after being defeated for reelection in 1994, went on to make a substantial amount of money in the dot.com explosion of the 1990s, returned to politics in 2000, narrowly defeating a Republican incumbent for a U.S. Senate seat from the state of Washington. Blanche Lincoln retired from the House at the end of the 104th Congress but then two years later ran for and won a Senate seat representing Arkansas. Four other Democrats chose not to seek reelection at various points over this time period and two lost later reelection attempts.

None of these seven female representatives served in the Democratic Party leadership caucus in the 112th Congress; two were ranking members of committees. Eddie Bernice Johnson was ranking member of Science, Space and Technology and Nydia Velázquez served as ranking member of Small Business. For a comparative perspective, 25 percent of 87 men initially elected to the U.S. House in 1992 were still members in the 112th Congress. One, James Clyburn of South Carolina, was a member of the Democratic Caucus leadership, four Republicans chaired committees, and one Democrat served as ranking committee member. The numbers are small for meaningful statistical comparative analysis between the sexes but this limited accounting does not suggest a particularly substantive male advantage or greater staying power. (Three of these male members were subsequently elected to the U.S. Senate and one was elected governor of his state.)

This chapter compares the career paths of the men and women who won seats in the U.S. House in the nine election cycles after the 1992 election. Chapter 8 then investigates trends in female congressional leadership. Between 1993 and 2010, 7,990 nonincumbent male and 1,360 nonincumbent female Democratic and Republican candidacies were undertaken for election to the U.S. House of Representatives. Of all of these contenders, 494 men and 97 women won seats in that body. This chapter surveys the demographics of these winners and the ways in which the 97 female victors have diversified the body of the House beyond their sex in terms of their backgrounds and life experiences. An accounting of the characteristics and routes to office of the male and female victors contributes to knowledge of gender and political leadership in the contemporary era. In addition to a wider diversity of demographic characteristics, distinctive backgrounds and experiences of the female winners could contribute to a more expansive approach to agenda setting and lawmaking and contemporary descriptive representation.

I earlier described the women elected to the U.S. House in the 1972 through the 1992 elections as a "new breed" and a "third wave" of woman climbing the political ladder and acquiring credentials to run sophisticated campaigns for election to the national legislature (1994, 73). As noted in earlier chapters, Irwin Gertzog has characterized these women as being "strategic actors" (2002). Strategic political candidates are ambitious, experienced, rational, and skillful, he states. In their research on women candidates, Ondercin and Welch have described strategic candidates as primarily running for an open seat in the legislature. Such candidates have identified significant sources of funding for their races and have had the right experience to be able to run a credible race (2005, 63). Gertzog, too, views running in open seat races as an indicator of a strategic candidacy.

Political commentators have come to characterize female congressional candidates as being "fierce and well-financed competitors in a large number of the country's hottest and nastiest races" (Leonard 2000). In the 2004 election cycle, they were described as "the most capable group of women candidates yet" (Chaddock 2004). In the latter article Karen White of EMILY's List is quoted as stating that "the women who are running this year are tough as nails. These are women who know how to raise money, put together the campaign operation, and have the political and constituent bases. . . . In the early 1980s, women were the anomaly, the underdog. These are leading candidates."

The contextual news media descriptions summarized in chapter 2 noted the significance students of politics have attributed to the political pipeline for current women representatives. Journalists have also described them in political science research terms such as Mary Leonard's depiction of U.S. Representative Anne Northup in her 2000 analysis of Northup's race against Eleanor Jordan described in chapter 4. According to Leonard, "Northup, 52, represents the *new breed* [emphasis added] of female politicians. A veteran state legislator, she ran for the House in 1996 and raised more money than the Democratic incumbent. She used saturation

TV advertising to tout her name (she comes from a well-known Louisville family), her record (probusiness, antiabortion rights), and her family values (she is Roman Catholic, married, and has six children)."

The newsworthiness of headlines and research focused on the idea of a "new breed" and women being strategic politicians in the contemporary era may be puzzling. We might assume that women seeking election to the national legislature would always have been strategic and must always have had substantial resources in terms of qualifications if they had the "audacity" to step outside of traditional stereotypes and challenge the idea that politics was a man's profession. But that has not always characterized female candidates.

As most of us are familiar based on many historical studies, the election of women to the U.S. House in the years prior to the second women's movement represented a different demographic. Few women were elected, never more than a very small percentage of the membership. A good proportion of these representatives were widows of newly deceased members nominated by their local party organizations for a variety of reasons. Prior to 1962, nearly one-half of the women (45%) had obtained their seats on the death of their husband (Ondercin and Welch 2005). Widows have represented 20 percent of the women who have been elected to the U.S. House since 1917 when the first woman, Jeannette Rankin, won a seat. Rankin was not a widow but an activist in the women's suffragist movement. The widows proved to be a diverse group in their ambitions and careers (Palmer and Simon 2008). They have also declined as a proportion of the female membership in the contemporary era.

From an historical perspective Irwin Gertzog has chronicled a second distinctive group of women elected to the U.S. Congress. This group was distinguished as coming from families belonging to the country's socioeconomic elite. Some were social elites, "women whose families were among the most respected citizens in their communities and states, in some cases enjoying national reputations." Others benefitted from significant wealth, according to Gertzog's accounting. A third group "profited from political connections" (2002, 100). Their proportion, however, among women elected to the U.S. House declined toward the end of the 20th century to just 13 percent of the 74 women elected between 1984 and 2000, according to Gertzog. He concludes that "other background characteristics, notably prior electoral success, have come to replace widowhood and elite membership as the principal passports to congressional service. . . . Consequently, the successes of modern congresswomen are linked at least as much to their track records in public office as to their political pedigree, and they come to Washington with all of the qualities we expect in strategic politicians" (102). He cites literature that has found that

> women serving in state legislatures are as ambitious as male legislators, with more of them considering politics a career than their male colleagues, and a large proportion stating plans to seek reelection. Among those who run or seriously consider contests for the House, women weigh both strategic and personal factors, not automatically allowing gender, marital status, or the psychic cost of running to deter candidacy. Moreover, there is evidence that in recent years more women with children are running for office in spite of their motherhood. In short, contemporary women politicians are as ambitious as men. (104; see also Fulton et al. 2006)

Thus, by the millennium, according to Gertzog, "political women are no less likely than men to be strategic politicians" (104). In his analysis, he operationalizes the concept of strategic politicians as individuals who have held elective office and who run in open seats. The application of the concept of strategic politicians to would-be and successful female national officeholders has been noted throughout this work. As the strategic politician concept has been developed and applied to female candidates it would suggest a growing commonality between male and female members of the U.S. Congress. This growing professional political commonality, as with other aspects of their campaigns analyzed in earlier chapters, points to a diminished gendered nature to congressional life.

But contemporary female members of Congress, in addition to being professional politicians, may contribute to diversity within the legislative body beyond their sex through their career backgrounds and professions, earlier substantive interests, and family lives. Younger women being elected to the national legislature while raising families would expand role models for other women, especially young women. There is historical merit to extending a descriptive analysis of the political experience and professional accomplishments to current female members of Congress and would-be members. The attention placed on aspects of descriptive representation in this chapter is built on the analysis in *A Woman's Place*, which compared the backgrounds of the men and women elected to the U.S. House during the feminist era. Other scholars, too, have focused on the types of women who have achieved elected leadership positions as important in understanding democratic politics (see, for example, Palmer and Simon 2008).

Traditionally, the typical U.S. representative has been a middle-aged

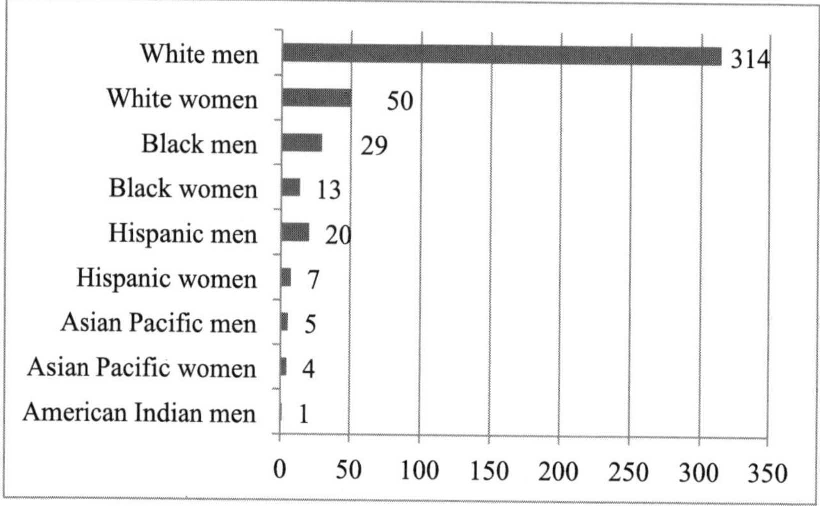

Fig. 7.1. Racial and Ethnic Diversity, 112th Congress (2011–12). (Data from Congressional Research Service.)

individual. The average age of members of the U.S. House in the 112th Congress was 56.7 years. New members had a mean age of 48 years (Manning 2011). U.S. representatives have tended historically to be lawyers with previous elected office experience. White men have long dominated in this system and they continue to do so. In the 112th Congress they constituted 72 percent of the membership of the U.S. House. Figure 7.1 provides a picture of the racial, ethnic, and gender diversity of the U.S. House at the beginning of the 112th Congress based on the results of the 2010 election. But within this overall white male dominance, women and minorities have become the majority of the Democratic Party Caucus in the House, illustrating a changing dynamic to the descriptive nature of that body.

Routes to House Membership and Retention of Seats

Of the 92 nonincumbent candidates who won during the first election cycle of this study, 1993–94, including special election victors, only 19 percent, three women and 19 men, were still U.S. representatives at the beginning of the 112th Congress after eight subsequent elections. Of all of the representatives elected from 1993 through the special elections of the 111th Congress, 49 percent, nearly one-half, were still members in the

112th Congress (48% of the men and 52% of the women). Approximately one-half of the membership serving at the end point of this study were elected in this contemporary era.

At the same time, nearly one-quarter of both the male and female representatives of this cohort had lost their seats in reelection attempts (24% of both sexes). Male members were slightly more likely than the female members to have retired (11% to 8%). Twenty-six of the male members and three of the female members had been elected to the U.S. Senate or to governorships. Table 7.1 traces the full panoply of postinitial House election career trends for the men and women elected during this time period. As this table indicates, few differences are evident in the tenure of the contemporary men and women elected to the U.S. House. They are moving up in seniority, moving up either through progressive ambition, unwillingly moving out as reelection victims, leaving to pursue other careers, or to retirement in similar trajectories.

As an aside, the 110th Congress was unusual in that four female members died during it. Prior to this time, only two female members had died in office: Sala Burton had died in 1987 and Patsy Mink died in 2002 while seeking reelection, as chapter 4 chronicled.

The route these contemporary members took to win a seat in the U.S. House of Representative was primarily, and not unexpectedly, through winning open seats, as noted in chapter 3. Over two-thirds of newly elected members, 69 percent of the men and 67 percent of the women, became representatives by winning an open seat. An additional 29 women (29%) and 143 men (29%) defeated incumbents to become U.S. representatives. Four women, all Democrats (4%), and 13 men (3%) won after an incumbent was defeated in a primary. (Not all of these were instances in which

TABLE 7.1. Legislative Careers of Members Elected from 1993 to 2011 by Sex

Status	Men	Women
Representative in 2011	41%	45%
Retired	9%	6%
Defeated for Reelection	20%	22%
Sought Other Office (governor or senator)	11%	6%
Resigned	1%	—
Received Executive Appointment	<1%	2%
Appointed to the Senate	<1%	1%
Newly Elected in 2010	16%	13%
Died in Office	<1%	4%
N	494	97

Source: Data compiled by the author.

the ultimate victor had defeated the incumbent in a party's primary.) Two of the four women whose route to Congress involved beating an incumbent in a primary defeated other women. Denise Majette (D-GA) defeated Cynthia McKinney in a 2002 primary and Carolyn Kilpatrick (D-MI) beat Barbara Rose Collins in 1996. In 2000, Hilda Solis (D-CA) defeated Matthew Martinez and in 2008 Donna Edwards defeated Albert Wynn in Maryland's 4th district.

Donna Edwards's effort to win a seat in the U.S. House is an intriguing illustration of female members bringing greater career diversity to Congress. Donna Edwards, with no prior elective office experience, challenged Rep. Wynn in the Democratic primary in 2006. Rep. Wynn won the primary by less than 3,000 votes. Not deterred, Edwards declared in her concession statement that "I look forward to continuing to be a voice for accountability and for change." In its editorial endorsing her in 2006, the *Washington Post* described Edwards as "tough, articulate and knowledgeable, she is one of the smartest and impressive newcomers to Maryland politics." Two years later she resoundingly defeated Rep. Wynn by 22 points in the Democratic primary. She subsequently won a special election to fill his seat when he resigned from Congress to become a lobbyist. She then won the general election as the incumbent.

Rep. Edwards's career prior to entering Congress is notable in reflecting upon the distinctive experiences women could bring to the national legislature that are not always captured in quantitative analyses. Donna Edwards has a law degree, which is a traditional credential of national lawmakers. But what makes her distinctive in terms of the experience she has brought to Congress is that she had been the cofounder and executive director of the National Network to End Domestic Violence and had headed the Center for New Democracy, a nongovernmental organization. Immediately preceding her election to Congress she worked as the executive director of the Arca Foundation in Washington, DC, a liberal political advocacy group. Rep. Edwards had also once worked as a clerk for Rep. Wynn when he was a member of the Maryland House of Delegates. She began her career at the United Nations Development Program and had been a systems engineer for Lockheed Corporation with NASA's shuttle program in the 1980s.

Clearly she brought a multifaceted professional and issue-oriented experience to national politics, one that would put an important voice regarding the distinctive concerns of women on its agenda and its deliberative function. Not having held elective office prior to winning a seat in the U.S. House of Representatives, Rep. Edwards lacked one of the main credentials of strategic candidacies but at the same time she had extensive leadership, political ,and professional credentials that she brought to her campaign.

Partisan Routes to Office

Based on earlier analyses of this work that have repeatedly shown the lagging presence of Republican women as candidates for a seat in the U.S. House it is not surprising that the majority of the women who won new seats during this period were Democrats (61%) while the majority of men who won were Republicans (63%). The route to victory, however, was similar across party and sex as table 7.2 shows. Prior to the 2010 election, GOP victors were more likely than Democratic winners to have won open seat races to claim their seats in the U.S. House but Republican challengers' victories in 2010 eliminated this partisan difference.

Nearly one-third (31%) of the open seat victories resulted in a partisan turnover as opposed to partisan continuity. Democratic male open seat victors were twice as likely to take seats away from Republicans than Democratic female winners were; 30 percent of Democratic male victors won a Republican seat compared to 15 percent of the female winners. The difference is accounted for by the larger proportion of female Democratic victors who were women of color winning open seat contests in majority-minority districts which I discuss more thoroughly later in this chapter. These districts tended not to have any Republican history and in many cases were new districts created after redistricting. Among Republican open seat winners, female victors were slightly more likely to have won a Democratic seat, by 36 percent to 32 percent of the Republican male winners. Gender and race mingled in partisan transfers of power.

TABLE 7.2. Method of Entry to the U.S. House, Male and Female Victors by Party, 1993–2010

	Democrats		Republicans	
	Men	Women	Men	Women
Open Seat	66%	66%	70%	66%
Incumbent Challenger	30%	27%	28%	34%
Incumbent Lost in Primary	2%	2%	3%	—
N	182	59	312	38

Source: Data compiled by the author.

Summary

In their 2012 *Women & Congressional Elections,* Palmer and Simon conclude that "the vast majority of women in Congress now seek long careers and are gradually accumulating the leadership roles and influence that come with long term service" (2012, 226). Trends reported to this point in this chapter parallel that conclusion, showing that routes to power and retention of those positions were more similar than dissimilar for the men and women elected to the U.S. House from 1993 through the 2010 election. However, opposed to this individual "careerism" in the U.S. House is substantial turnover in membership that is also characteristic of this legislative body for both sexes.

As the data on the presence of male and female legislators first elected to the House in the 1992 and 1994 elections reported earlier indicate, only a minority were still serving as the 112th Congress, which commenced after the 2010 election. Examined from this latter perspective, movement out of the legislature, both through defeat and personal decisions, has served as a limitation on women achieving a more substantial presence as U.S. representatives in addition to their lesser presence in opportune races for newcomers as found in chapter 3. Yet at the same time female representatives have become as much careerists as their male counterparts.

Demographic Characteristics of Contemporary House Members

Race and Ethnicity

The election of women to the national legislature during this period not only affected the gender balance of the legislature, it also increased the institution's racial and ethnic diversity. Of the 97 women elected to the House between 1993 and 2010, 24 or one-quarter were members of a minority racial or ethnic group. Seventeen of the 97 women were African American, four were Latina, and three were Asian American. At the same time, only 6 percent of the newly elected male legislators were minorities, one area in which a substantial gender gap has emerged in the contemporary era.

The African American female members in the 112th Congress (2011–12) also make up a substantially larger percentage of the African American membership than white women make up of white membership. African-American women are nearly one-third of African American membership (31%) while white women are only 14% of white membership. All of the women of color but one elected to the U.S. House during this time period were Democrats. Among the 350 Republicans elected during this period only one was a woman of color, Jaime Herrera Beutler, a Latina elected in 2010 from the state of Washington. Three Black Republican males also won election to the U.S House in 2010.

In her book *Black Faces in the Mirror* (2003), Katherine Tate provided evidence that Black women were more likely to enter politics at higher rates than White women, and that Black women can benefit from a Black-and-women's vote coalition. Also the creation of majority-minority districts was significant in the election of Black women to Congress. According to Tate,

> the single most important fact that explains the higher percentage of Black women serving in the U.S. Congress is the new opportunities created by the Voting Rights Act in providing new majority-Black districts from which to run. . . . With rare exceptions, almost all the Black women who have been elected to the U.S. House of Representatives have been elected in new majority-Black districts. The largest surge in the numbers of women occurred in 1992 when thirteen new Black lawmakers were added to the House, all because of the new Black districts that had been created. Among the thirteen new Black members, five were women. (64–65)

The surge Tate describes occurred just prior to the election cycles under investigation in this study. It stressed the distinctive impact of the 1990 census and resulting creation of a number of majority-minority districts for the 1992 election and beyond. The 2000 census and resulting reapportionment of congressional districts did not have the same racial impact in the creation of new districts although continuing demographic changes in the racial and ethnic makeup of the population are creating more opportunities for minorities to be elected to Congress. Twenty-seven districts were majority African American in this decade. Seven of these districts had a female representative (26%). The other African-American female representatives were elected from districts with a majority of minorities. None of the 17 African-American women elected to the U.S. House during the nine election cycles of this study represented predominately white districts.

Age, Marital Status, and Motherhood

Most new members of the House arrive in the chamber between the ages of thirty-five and fifty-five, so there is a relatively narrow window in each prospective candidate's life when he or she will be "ripe" for a congressional campaign (Gaddie and Bullock 2000, 53). Traditionally women have tended to enter politics at an older age than men. The primary explanation for this difference has been that women tended to delay the start of their careers until their children were in school. Thus, as legislators they would on average be older than their male counterparts. Women have also found that they have been discouraged from running for office with young children and would receive criticism on the campaign trail if they tried it. But that impediment seems to have been diminishing as cultural attitudes at-large are evolving and perhaps have even become more accepting within the conservative community as a consequence of Sarah Palin's 2008 vice-presidential campaign with five children, one a newborn with Down syndrome, and her subsequent campaign to elect "mama grizzlies" to public office. Chapter 4 illustrated the 2010 South Dakota race between Stephanie Herseth Sandlin and Kristi Noem who were both mothers of young children. They prominently featured their children in their campaign ads.

The average age of members of the House at the beginning of the 112th Congress, as noted earlier, was 57 years old. Given the high reelection rates and the long careers of members, the legislative bodies have become older in recent congresses. The individuals who were elected to the House between 1993 and 2010 ranged in age at the time of their election from 26 to 68. The average age of the men elected to the House during this time period was 47 and the average age of the women was 50. Nine of the men, 2 percent of the total, were in their 20s when they were first elected. No woman has yet broken the 30-year-old age barrier. The male "20-somethings" included Patrick Kennedy (D-RI), son of Senator Ted Kennedy, and Harold Ford Jr. (D-TN), son of long-time representative Harold Ford Sr., who assumed his father's seat. With his election to the House in 2008, Aaron Shock (R-IL) became the youngest person elected to the House during this period at age 26. Only two of the nine men elected while in their 20s were married and only one, Randy Tate (R-WA), elected in 1994, had a child. So for the most part, they were young eligible bachelors. Indeed, Shock even created a sensation when he posed bare-chested on the cover of the June 2011 *Men's Health* magazine.

Elected as a U.S. representative at the age of 32 in 2010, Jaime Herrera Beutler (R-WA) was the youngest woman elected to the House during this period and the youngest woman ever elected. She had an impressive political career prior to winning a U.S. House seat. A graduate of the University of Washington, she had been a senior legislative aide to U.S. Representative Cathy McMorris Rodgers (R-WA) and had been elected a state representative in Washington State. Prior to Herrera Beutler's election, Linda Sanchez, elected from California's 39th district in 2002 at the age of 33, had been the youngest woman elected. She is the sister of Representative Loretta Sanchez, making them the only sisters to serve in the House.

Although no female member of the House has broken the under-30 age barrier, examples of their entry into the elective office arena at earlier ages do exist among the most recently elected lawmakers. Debbie Wasserman Schultz became Florida's youngest-ever elected female legislator when she was elected to the Florida House at the age of 26. Cathy McMorris Rodgers began her career as a representative in the Washington House at the age of 24 and Gabrielle Giffords was also the youngest female ever elected to the state Senate in Arizona.

In addition, while they lost their election bids, three women in their 20s were major party nominees in 2004. A political action committee has even been formed to encourage the election of younger women to national office, the nonpartisan Women Under Forty PAC. In the 2010 election this PAC contributed a total of $12,250 to eight women seeking election or reelection to the U.S. House. Five of the recipients were Democrats and three were Republicans.

Table 7.3 compares the average ages of newly elected male and female members of the U.S. House in the contemporary era with that of various cohorts elected in the years since the emergence of the second women's rights' movement. The mean age difference between the men and women elected to the U.S. House during these periods has tended to be relatively stable. The age gap between the sexes has not narrowed over the course of these recent elections. First-term male members have continuously been approximately three years younger on average than first-term female members.

TABLE 7.3. Trends in the Average Age of Newly Elected Members of the U.S. House by Sex

	Women		Men	
Election Years	Average Age	Number	Average Age	Number
1968–1972	44	11	44	26
1974–1978	47	12	42	39
1980–1984	48	15	45	34
1986–1990	51	14	44	21
1992	49	24	43	86
1993–2010	50	97	47	494

Source: Data compiled by the author from *CQ Weekly Reports*.

Table 7.4 provides a comparison of newly elected male and female representatives in the nine election cycles of this study on a number of demographic characteristics and table 7.5 provides comparisons with earlier years. Table 7.4 first shows the age distribution of these elected officials by age groups and sex, illustrating the older age distribution of female members when first elected compared to the newly elected male members. The main sex differences are among the youngest and the oldest cohorts. Newly elected male members are younger and newly elected female members are older with large contingents of both sexes in the traditional midlife age range.

Marital Status

A substantial difference exists between the men and women elected to the U.S. House during this time period regarding their marital status. Women were substantially less likely to be married when they were elected, 65 percent to 88 percent of the men (table 7.4). They were more likely to be single (10% to 8%) or divorced (15% to 3%). The *CQ* profiles that are used to compile these figures provide information only on marital status at the time of initial election to the U.S. House. It may be the case that the divorce rate among the male members may actually be higher than suggested in these figures but that they were more likely to have remarried than their female counterparts, an interesting topic for a future sociological study.

Table 7.5 compares the marital status of newly elected male and female members for the contemporary period with its immediate preceding eras. No dramatic changes present themselves, but the percentage of divorced female members has increased somewhat, especially if we were to include the 1992 winners with the women elected since that famous election. In addition, two of the four congressional widows in this analysis have remarried since becoming members of the U.S. House.

The election of Black women to the U.S. House primarily accounts for the sex difference in members' marital status. As Katherine Tate has stated in *Black Faces in the Mirror*, "perhaps the single most striking difference between Black women members and all other members of the House relates to their marital status" (2003, 46). Up through the 2000 election, only one-third of the Black women elected were married when they entered Congress. This marital status statistic matched that for Black women in the general population in the 1998 Current Population survey that Tate reported.

TABLE 7.4. Demographic Characteristics of Newly Elected U.S. Representatives by Sex, 1993–2010

	Women		Men	
Characteristic	%	*N*	%	*N*
Age				
25–29	—	0	2	9
30–34	4	4	7	32
35–39	12	12	14	68
40–44	9	9	20	97
45–49	19	18	19	92
50–54	25	24	20	98
55–59	22	21	13	63
60 and Older	9	9	7	35
Education				
High School or Less	3	3	2	11
Some College	3	3	4	19
Associate's Degree	5	5	3	14
Bachelor's Degree	27	26	25	125
Master's Degree	22	21	15	72
MBA	3	3	4	20
PhD	5	5	4	21
Law Degree	31	30	37	148
MD/Dentist/DVM	1	1	6	27
Elected Positions Held				
None	27	22	36	145
School Board	—	0	2	5
City Council	4	3	3	13
City Official	—	0	1	4
Mayor	2	2	3	10
County Board	5	4	4	18
County Official	1	1	3	14
County Executive	—	0	.2	1
State Representative	26	21	22	90
State Senator	25	21	19	77
State Supreme Court	1	1	.5	2
Statewide Office	5	4	4	17
Lt. Governor	2	2	.5	2
Former House Member	2	2	2	7
Marital Status				
Single	11	9	9	35
Married	64	53	87	353
Divorced	15	12	4	16
Widowed	8	7	.2	1
Same Sex Partner	1	1	—	0
Engaged	1	1	—	0

Source: Data compiled by the author from *CQ Weekly Reports*.

If anything, the marital distinctiveness of the Black women who have entered the U.S. House between 1993 and 2010 continues this distinctiveness; 30 percent (5 of 17) of this group of female members were married at the time of their entrance into Congress. For a comparative context, 77 percent of Black men elected during this period were married as were 71 percent of white women.

The four congressional widows elected in this time period have all sought reelection and have been making a career for themselves in the

TABLE 7.5. Demographic Trends

	1968–1990		1992		1993–2010	
	Women (%)	Men (%)	Women (%)	Men (%)	Women (%)[a]	Men (%)
Marital Status						
Single	12	8	8	7	10	8
Married	58	87	67	83	65	88
Divorced	8	3	25	11	14	3
Widowed	8	3	—	—	8	.2
Congressional Widow	15	—	—	—	6	—
Same Sex Partner					1	—
Previous Elective Positions						
None	42 (34)	24	25	26	26 (23)	36
School Board	4 (5)	1	—	1	—	1
City Council/Other City Office	10 (11)	8	17	7	5	4
Mayor	2 (2)	3	—	6	2	3
County Legislator	2 (2)	3	8	2	4	4
Other County Office	2 (2)	1	—	2	1	2
State Representative	14 (16)	23	21	22	28 (29)	23
State Senator	17 (21)	19	25	27	25 (26)	18
Statewide	4 (5)	4	—	3	6	4
Judicial	—	4	4	2	1	2
Former U.S. Representative	2 (2)	7	—	—	2	2
Education						
High School or Less	0	2	—	2	3	2
Some College	23	8	8	4	3	4
Associate's Degree	n/a	n/a	n/a	n/a	5	3
College Degree	29	24	38	17	27	25
Postgraduate Work	10	5	13	1	n/a	n/a
Master's Degree	19	12	25	14	25	19
Professional Degree	2	8	—	8	1	6
Law Degree	17	43	17	54	31	37

Source: Data compiled by the author from *CQ Weekly Reports.*
Note: Figures in parentheses exclude congressional widows.
[a]One woman listed being engaged.

U.S. House. The most recent widow, Doris Matsui (D-CA), was elected to take her husband's place in early 2005. Rep. Matsui was 60 years old at the time of her election. Prior to becoming a U.S. representative, she had served as deputy director of liaison in the Clinton administration and as director of government relations for the law firm of Colleen, Shannon and Scott, a Washington firm that represents medical technology, telecommunications, and financial organizations, from 2000 until resigning to take her seat in Congress. Although a substantial political actor in her own right, Rep. Matsui took the somewhat old-fashioned widow's route to the House but is a careerist in her position as a national legislator.

Only one of the four female members who died during the 110th Congress was married at the time of her death, Jo-Ann Davis (R-VA). Her husband, Chuck Davis, a retired firefighter, vied in the Republican caucus to be that party's nominee in the special election to take her seat. However, the party officials instead chose State Delegate Robert Whitman to be their nominee, and in the safe Republican district he ultimately won the seat. Had Chuck Davis prevailed he would have been the first widower to follow this route to Congress. (John Mink would have only served the last few weeks of Rep. Patsy Mink's term at the end of the 107th Congress had he won that special election described in chapter 4. He did not seek the nomination to replace her in the next Congress.)

Motherhood

"Moms in the House, with Kids at Home," headlined Lyndsey Layton's 2007 *Washington Post* article on women in the U.S. House and Senate. Layton characterized these women, ten of them raising children under 13, as a select group. (Two new women elected to the 112th Congress also had children in this age group.) The article focused on how they balanced motherhood with politicking and lawmaking. Little mention in the article was made of their having had to face criticism along the campaign trail or having had to face and overcome discrimination in seeking such a high-powered position while caring for young children. Although such an article would not have been a news piece for a comparable set of male representatives and senators, it set a positive tone while highlighting gender. The article centered on these female lawmakers' coping mechanisms and the support they have given to one another. Layton writes:

> They reside on a shaky high wire, balancing motherhood with politicking, lawmaking, fund-raising and the constant shuttle between

> Washington and their home states. . . . And they all live with a reality possibly even more difficult: The public will scrutinize and judge the mothering choices these politicians make. It is this that sets them apart from other professional women and their male counterparts in Congress, and the 10 in the group are keenly sensitive to it. If they have private moments in which they question the work-life balance, most are reluctant to reveal them. Instead, they say their kids benefit from the special opportunities—picnics at the White House and VIP tours of landmarks—and get early exposure to public service. One boasted that her daughter, when she was 11, could rattle off an explanation of the Medicare "doughnut hole."

Several of these representatives and senators expressed determination to show that a woman can raise a family while serving in Congress. Nearly all said they feel compelled to use their own perspective as the tiny minority of working mothers in Congress to represent the 70 percent of mothers who have school-age children and jobs outside the home.

Giving birth while serving in the national legislature is no longer a media phenomenon. Eight women have had a baby while serving as a U.S. representative. Five babies have been born to female members since 2007. The 111th Congress, however, experienced a new first in this regard. Linda Sanchez, 40, gave birth in May of 2009. What made her experience unique was that she was the first female representative to be openly pregnant out of wedlock. She and her boyfriend subsequently were married prior to her giving birth. Although her experience received much media attention, little consternation was expressed in the mainstream print media and she won reelection with 64 percent of the vote in the 2010 election. Just after the 2010 election, Rep. McMorris Rodgers gave birth to her second child, becoming the first member of Congress to give birth twice while in office.

Educational Backgrounds

Not surprisingly the men and women elected to Congress have high degrees of formal education. Only 14 (2%) of the 591 newly elected members of the time frame of this study had a high school degree or less, three female and 11 male representatives (table 7.4). Considering all of the members of the 112th Congress, 26 (6%) had no education beyond high school. At the other end of the educational spectrum, 66 percent of the men and 62 percent of the women have postbaccalaureate degrees. (Congressional

Research Service's *Profile of the 112th Congress* indicates that, overall, 66 percent of its House members have postbaccalaureate degrees.)

The sexes were similarly highly educated with 5 percent of each group having a PhD. Overall, 18 representatives in the 112th Congress have PhDs (4%) and 167 members (36%) had law degrees. The percentage with law degrees among the newly elected members in this study is similar to the U.S. House at large. A total of 213 of the 591 elected during the nine election cycles of this study had law degrees, 37 percent of the men and 31 percent of the women. Law degrees have increased among the women elected to the U.S. House and have decreased among male members recently elected compared to earlier cohorts. Thus, gender differences in this domain have greatly lessened through the movement in different directions of the sexes. The biggest educational differences lay in the greater percentage of female lawmakers who have master's degrees while the male lawmakers are more likely to have medical degrees. One female member, Nan Hayworth, elected in 2010, had a medical degree and has been a practicing physician. She is an ophthalmologist.

Summary

This investigation of a number of demographic characteristics highlights both similarities and differences between the men and women elected to the U.S. House in the 1990s and since the millennium. Women still tend to be slightly older on average than their male counterparts. The difference is not large and younger women are being elected and the prominence of female representatives with young families whom they highlight in their campaigns is a changing cultural phenomenon. They are also less likely to be married or currently married than the male representatives. Further, male and female U.S. representatives have similar high rates of formal education.

Precongressional Careers

Political Experience

Writing in 1990 about political amateurs in Congress, David Canon noted that an average of one-fourth of the members have had no previous public office experience and some years more than half have had no elective experience (1990, xii). Canon highlighted celebrities as a distinctive group of amateurs seeking seats in the national legislature in *Actors, Athletes and Astronauts*. Successfully recruited celebrities have all been men. Few female celebrities have been recruited to run. Preeminent possibilities would be someone like Oprah Winfrey who indeed has been mentioned for national office but who has consistently stated she would not be a candidate for public office. Other possible "stars" would include athletes such as Billy Jean King, Mia Hamm, Rebecca Lobo, astronaut Mae Jamieson, and such politically active actresses as Susan Sarandon or singers Joan Baez and Barbra Streisand. It is something to consider.[1]

At the same time prior office-holding experience has been deemed to be more important for women in their quests for national office than for men. Given the emphasis on the "strategic" nature of their candidacies as a group we would expect women elected in the contemporary period to have been primarily experienced candidates, perhaps more so than their male counterparts. Chapter 3 stressed the greater prior elective office experience of female candidates vying for an open seat nomination.

In the period from 1968 through 1990 the women elected to the House, excluding widows, contrary to expectation were less likely to have previously held elective office than their male counterparts. In contrast, in 1992, the "year of the woman," three quarters of both the men and women elected to the House had held elective office. Comparing all of the men and women elected to the House after 1992 through the 2010 general election, we find that the female representatives, excluding the four widows, were substantially more likely than their male counterparts to have held elective office, 77 percent to 64 percent, consistent with expectations.

Climbing the political pipeline by obtaining credentials from lower level office-holding is most characteristic of the successful contemporary female U.S. representatives. Table 7.4 shows the distribution of the prior political office-holding experience of the men and women elected in this era. Over one-half of the female representatives (51%) had served in their state legislatures either as a representative or senator compared with 41 percent of the male representatives. The greater prevalence of prior office-holding experience among women legislators is perhaps one of the major gender differences in the composition of the contemporary national legislature. As shown in the analysis of the backgrounds of individuals seeking open seat nominations, women without previous elective office experience are less likely to join the pool of candidates. It is not just a matter that successful female candidates need this credential more than male candidates but that without it they are less likely to run in the first place. African

American female members are also notable in the extent of their previous elective office experience. Only two of the 15 African-American female representatives had not previously been elected to public office, Donna Edwards, whose career was described earlier, and Terri Sewell, elected in 2010 from Alabama's 7th district.

The men and women who won election to the House through an open seat victory were more likely to have had prior elected office experience than those who beat incumbents. Among the male winners, 69 percent of the open seat victors had previously held elective office compared to 49 percent of those who had defeated an incumbent. Among the female victors 83 percent of those winning open seats had held elected office compared with 48 percent of those who had defeated incumbents.

Occupational Backgrounds

Congressional Research Service's *Membership of the 112th Congress: A Profile* lists business first followed by public service/politics then law as the dominant declared professions of U.S. House members serving in that Congress. Business experiences and the law profession have been the dominant occupational backgrounds of members of the national legislature historically. People engaged in these activities have also constituted a large segment of the purported pool of eligible potential candidates for elective office. They were two of the major categories from which Lawless and Fox drew their sample of potential public officials in *It Takes a Candidate* (2005), the prominent contemporary study of gender and political ambition. Census data on the presence of women in these two eligibility pools are available to provide a sense of the extent to which women are in positions to be recruited to run and the likelihood they will campaigns for a seat in the U.S. House.

Women owned 7.8 million nonfarm U.S. businesses operating in the 50 states and the District of Columbia in 2007, 28.7 percent of all nonfarm businesses in the United States. Women-owned firms employed 7.6 million persons and generated $1.2 trillion in receipts. Such ownership had increased 20 percent since the previous tabulation in 2002 (U.S. Census Bureau 2007). Women make up 16 percent of Fortune 500 leadership according to Catalyst's *Statistical Overview of Women in the Workplace* and women comprise 51.5 percent of managerial, professional, and related positions (Catalyst 2011). In 2009–10, women were 47.2 percent of J.D. students, 31.5 percent of all lawyers, and 19.5 percent of law firm partners. (Catalyst 2012). We know, too, that during the time period under consideration in this study, women have constituted nearly one-quarter of state legislators with wide variation across the states.

Women also now surpass men in gaining advanced degrees as well as bachelor's degrees, according to U.S. Census Bureau figures released in 2011. Among adults 25 and older, 10.6 million U.S. women have master's degrees or higher, compared with 10.5 million men, and roughly 20.1 million women have bachelor's degrees, compared with nearly 18.7 million men (Yen 2011).

Legal and business professions have dominated the occupational backgrounds of national political leaders. However, an examination of the employment histories of members of the U.S. House show eclectic, sometimes colorful, and varied career paths to national public office. Comedian Al Franken's election to the U.S. Senate in 2008 perhaps stands out as the most "colorful" and most different "professional" credential. At the same time, news media campaign stories regarding Sean Duffy's campaign for Wisconsin's open 7th district seat in 2010 often noted his background as a reality TV performer and lumberjack champion. But he also had a legal background and was county prosecutor when he successfully won election to the U.S. House. In his *CQ Weekly*'s profile upon election, Duffy listed the following occupations: county prosecutor; lawyer; bus driver, professional timber sports competitor, reality show personality.

Vicky Hartzler's list of occupations as farmer, rancher, farm equipment dealership owner, homemaker, and teacher provides an example of the multiple career background of a successful congressional female candidate. She had also been a Missouri state representative in the 1990s. Hartzler defeated long-time Democratic incumbent Ike Skelton in 2010 in Missouri's 4th district to win her U.S. House seat. One might be particularly curious about the occupational background that Rep. Michelle Bachmann listed when first elected to the U.S. House given the nature of her campaign for the Republican Party presidential nomination in 2011. She listed homemaker and U.S. Treasury Department lawyer in her *CQ Weekly* profile.

Table 7.6 lists the occupational backgrounds of the individuals elected to Congress based on the occupations *CQ Weekly* has provided in its profiles of newly elected U.S. representatives immediately following an election. Its listings provide a standard, longitudinal method of cataloging occupational backgrounds and as indicated in the previous paragraph multiple occupations are included. They are informative. Incumbents' official websites provide even fuller qualitative pictures of their backgrounds although obviously written to reflect as positive an image of the incumbent as possible. Consider, for example, the varied career of Dan Maffei, elected in 2008 from New York's 25th district. *CQ Weekly* lists his occupations as investment firm executive; political consultant; congressional aide; and television reporter and producer. Consider the description for Debbie Halvorson, also elected in 2008. She had been a cosmetics saleswoman, homemaker, apartment property manager, and driving instructor, according to her profile. Rep. Halvorson also was a state senator when she ran for Congress in 2008 and a member of the Democratic Party leadership team in the state senate in Illinois.

If one goes to Rep. Maffei's official website, you learn that as a congres-

TABLE 7.6. Precongressional Occupations (in percentages)

Occupation	Men	Women
Lawyer	33	28
Business Executive/Owner	27	21
Company Employee/Manager	20	22
Public Official (elected)	17	14
Teacher/Professor	11	22
Exec/Legislative Aide	11	13
Real Estate	5	4
Public Administrator	2	7
Nonprofit Executive	2	5
Homemaker	0	6
Lobbyist	2	2
Accountant	1	2
Law Enforcement	1	2
Military	1	2
Pilot	1	0
Journalist	1	0
Athlete/Sportsman	1	0
Manual Laborer	1	1
Political Activist	1	1
Minister	1	0
Presidential Appointee	1	1
Sports Coach	.5	0
Gubernatorial Aide	.4	0
Social Worker	.4	0
Foreign Service Officer	.2	0
Prison Guard	.2	0
Peace Corps/VISTA Volunteer	.2	0
Law Clerk	.2	2
Party Official	.2	0
State Cabinet Member	0	1
Artisan	.2	0
Rehabilitation Specialist	.2	0
International Justice Consultant	.2	0
N =	494	97

Source: Data compiled by the author from *CQ Weekly Reports*.

sional aide he worked for former U. S. senators Daniel Patrick Moynihan and Bill Bradley and served as a senior staff member of the House Ways and Means Committee and that he had been senior vice-president of Pinnacle Capital Management, LLC. He had been a television reporter in his hometown of Syracuse and a member of the Communication Workers of America union. (He had also earned a master's degree from the John F. Kennedy School of Government at Harvard University.)

What we learn from Rep. Halvorson's website is that she began her public service as Crete Township clerk in 1993. She had been a small businesswoman for 14 years before entering public service and had "spent time as a lecturer at her alma mater, Governor's State University." Her "small businesswoman" experience involved being a saleswoman for Mary Kay Cosmetics, which provided her with a large network of contacts (Conrad 2008). She beat an 18-year incumbent to win her first term as a state senator after being recruited to run by Democratic state Senate leader Emil Jones. The DCCC also recruited her to run in the open 11th congressional district in 2008. These biographies illustrate the multifaceted precongressional careers representing many different experiences that often are not captured in quantitative listings. For a systematic comparative analysis of the prior occupations of the men and women who were elected to the U.S. House in these contemporary election cycles, however, I use the *CQ Weekly* listings.

Up to three positions from the *CQ Weekly* profiles were coded to compose a picture of the occupational backgrounds of the men and women elected to the U.S. House from 1993 through 2010. Thirty-six categories have been included. An attempt was made to both reflect the level of diversity in the occupational backgrounds of the members while grouping occupations into a smaller set of categories for comparative analysis purposes. A few categories necessarily, therefore, group together a type of occupational position that ranges greatly in terms of authority and the amount of resources or personnel over which lawmakers had control in their precongressional careers. An example is the categorizing of business owners, which could mean running a fairly small family business to being the head of a major corporation.

For the 110th Congress (2007–08), Paul Herrnson calculated that 27 percent of House members listed law as their occupational background, 22 percent had been employed in business or banking, and 25 percent were in politics or public service (2008, 58). I noted earlier the predominant occupations for members of the U.S. House in the 112th Congress. Herrnson's and Congressional Research Service's listings, which are based on

Congressional Quarterly figures, provide comparative benchmarks for the whole U.S. House membership with this study of newly elected members in the contemporary era. For example, while *CQ Weekly* lists 13 members as having provided homemaking as an occupational background in the 112th Congress, six of the 97 women elected to the U.S. House between 1993 and 2010 included homemaker as one of their prior occupations. All of these recently elected female members who included homemaker in their profile were seasoned politicians at the time of their election to the U.S. House and media coverage of their campaigns only described them in terms of being a state senator or state representative or a local businessperson. They were not profiled as "moms" running for office.

The biggest difference in prior occupations between the sexes among this cohort was in the education profession. The female House members were 10 percent more likely to have had a background in this occupational area than the male members. The male members were 6 percent more likely to have been business owners and 5 percent more likely to have been lawyers.

Both sexes bring a variety of backgrounds to the legislative process and while most have had previous elective office experience—female members more than the male members—their work experiences are broad and eclectic as suggested by the anecdotes that introduced this section. Diverse career paths describe both male and female members' routes to national office-holding. They apparently are becoming more similar than different as one might have suspected based on the strategic politician, new breed, and third-wave characterizations of contemporary female public office seekers. But behind those similarities we find a host of life experiences that each sex brings to the legislative process as in-depth qualitative profiles illustrate. A special look at the Republican women in the 2010 election and the 112th Congress provides a distinct lens on these life experiences and their articulation in the early days of the most recent Congress.

The partisan gap in women's candidacies and membership in the U.S. House in the contemporary period has been one of the themes of this work. Why more Republican women have not been as engaged in the campaign process has been a political puzzle, but as described in chapter 2, a story line of the 2010 election was the emergence of assertive conservative women candidates seeking Republican Party nominations for the House, Senate, and governorships. All of the incumbent female Republican U.S. representatives were reelected and nine new Republican female winners joined them. The Republican press release issued after the election noted in chapter 2 touting 2010 as the "year of the Republican woman" cited the diversity of backgrounds and geographical representation of their female candidates and winners. Sarah Palin's campaign to elect more women to public office highlighted motherhood in her call for "mama grizzlies" to assert themselves on the campaign trail.

This growth in conservative women's candidates promoted both inside and outside the Republican Party organizational structure presents a new lens on the descriptive nature of female politicians. Marin Cogan in a June 20, 2011, Politico.com piece titled "GOP Freshmen Women Go on Offense" captures this new phenomenon. She characterizes the first-term Republican women in the 112th Congress as a new weapon in the Republican messaging arsenal, "a growing, influential caucus of younger GOP women intent on fighting back against Democratic claims that the party is anti-woman." She says this new group does not fit the traditional model of women who run for office: "Rather they are rock ribbed, younger, conservative working mothers, a new breed of GOP representative the Republican male leaders are more than happy to have deployed on the front lines, to act as the public face for a party that still suffers from a gender gap in their rank-and-file."

On June 21, 2011, U.S. Representative Cathy McMorris Rodgers, vice chair of the House Republican Conference, led 14 Republican female members on the House floor for a GOP Women's Special Order. The special order, "I Am a Republican Woman," highlighted members' backgrounds, their personal stories and policy objectives, and the Republican agenda to create jobs. Each woman spoke for one to three minutes.

Although conservative political thinkers have decried identity politics, the comments of these female Republican representatives stressed identity in their remarks as to why they were a "Republican woman." They emphasized their motherhood while also underscoring their professional status and careers before coming to Congress. Of the 14 women who participated in this special order, ten highlighted motherhood and grandmotherhood and talked of their children. McMorris Rodgers talked of coming "home every night to two beautiful children." Rep. Roby spoke of addressing the question of "why in the world would a 34 year old woman with a six year old and a two year old run for Congress?" We learn from Rep. Buerkle that she is the mother of six children and grandmother of 11. Rep. Ros-Lehtinen stated, "I'm a daughter. I'm a mother. I'm a grandmother." They also spoke of their experience as nurses, small business owners, physicians, farmers, educators, and attorneys. What they did not talk about were social issues but rather creating jobs and limiting government spending and regulations. They put a distinctive gendered spin on their policy advocacy.

It was one that stressed the unique experiences of their roles as women that made them strong, credible advocates for the economic policies of the Republican Party, rather than emphasizing their similarities with men. Rep. McMorris Rodgers's opening remarks illustrate this theme:

> While our backgrounds and professions may be different, one thing is not: We are all conservative reformers committed to leaving American better for our children and grandchildren. After all, women in this country know better than anyone the affects of harmful economic politics. Why? Because two out of three businesses are started by women. Women-owned businesses are the fastest growing segment in the United States economy and they generate over $3.5 trillion in revenue a year. Women manage 83 percent of household income, spend two out of three health care dollars, and make up the majority of health care providers in America. (*Congressional Record* 2011)

This emphasis on the particular characterization of their backgrounds and its connection to their policy orientations in Congress that this group of women has brought to national politics is a distinctive aspect of both descriptive and substantive representation. Chapter 8 expands on ideas about representation and the movement of female legislators into positions of leadership from which they can affect public policy.

The Geographical Representation of Women in Congress

In the 2010 election Republican Martha Roby narrowly beat Democratic incumbent Bobby Bright in Alabama's 2nd district. In Alabama's 7th district, Democrat Terri Sewell won an open seat victory to become a U.S. representative. They were the first women to represent Alabama in the U.S. Congress and Sewell was simultaneously the first Black woman to represent Alabama. Roby had been endorsed by Sarah Palin and by Maggie's List, a group that had formed in 2010 to support conservative female candidates, as noted in chapter 6. On the Democratic side, EMILY's List had endorsed Sewell.

Both of these women are lawyers. Martha Roby had been an Alabama state senator and member of the Birmingham City Council. Terri Sewell had not previously run for public office but she had extensive political experience. She had worked for U.S Representative Richard Shelby and U.S. Senator Howell Heflin. Also her mother had been the first Black woman elected to the Selma City Council. Martha Roby's father is chief judge of the United States Court of Appeals for the Eleventh Circuit. Roby had received a bachelor's degree in music from New York University and obtained her law degree from Samford University in Birmingham. When she ran for Congress in 2010, Roby was the mother of children aged two and six.

Sewell, single, had graduated from Princeton University and received her law degree from Harvard Law School. She won the Afro-American Thesis Prize for her Princeton senior thesis, "Black Women in Politics: Our Time Has Come." Sewell had also received a master's degree from Oxford University and has had her master's thesis, *Black Tribunes: Race and Representation in British Politics*, published.

An interesting gender sidelight that focuses on social conservatism from Martha Roby's 2nd district primary contest occurred when the Concerned Women's Political Action Committee, which had endorsed her, attacked her opponent Rick Barber for hosting nightly poker tournaments in the pool hall he owned, apparently in violation of state law (Frontrunner 2010). Concerned Women PAC CEO Penny Nance issued a statement noting that "[s]o often serious addictions start quite innocently. . . . That's why we would question the judgment of any candidate who would promote gambling at any level in their personal lives" (Isenstadt 2010). Roby soundly beat Barber in a runoff.

The description of the election of these two women to the U.S. House illustrates the expanding geographical representation of women in the U.S. Congress. The underrepresentation of women in the national legislature has been related to political geography. Palmer and Simon note that "female representatives are not randomly distributed across the country" (2008, 177) and in his work Richard Fox has found that "[w]omen have not been equally successful running for elective office in all parts of the United States" (2010, 196). He reports that more than one-third of the states had no women serving in the U.S. House in 2008 (199). From a regional perceptive, since the late 1990s only the West "shows clear gains for women" (198).

Geography is significant for representation for a variety of theoretical reasons. The local visibility of women in political leadership positions serves a symbolic importance to constituent women, as noted in chapter 1. They serve as role models to girls and young women. Then, too, women in different areas of the country may have diverse concerns that need to be articulated in national public policy discussions on which female representatives from their districts can take the lead. If women are more likely to run and win in particular types of districts this bias indicates a continued economic and social context to women's political leadership and is reflective of a gendered electoral process.

In *A Woman's Place Is in the House*, a few district demographic characteristics were related to the nomination of women for a seat in the U.S. House. Women were less likely to be nominated in southern districts. Democratic women were more likely to be nominated in higher income districts while urban populations were more likely to nominate Republican women than less urban districts. Overall, the bivariate data analyses from that study using rather general characteristics suggested that constituency context seems to have had only a modest impact on the presence of women as candidates and nominees for the U.S. House during the feminist era (1994, 139).

Exploring constituency and geographical factors from a much longer time perspective and in much greater detail Palmer and Simon have constructed a woman-friendliness index as noted earlier in this work. They sought to answer the question "Can we identify the districts that are more likely to elect women" (2008, 177). Their woman friendliness index was not only significant from a political science research perspective but also captured the imagination of political pundits and activists, receiving substantial media attention, which in turn affects public knowledge and discussion. For example, the nationally syndicated columnist David Broder (cited in chap. 2) publicized their research in a "Narrowing the House's Gender Gap" column (2006). He concluded his column, which included an interview with Palmer and Simon, with a suggestion about its practical political use to states:

> Demographic changes now underway will increase the number of districts where women can compete. But the radical suggestion from Palmer and Simon is for states to use this knowledge of what makes a district 'woman-friendly' in the next round of redistricting, after the 2010 Census, to increase substantially the number of women in Congress. As women in state legislatures position themselves for the coming redistricting battles, that's something they can keep in mind.

Palmer and Simon's research is the most comprehensive analysis of the effect of district characteristics on the election of women to Congress. To answer their questions about the effect of district profiles, they constructed a list of geographical and constituency characteristics found to be related to partisanship and electoral success in congressional districts and characteristics thought to be related to the election of women. They then constructed measures of "core" Democratic and "core" Republican districts determined by whether that party's candidate had won in at least four of the five elections in a ten-year Census cycle. The characteristics of core districts electing only men were compared to those electing a woman during a decade. They found that characteristics that make a district women-friendly are not identical to those associated with party victories.

Female Democratic House members tended to win election in districts that were more liberal, more urban, more diverse, more educated, and much wealthier than those won by male Democratic members of the House. "They come from much more compact, 'tonier,' upscale districts than their male counterparts," Palmer and Simon wrote. These results, they find, hold only for white women. African American female representatives, all of whom have been Democrats, represent districts that are quite similar to those that African American men represent (2008, 178).

Female Republican House members also were found historically to represent distinctive districts. "Female Republican House members tend to win election in districts that are less conservative, more urban, and more diverse than those electing male Republicans; they come from districts that are 'less Republican,'" Palmer and Simon reported. However, in their most recent analysis, which examined elections from 2002 through 2010, they report that the distinctiveness of those districts electing Republican women disappears. One of the most dramatic shifts they cite regards the election of Republican women from the South: "By the 2002–2010 period a third of all Republican women in the House were from the South virtually equal to the proportion of men" (2012, 206).

How then have women's experiences in the most recent election affected questions of political geography and geographical representation? Examining the 112th Congress, over half of the states had a female representative although they only represented 17 percent of the 435 districts. California disproportionately impacts the numerical representation of women in the U.S. House in contemporary times. With its 53 representatives, California dominates the legislature numerically. Nineteen of the 53 representatives from California were women, 36 percent of the delegation and 26 percent of all the women in the U.S. House in the 112th Congress.

Just as women have incrementally increased their presence in the national legislature, their geographical representation has incrementally expanded as the story of Martha Roby's and Terri Sewell's elections has illustrated. One more state, Alabama, in 2011 joined the ranks of states having had female representation in the Congress in the contemporary era. If we span the country for the last two decades, the 103rd to the 112th Congress, from 1992 to include the "year of the woman" election to 2011, of the 435 districts, 134 have had a female representative, or 30 percent of all of the districts. Ten states have not had a female representative between 1993 and 2011. But two of those states (Alaska and Louisiana) have a female U.S. senator, and three others have elected a woman as governor (Delaware, Montana, and South Carolina). Nebraska and Vermont, which have had no women in any of these positions during this time period, did have women governors immediately preceding it. Iowa, North Dakota,[2] and Mississippi are the only three states not having elected female leaders to either govern it or represent it in the national legislature.

Thus, although the election of women is more commonplace in some areas of the country than in others, throughout the nation women and girls have role models of female political leaders. If electing women to these offices is a political innovation, as Ondercin and Welch (2005) describe them, then innovation has primarily given way to the routine or the ordinary from a broad sweep of the country perspective as far as the election of women to political leadership positions is concerned.

I take one final assessment of trends in district representation by returning to Palmer and Simon's "friendliness" index based on 11 demographic characteristics (2008, 204). The question is whether the women elected since the millennium expanded women's representation in districts beyond the areas categorized as friendly or have the women who have been elected in the most recent cycles primarily enhanced representation in the group of districts having "friendly" demographic characteristics. Palmer and Simon show that the district demographic characteristics indicate growing "friendliness" toward women candidates over time (2008, 209–10).

Women have been elected in 55 districts that previously had not had a female representative in the first decade of the 21st century. Forty-one women were newly elected from 2002 through 2008, 13 Republicans and 28 Democrats. Using Palmer and Simon's "friendliness" chart, only one of the Republican women was elected in a district scoring more than five on the friendliness to Republican women scale, Katherine Harris in 2002 in Florida's 13th district, while seven of the 28 Democratic women (25%) were elected in districts rated as friendly, having a score of six or more, while 75 percent were elected from districts scoring in the bottom half of the friendliness districts. The women being elected to Congress consequently in the most recent elections have expanded the range of districts sending women to the U.S. House, enhancing the scope of "friendliness" and contributing to gender becoming less of a factor in these elections, as Palmer and Simon's 2012 update on female Republicans being elected from the South also shows.

Conclusion

From a descriptive perspective contemporary female elected officials are more similar than different from their male colleagues. They continue to be older on average and less likely to be married when elected but their educational and occupational backgrounds have merged at least from a quantitative perspective. Male and female representatives tend to act strategically in seeking national office. Female U.S. representatives are even more likely to have elected office experience and less likely to be amateurs (loosely defined) than their male colleagues. On that one dimension they are more "qualified." At the same time, these women who have been elected to the U.S. House in recent elections have also created greater diversity in breaking demographic barriers. Many of these women were the first woman elected from their congressional district and some were the first woman elected to Congress from their state. In addition to these national level firsts, they were pioneers earlier in their political careers. I conclude this chapter with a list of these diverse firsts among contemporary female members of the U.S. House.

Firsts among the Women Elected to the U.S. House

- Ileana Ros-Lehtinen (R-FL), the first Latina to serve in the Florida State legislature and the first Cuban American woman elected to Congress (1989–)
- Lucille Roybal-Allard (D-CA), the first Mexican American woman elected to Congress (1992–)
- Nydia Velázquez (D-NY), the first Latina to serve on the New York City Council and the first Puerto Rican woman elected to Congress (1992–)
- Loretta and Linda Sanchez (D-CA) are the first sisters elected to Congress.
- Hilda Solis (D-CA, 2000–2009), the first Latina elected to the state senate in California
- Patsy Mink (D-HI), the first woman of color elected to the House and the first Asian American woman (1964–1976; 1990–2002)
- Juanita Millender-McDonald (D-CA), the first African American woman

elected to the Carson City, California, city council and in 1991 served as it mayor pro tempore.

- Eddie Bernice Johnson (D-TX), the first African American woman from the Dallas area ever to hold public office when she was elected in 1972 to the Texas state legislature.
- Gwendolynne Moore (D-WI), the first African American woman elected to the state senate in Wisconsin in 1992
- Maxine Waters (D-CA), the first woman in California history to be elected to a whip position in the state legislature. She later became chair of the Democratic Caucus in the state assembly.
- Diane Watson (D-CA), the first African American woman elected to the state senate in California in 1978
- Candice Miller (R-MI), the youngest supervisor in Harrison Township history, elected in 1980
- Debbie Wasserman Schultz (D-FL), the youngest woman elected to the Florida state legislature when she was elected at age 26
- Gabrielle Giffords (D-AZ), the youngest woman ever elected to the Arizona state senate when she was elected in 2003 at the age of 33
- Judy Chu (D-CA), the first Chinese American woman elected to the U.S. House
- Tammy Baldwin (D-WI), first out-lesbian elected to the U.S. House

EIGHT

Gender, Policy Making, and Leadership

Descriptive and Substantive Representation

The entrance of nine new conservative Republican female representatives in the 112th Congress, which was spotlighted in chapter 7, plus the conservative gender identity politics Sarah Palin trumpeted in the 2010 election set the stage for women's issues and gender to come to the center of policy making in the 112th Congress in contradictory, acrimonious, and polarizing ways with female legislators in the forefront of the debates. Rather than attention being paid to the ways in which female members of the two parties had come together across the aisle to create greater equality for women in federal policies through the Congressional Caucus for Women's Issues (CCWI) in earlier congresses, the 112th Congress will be known for the polarizing leadership of Democratic and Republican female members on a variety of issues, policies distinctly focusing on women such as violence, reproductive health care, and access to contraceptives, and the impact of more general economic policies on women. A major theme of both congressional and presidential politics in 2012 was whether a "war on women" was being waged and by whom. Democratic and Republican female legislators saw themselves as representing women although they articulated the concept of representation in quite opposing fashion. They also viewed the substantive nature of that representation in quite distinctive terms based on their rhetoric and votes.

The election of women and their performance in office raise political puzzles for social science research. The seminal collection of articles on the impact of female representatives in the U.S. national legislature asked the question "Are women transforming the U.S. Congress?" (Rosenthal 2002a). How can empirical researchers answer such a question—yes, no, in some ways, to some degree in some contexts? First the concept of transformation needs to be defined. As with so many abstract political concepts it has multidimensional aspects and what constitutes transformation has diverse theoretical bases for different scholars. The research presented in the chapters of *Women Transforming Congress* edited by Cindy Simon Rosenthal in 2002 considered transformation in terms of substantive representation regarding public policy and in terms of institutional change regarding the structure and function of the organization.

The impact of female legislators has been much greater on policy change than on changing the nature of the institution. Rosenthal's concluding chapter argues that policy changes have occurred but institutional transformation seems elusive (447). Congresswomen, along with other actors, have contributed to transforming the congressional public policy agenda and reshaping institutional and political responses to women as a constituency. As Rosenthal states, "The consideration and accommodation of feminalist concerns have altered the agenda, changed the context of policy debate, and affected legislative outcomes regarding reproductive policy, cancer and health care, welfare reform, civil rights, and criminal and economic affairs" (446).[1]

It is much more difficult to even conceive of how or why women as a group would come together to change the institution, its norms, and modes of operation, even though scholars have shown that they conceive of and perform leadership differently from men (see Rosenthal 1998; Kathlene 1994, 1995). They may have benefited in their elections from perceptions of being outsiders who would clean up the system but the lower level office-holding experience of many contemporary female national lawmakers suggest they have learned to operate in organizations with similar hierarchies (although with greater variation) and have experienced power and leadership in a similar fashion as their male colleagues. In addition, the campaign support of congressional party organizations described in chapter 6 provides incentives for going along with institutional arrangements as well as being able to claim credit back home for policy initiatives. Female members have not taken the lead, for example, in eliminating earmarks but rather, as Anzia and Berry (2011) have shown, have been better at "bringing home the bacon." They have also become leaders in raising and distributing money to fellow partisans' campaigns so we should not expect them to be leaders in reforming the campaign finance system. But still how has the incremental increase in the number and tenure of female members made a difference in the contemporary Congress?

Party Leadership in Congress

Chapter 6 described the movement of female members of the two parties into campaign leadership posts. The campaign committees are part of the overall leadership structure within the party organizations in both the House and the Senate. In addition, leadership importantly consists of positions in the governing and policy-making organizations of the parties and service as chairs and ranking members of these bodies' policy-making committees. Moving beyond a focus on getting elected to the national legislature, analyzing the extent to which women have gained access to positions of institutional power within the committee systems and party leadership structures is essential to a consideration of their "critical presence" and ability to affect policy making.

Historically, women have filled 53 Democratic Party Caucus leadership positions and 25 Republican Conference leadership positions in the U.S. House, counting both elected and appointed posts, a tiny fraction of all the positions available since women first achieved election to Congress. The first woman to serve in such a position was Connecticut representative Chase Going Woodhouse, who served a single term as secretary of the Democratic Caucus in the 81st Congress (1949–51). Illinois representative Lynn Martin became the first Republican woman elected to a House leadership position when she won the vice chair post in the Republican Conference in the 99th–100th Congresses (1985–89).

By far the most significant event in women's legislative political leadership history in the United States was the "breaking of the ultimate marble ceiling" that occurred when Nancy Pelosi was elected Speaker of the U.S. House of Representatives at the beginning of the 110th Congress in 2007. Rep. Pelosi had moved up the party organizational hierarchy, first being elected party whip in 2001 and then chair of the Democratic Caucus (or minority leader) in 2003. Her Democratic colleagues unanimously reelected her Speaker of the House in the 111th Congress. By extension she became the most politically powerful woman in American government, second in line for the presidency.

After the Democrats lost control of the House, her party caucus still elected Rep. Pelosi its leader although not unanimously and not without dissension. Members had concern about her being a lightning rod for conservative criticism and the party's loss of its control of the House in the 2010 election. The Campaign Media Analysis Group reported that more than $65 million was spent on 161,203 ads targeting Rep. Pelosi during the 2010 election year (Steinhauser and Livingston 2010). Karen Tumulty in the *Washington Post* (2012) reports that she "was portrayed as, among other things, a cackling witch." The Democratic Caucus elected her minority leader by a vote of 150 to 43 for Heath Shuler, a conservative Democrat in his third term from North Carolina.

Pelosi had won the minority leadership position that put her on track to become Speaker on a vote of 177 to 29 against Harold Ford after the 2002 election. At the same time, Rep. Deborah Pryce of Ohio made leadership history within the Republican Party with her election as conference chair, the fourth-ranking post in the GOP leadership. She had moved up the ranks from conference secretary to vice-chair before her election as conference chair, which she won by a vote of 133 to 61 for J. D. Hayworth and 28 votes for Jim Ryun. She served in this position for two congresses. Jonathan Riskind described her election in an Ohio *Columbus Dispatch* piece as being the result of her fund-raising prowess (as with Rep. Pelosi):

> U.S. Rep. Deborah Pryce doled out more than $1.1 million in campaign cash for the 2002 election, but more than half went to help other GOP candidates across the country, according to a new computer analysis for *The Dispatch*. The political largesse is a big reason why the Upper Arlington Republican has risen in the House hierarchy. After the fall election, colleagues appointed her GOP conference chairwoman—the highest position ever held by a Republican woman. Republicans grateful for more than $630,000 that Pryce gave to candidates nationwide—directly and through party organizations—say that kind of partisan zeal deserves to be rewarded. That wasn't the only factor in her successful leadership bid, but it certainly played a major role, they say. (2002)

Beyond these two historical cases, how extensive has the movement been among the female members of the U.S. House into leadership positions? As women's presence has grown to 17 percent of the membership have women risen to 17 percent or more of the leadership? Lack of seniority has limited women's advancement as well as gender bias and tenure must be taken into account in assessing leadership attainment. Rep. Pelosi, for example, had served for 20 years in the House before becoming Speaker.

(John Boehner had also served 20 years when he attained the speakership in 2011.) The overall average length of service for representatives at the start of the 112th Congress was 9.8 years or 4.9 terms (Manning 2012). The mean and median number of years in the U.S. House for the female members was 11 years. Therefore, tenure as an impediment in previous congresses for female members gaining leadership has lessened as a factor in recent leadership appointments. Indeed, Swers and Larson contend that "as women first elected in the 1990s have gained seniority, their access to institutional power has increased, enhancing their ability to shape policy outcomes" (2005, 121).

Marcy Kaptur (D-OH) is the dean of the female delegation with 28 years of service at the beginning of the 112th Congress. The most senior Republican woman in the U.S. House is Ileana Ros-Lehtinen, serving her 11th term. Six of the 14 Democratic women in the top third of seniority were women of color. They have not moved into top elected leadership positions but within the Democratic Caucus they do serve on its Steering and Policy Committee. Additionally, Juanita Millender-McDonald was appointed chair of the House Administrative Committee in the 110th Congress, the first woman of color to chair a congressional committee, although it is not a power committee.

Tenure, or seniority, in general has also declined as *the* factor in climbing the leadership ladder. Especially in the contemporary congresses since Newt Gingrich's ascension to the speakership in 1995, movement quite rapidly into leadership positions has become more characteristic of the party organizations and it has become more dependent on leadership selection rather than on seniority. Chapter 6 showed how quickly Debbie Wasserman Shultz moved into a prominent role in the DCCC, for example. On the Republican side, Cathy McMorris Rodgers was elected vice-chair of the Republican Conference in 2008 at the beginning of her third term in Congress after having served only four years in the institution. Minority Leader John Boehner selected her to run. She faced no opposition. The press release her office issued upon her election highlighted the image the party was attempting to project. Its opening sentence read, "As a new mother and second youngest woman Member of Congress, my unique perspective will help our party as we build coalitions, redefine our agenda and develop and spread our party's message."

By the middle of the first decade of the 21st century, journalists were beginning to highlight the rise of women into influential positions in Congress, describing their "skyrocketing influence" (Stevens 2005) and their "increased clout" (Giroux 2007). Allyson Stevens quoted Rep. Hilda Solis as stating in 2005 at the beginning of the 109th Congress, "We aren't just tokens anymore. We're on committees. We're ranking members on committees. We're even on 'Meet the Press.'" The 15 percent of women in Congress held "a higher percentage of leadership positions, giving them a greater ability to shape their parties' agenda, steer legislation through Congress and attract media attention to their priorities," Stevens reported.

Political scientist Cindy Simon Rosenthal has taken a more analytical approach toward the question of women's progress running for and winning leadership positions in the contemporary Congress. Congressional leadership studies had suffered from a lack of a gender analysis, she argued. Writing in 2008, she concluded that women's presence was exceptional in three senses of the word: being a rare occurrence, deviating from the norm, and being held to higher standards and expectations (2008, 197). Thus, she analyzed the tenure, entrance into leadership contests, contested nature of those contests, and the ideological scores of candidates and winners compared to party mean and median scores for male and female members within both parties. Would-be female leaders had had to engage in more contested elections and have tended to be more liberal members of their caucus or conference, her analysis found. Her data included leadership contests in congresses from 1975 through 2007.

Recent Party Leadership

Table 8.1 incorporates and extends Rosenthal's analysis of the presence of women in leadership into the three most recent congresses. It presents data on the number and percentage of women in the Democratic Caucus and Republican Conference and as a percentage of various leadership positions in the 110th through the 112th Congress.

In each of these congresses, women were approximately 10 percent of the Republican Conference and between 21 to 25 percent of the Democratic Caucus.[2] Women have less seniority especially within the Republican Party. Given the massive losses within the Democratic Party in the 2010 election, women's percentage of the senior members increased even though their numbers did not grow. It should be noted that the 1992 election was not just the "year of the woman" substantially increasing female representation in the U.S. House, but that six women of color were elected in that election and women of color now are a core of the senior members of the Democratic Party. They are six of the 14 women in the top third of the senior members as noted earlier. The Democratic Party has a much more expansive leadership structure and women have been substantially included under Rep. Pelosi's leadership although she is the only elected female member of the leadership (Swers 2008). Counting both elected and appointed positions, women were overrepresented in leadership compared to their membership numbers.

The Republican Party has fewer leadership positions and recently within the party women have not fared very well. Only one woman in each of these congresses has been elected to a Republican Party leadership position, vice-chair of the conference, while two women have served on the steering committee in two of the congresses. Having Rep. McMorris Rodgers as its conference vice-chair meant that 14 percent of the elected Republican leadership was female, indicating a slight overrepresentation relative to women's numbers in the party membership, although it only meant a jump from no women to one woman in an elected leadership position and not to one of the top four positions.

Texas Rep. Kay Granger was elected Republican Conference vice-chairman for the 110th Congress. She won a contested election, beating Rep. Steve Pearce of New Mexico, 124 to 63, to assume that post. In the

TABLE 8.1. Women's Presence in Leadership Positions, 110th–112th Congress

Congress	% Women in Conference Membership	% Women in Top Third of Party Seniority	% Women in Party Steering Committee	% Women in Party Leadership	% Women in Chairs and Ranking Minority Members
110th					
Democrats	21.1	15.4	30	38.9	19
	(50/232)	(12/78)	(15/50)	(7/18)	(4/21)
Republicans	10.4	6	7.1	12.5	4.8
	(21/202)	(4/67)	(2/28)	(1/8)	(1/21)
111th					
Democrats	22	16.5	35.3	33	14.3
	(56/255)	(14/85)	18/51	6/18	(3/21)
Republicans	9.5	6.7	3.6	12.5	4.8
	(17/179)	(4/60)	1/28	(1/8)	(1/21)
112th					
Democrats	25	22	37.2	31.6	19
	(49/193)	(14/63)	19/51	6/19	(4/21)
Republicans	10	8.6	7.4	11	4.8
	(24/242)	(7/81)	2/27	1/9	(1/21)

Source: Data compiled by the author from Cindy Simon Rosenthal, "Climbing Higher: Opportunities and Obstacles within the Party System," in *Legislative Women: Getting Elected, Getting Ahead*, ed. Beth Reingold (Boulder: Lynne Rienner, 2008), 197–220 and www.house.gov.

111th Congress, Cathy McMorris Rodgers replaced Granger in that post. According to political reports, Rep. Granger chose not to seek reelection to that position while she mulled a run for the U.S. Senate if Kay Bailey Hutcheson relinquished her seat to run for governor of the state.

Marsha Blackburn of Tennessee also sought the Republican Conference chair position for the 110th Congress in a four-way race but received few votes in the balloting. She was reported to have "spent the better part of the year laying the groundwork for her campaign, including frequent radio and TV appearances." One member contended that Blackburn's eagerness could have also led to her failure, stating that "Marsha worked really hard, but there was just this perception that Marsha was in it for Marsha, and not for the team" (Davis 2006). One has to wonder about the suggestive sexism in this comment as a broader reflection on the party. Rep. Blackburn is a staunch conservative so certainly not out of the mainstream of the party, a plus in a leadership bid. Certainly aggressive bids for leadership positions are hardly unknown. Rep. McMorris Rodgers also has consistently cast conservative votes in the U.S. House. As will be detailed later in this chapter within the contemporary polarized Congress, Republican female members of the U.S. House have in general become reliable conservative voters within the party conference.[3] Moderate Republican women have pretty much disappeared.

In the 112th Congress, after regaining the House majority Republicans added a position for a first-term member to be part of the leadership team. Since first-termers were a large contingent of its membership elected from the raucous campaigns of 2010 and the antiestablishment prominence of the Tea Party, Rep. Boehner decided to allow the new members to elect one of their own to his leadership team. Rep. Kristi Noem (R-SD) and Rep. Tim Scott (R-SC), a woman and an African American, sought this post. Boehner decided, most likely because of the importance of the party's need to reach out to these two demographic groups, to appoint both of these individuals to the leadership team.

Committee Leadership

The second side of leadership within the national legislature is service as either chair of a committee or a ranking member if one is in the minority party. Few women have chaired congressional committees. Most prominent has been Democrat Louise Slaughter who chaired the Rules Committee in the 110th and 111th Congresses. Pelosi appointed her to that position when she became Speaker. The Rules Committee, once a powerful bastion of independence within the House, has now become an arm of the House leadership. The Rules Committee is a key actor in the structuring of floor activity, setting the terms of floor consideration of a proposed bill.

Rosenthal suggests that women did not fare "well in securing committee posts until the 110th Congress. During the recent era of Republican rule of the House (1995–2006), women did not benefit from the conference policy of term limits on committee chairs and the declining importance of seniority. The only Republican woman to chair a full committee during 12 years of GOP rule was Jan Meyers (R-KS) who oversaw the unheralded Committee on Small Business in the 104th Congress (1995–1996) " (2008, 201). Prior to the 110th Congress, six women had held 14 committee chair positions through all of the congresses. Mae Ellen Nolan (R-CA) was the first to chair a committee when she served as chair of the Committee on Expenditures in the Post Office Department in the 68th Congress (1923–25). (See the Center for American Women and Politics Fact Sheet available at their website.)

Tables 8.1 and 8.2 present data on the presence of women in committee leadership positions since the beginning of the Pelosi era, the three most recent congresses. Currently the U.S. House has twenty-one committees, two joint committees, and two select committees. Not all committees are considered equal in terms of power and influence over substantial public policy. Consequently they are not all seen as desirable assignments. Thus, table 8.2 singles out women's presence on the more prestigious committees.

Speaker Pelosi expanded women's influence in the House by appointing four women to be chairs of committees, most significantly making Rep. Slaughter chair of the Rules Committee. The other assignments were as chairs of committees with less status. Nydia Velázquez was named chair the Committee on Small Business, Juanita Millender-McDonald would chair the House Administration Committee, and Stephanie Tubbs Jones was assigned to chair the House Ethics Committee. Republican Ileana Ros-Lehtinen served as ranking member on the Foreign Affairs Committee.

In the 111th Congress women chaired three committees. Reps. Slaughter and Velázquez maintained their chair positions and Zoe Lofgren (CA) became chair of the Committee on Ethics taking over after the death of Rep. Stephanie Tubbs Jones in 2008. Rep. Millender-McDonald also had died. In addition, Rep. Carolyn Maloney (NY) chaired the Joint Economic Committee. Rep. Ros-Lehtinen continued to be the lone female Republican serving as ranking member on a committee. In the 112th Congress with the Republicans once again in the majority, Rep. Ros-Lehtinen became chair of the Foreign Affairs Committee. She is the sole Republican female chairing a committee. No other Republican female member vied for any of the contested committee chair positions for the 112th Congress.

Four female Democrats joined Rep. Ros-Lehtinen as ranking members in the 112th Congress. Rep. Slaughter and Rep. Velázquez reverted to ranking member on the committees they had been serving as chair. In addition Rep. Eddie Bernice Johnson was appointed ranking member of the Science, Space and Technology Committee, and Rep. Linda Sanchez was appointed ranking member of the Ethics Committee. Female members did not appear to be involved in any contests for ranking member.

Table 8.2 also describes women's membership on the more prestigious committees and therefore the most sought after seats in these three most

TABLE 8.2. Women's Membership and Leadership on Power Committees, 110th–112th Congress

	Democrats		Republicans	
110th Congress				
Power Committees' Membership				
Rules	5/11	(45%)	0/4	(0)
Appropriations	8/38	(21%)	2/29	(7%)
Ways and Means	3/25	(12%)	0/16	(0)
Energy and Commerce	8/30	(27%)	3/25	(12%)
111th Congress				
Power Committees' Membership				
Rules	3/10	(33%)	1/4	(25%)
Appropriations	6/36	(17%)	2/22	(9%)
Ways and Means	3/26	(12%)	1/15	(7%)
Energy and Commerce	10/36	(28%)	3/23	(13%)
Committee Chairs/Ranking Members	3/22	(14%)	1/22	(5%)
Subcommittee Chairs/Ranking Members				
Appropriations	3/12	(25%)	2/12	(17%)
All Committees	26/97	(27%)	5/97	(5%)
112th Congress				
Power Committees' Membership				
Rules	1/4	(25%)	1/8	(16%)
Appropriations	6/21	(7%)	3/29	(10%)
Ways and Means	1/15	(12%)	2/22	(9%)
Energy and Commerce	8/23	(35%)	4/31	(13%)
Committee Chairs/Ranking Members	3/22	(14%)	1/22	(5%)
Subcommittee Chairs/Ranking Members				
Appropriations	3/12	(25%)	2/12	(17%)
All Committees	26/97	(27%)	11/97	(11%)

Source: Data compiled by the author from www.house.gov.

recent congresses. Compared to their presence among the more senior members of the House as shown in table 8.1 neither party disproportionately fails to appoint women to these committees.

Subcommittees

Committees traditionally have varied in their "power" status and within committees some subcommittee chairmanships have been considered to be significant independent bases of power. For example, the Appropriations Committee, a power committee, which is charged with the initial allocation of federal dollars to fund projects throughout the country, has historically operated under a system of subcommittee autonomy with subcommittee chairs being known as "cardinals," of which there are 12, indicating their power and influence. In contemporary congresses, House leadership has played a more prominent role in assembling and steering legislation on important issues through the legislative process, often with a task force outside of the formal committee system or working across committees (Sinclair 2006). But still within this leadership hierarchy and with committees as work centers regarding the substantive nature of proposed bills, subcommittee leadership is a way for individual members to make a meaningful career in the House and be key players in making public policy and gaining power and influence.

Being a "cardinal" on the Appropriations Committee is a distinctive marker of influence. When she was nominated to serve as chair of the Legislative Branch subcommittee of the Appropriations Committee at the beginning of the 110th Congress and the start of only her second term in the House, Rep. Wasserman Shultz's office issued a press release emphasizing the importance of this assignment and making reference to her becoming a "cardinal." The press release stated

> On the first day of the new 110th Congress, the House Committee on Appropriations recommended Rep. Debbie Wasserman Schultz serve as a "Cardinal," chairing the Legislative Branch Subcommittee and to serve on the Financial Services Subcommittee on the Appropriations Committee. The subcommittees determine the Congressional appropriations of funds for particular parts of the federal government. Serving as the Chair of the Legislative Branch Subcommittee, Rep. Wasserman Schultz will oversee the subcommittee that determines the funding level for the entire legislative branch. . . . Rep. Wasserman Schultz will serve as one of only twelve

> Cardinals on the House Committee on Appropriations. The Committee is comprised of 37 Democrats and 29 Republicans. Members who have been recommended to chair a subcommittee are referred to as "Cardinals."

In addition to Rep. Wasserman Schultz, Rep. Rosa DeLauro chaired the Agriculture Subcommittee and Rep. Nita Lowey chaired the Subcommittee on State, Foreign Operations and Related Programs of the Appropriations Committee in the 110th Congress. Thus, there were three female cardinals with women leading one-fourth of the Appropriations subcommittees. No Republican female members served as ranking members of any of the Appropriations subcommittees. These three women continued their positions as Appropriations subcommittee chairs in the 111th Congress. In addition, two female Republican representatives were appointed ranking subcommittee members. Republican Kay Granger was appointed ranking member on the Subcommittee on State, Foreign operations and Related Programs and Jo Ann Emerson became ranking member on the Subcommittee on Financial Services and General Government. They became cardinals as chairs of these two subcommittees when the Republicans regained control in the 112th Congress.

Subcommittees in general are significant in the construction of laws and the chairs of these organizations can be quite influential in the legislative process. In the 111th Congress there were 97 subcommittees including select committees' subcommittees. Democratic female representatives chaired 26 of these subcommittees, 27 percent of the total number of chairs including first-termer Kathy Dahlkemper of Pennsylvania who chaired the Regulations, Health Care, and Trade Subcommittee of the Small Business Committee. Thus, women were slightly overrepresented as subcommittee chairs within the Democratic Party relative to their membership in the caucus (22%). Five Republican women served as ranking members on subcommittees, 5 percent of the ranking members. They were underrepresented since women were 10 percent of the Republican Conference.

Eleven Republican female representatives served as subcommittee chairs in the 112th Congress newly under Republican control. Their representation as subcommittee chairs matched their representation in the institution. In addition to chairing two Appropriations subcommittees, they chaired two Financial Services subcommittees and one Energy and Commerce subcommittee. The other subcommittee chair positions were on less prestigious committee. First-termers Renee Ellmers chaired the Health and Technology Subcommittee of the Small Business Committee and Ann Marie Buerkle chaired the Veterans Affairs Health Subcommittee. The Democratic women maintained their share of subcommittee leadership positions as ranking members on the same subcommittees that they chaired in the earlier two congresses.

Summary

Nancy Pelosi's ascension to Speaker of the U.S. House in January 2007 was a unique breakthrough in women's political leadership. It was a momentous event for female lawmakers and a symbolic one for women and girls in general. She immediately moved an activist agenda through the House. Even though from a comparative perspective female membership in the U.S. national legislature remained low, the independent and central role that Congress plays in policy making, as noted in the introduction, means that women in leadership positions have significant influence on national policy. The data presented in this chapter on women's presence in party and committee leadership positions in the most recent congresses show a lessening of bias against their achievement of power in the institution. Their presence in party organizational leadership positions and as committee and subcommittee chairs and ranking members closely matches or exceeds their presence among the membership. Democrat female members, a larger portion of that party's membership, have achieved more power positions than their counterparts in the Republican Party beyond Rep. Pelosi's distinct achievement.

Policy Representation

Movement into leadership positions is one significant facet of women's influence in Congress. The effect of their presence on the policy substance of the institution is a second indicator of their influence. An examination of female members' use of their presence and influence to affect policy making is in order. Irwin Gertzog, a longtime chronicler of the Congressional Caucus for Women's Issues, early in the millennium expressed optimism about the policy impact of women's increased influence within the House: "The growing number of women elected to the House, their increasing seniority and their selection for key party and committee positions will almost certainly help validate an expanded feminist agenda—even in the face of new and important national priorities" (2005, 176).

Of ultimate importance to their substantive representation are the votes they cast on the floor of the U.S. House as it considers the enactment of legislation. Contrary to Gertzog's prognosis of an expanded feminist agenda, what has occurred is growing polarization between the female members of the two parties along with the overall polarized nature of recent congresses. Indeed, the female members in the 112th Congress have been prominent in pronouncing very contrary visions of their parties regarding issues of special concern to women.

Roll Call Voting

A Woman's Place Is in the House reported that women legislators tended to cast more liberal votes in roll call voting on the floor of the House after controlling for party and constituency factors. There I concluded that data

> show women to be a continuing liberal influence in Congress as theory has suggested. Party is the main divide on political ideology in the U.S. Congress, and women within the parties reflect that divide, but Democratic women enhance the distinctiveness of the parties, making the Democratic Party more liberal, while Republican women, being less conservative than their male colleagues, mute the difference and help push the body in a more liberal direction. (1994, 158)

In more recent congresses, however, the distinctive policy representativeness of female members of the U.S. House compared with their male colleagues as reflected in roll call votes has diminished. Brian Frederick (2009) has pointed out that "recent changes in the broader political system at the national level raise significant questions concerning whether greater numbers of women in office makes a substantive difference in the legislative process in the fashion these previous studies have documented."

These recent changes have primarily centered on the heightened polarization of the congressional parties. Gender questions in this domain center on the effect this increased polarization has had on the votes female representatives have cast. Have they too become more polarized or are they still more liberal than their male colleagues? To answer these questions Frederick (2009) explored the roll call voting behavior of women in the U.S. House of Representatives from the 97th through 109th Congresses (1981–2006).

His trend analysis showed a movement away from a gender effect on roll call voting primarily as a result of the greater conservatism of the more recently elected Republican women than that of Republican female representatives of an earlier generation. Frederick states that "[s]teadily the average ideological position of Democratic women has grown more liberal while the average ideological location of Republican female House members has grown more conservative. . . . The growing liberalism of House Democratic women and the more consistent conservatism of GOP women has finally reached a point where women in the House are now actually more ideologically distant than their male colleagues" (185). By the 108th and 109th Congresses Republican women had become as ideologically conservative as their male colleagues.

Women may bring a distinctive voice to the legislative process but when it comes to ideology, as evidenced in roll-call voting in Congress, the same fundamental factors that drive all members of Congress—party and constituency preferences—influence their votes in the contemporary era. Moreover, as partisan polarization has intensified, these factors have overwhelmed sex as a predictor of ideological positioning in the U.S. House. Regardless of the increased number of women in the U.S. House this finding is supportive of the proposition that the strength of these other factors condition the link between descriptive representation and substantive representation. An analysis of *National Journal*'s Voting Records in the first session of the 112th Congress illustrates this point and sustains Frederick's earlier analysis.

Each year since 1981 the *National Journal* has constructed a database of votes on major economic, social, and foreign policy issues, rating them as a liberal or a conservative vote based on an analysis of the debates on these bills. Each representative is scored from 0 to 100 on overall liberalism and similarly on overall conservatism. In the first year of the 112th Congress, the mean liberal score for female Democrats was 83.8 and for Democratic males it was 76.0; the liberalism score for Republican males was 28.1 and for Republican females it was 25.5. These scores illustrate the vast distance between the female membership of both parties within an overall very polarized Congress. A similar lineup is found if one examines *National Journal*'s conservative vote scores. The mean score for female Democrats was 16.2; for male Democrats it was 24.0; for male Republicans it was 71.2 and for female Republicans it was 74.5. Female GOP members as a group, based on *National Journal*'s voting analysis, are now the most conservative group while female Democrats continue to be the most liberal contingent. Democratic women continue to make the Democratic Party more liberal but GOP women no longer moderate the general conservative ideology of the Republican Party. I now turn to examine whether this difference also characterizes votes on bills aimed at women's social and economic position.

Women's Issues' Voting

The significance of descriptive representation for substantive representation may be heightened, however, when votes on a subgroup of women's issues are examined as Frederick and others have suggested (see, for example, Norton 1999). In this context, bringing more women into the legislature should have an effect on social welfare and economic issues that have a distinctive impact on women and on proposals to advance women's rights, what have been labeled "feminist" legislation.

To address hypotheses about the trend in relationships between sex, party, and votes on women's issues, Frederick analyzed gender and support for women's issues based on the American Association of University Women's (AAUW) Legislative Priorities voting record scores. For several decades the AAUW has adopted a set of legislative priorities and constructed the Congressional Voting Record to provide citizens with information on how their legislators have voted on a set of priority areas. The areas have varied from Congress to Congress but have included education, reproductive rights, welfare reform, economic security, judicial nominations, tax and budget issues, civil rights, and affirmative action. Even though the AAUW is a progressive organization that often seeks governmental remedies in areas of concern to women and has sought to expand women's rights in a liberal direction, its Congressional Voting Record database provides a valuable tool to this study of gender in contemporary Congressional elections and lawmaking.

Frederick's analysis of the AAUW Congressional Voting Record supports the thesis of a decline in gender as being a major explanatory factor in casting votes on these pieces of legislation. As he concludes:

> Even on women's issues male Democrats are now about as liberal as female Democrats after other variables are accounted for. . . . Gender differences in the GOP conference on the AAUW scorecard almost vanished by the 109th Congress, when female Republican scored about 49 points lower, while male Republicans scored 52 points less than did male Democrats, all else equal. Earlier studies documenting greater liberalism on various issues among Republican women in the House were based on solid empirical evidence. How-

> ever, in more recent years this assumption was no longer valid as a new group of conservative female House Republicans elected to the House has diminished the distinctive influence of gender when it comes to votes on women's issues. (2009)

Figure 8.1 illustrates and expands Frederick's analysis of the AAUW Voting Record scores of male and female Democratic and Republican members of the U.S. House for each of the congresses included in this study including the first session of the 112th Congress. With the 111th Congress, AAUW began to include cosponsorship of legislation as well as actual floor votes in its Voting Record calculations, which may have affected the Republican scores. I have also included scores for the 103rd Congress for comparative purposes. The 103rd Congress was the last Congress in which the Democratic Party was in the majority prior to the 110th Congress and the first Congress after the "year of the woman" election. Clear party differences are readily observable with Democrats highly supportive of the AAUW agenda and Republicans much less so. One can also see that the Democratic female members were the most consistently strong supporters of the AAUW agenda with scores tending over 90 percent. Their Democratic male colleagues were not far behind with support scores in the 80s. The Republican female members were not too far behind in the 103rd Congress, voting for AAUW priorities 66.6 percent of the time, but then their support declined quite dramatically (though never as low as their male colleagues, as Frederick has shown in his more detailed statistical analysis). In the 109th and 110th Congresses, however, Republican male support climbed somewhat, perhaps reflecting an attempt to temper growing public discontent with the Republican Party. However, votes in the 111th and first session of the 112th Congress show a dramatic decline among both Republican male and female members when cosponsorship is added to the analysis. This figure provides a further illustration of the contemporary complexity of the relationship between descriptive and substantive representation from a gender lens and the decline of gender as a distinguishing voting factor in the contemporary U.S. House of Representatives.

The Lilly Ledbetter Fair Pay Act enacted into law in 2009 most clearly illustrates that "women's issues" still receive significant legislative attention and the divergence of the parties of these issues. It was the first bill President Barack Obama signed into law. The bill had become a rallying point for women's rights activists in the 2008 election. Lilly Ledbetter was a featured speaker at the Democratic National Convention and was honored

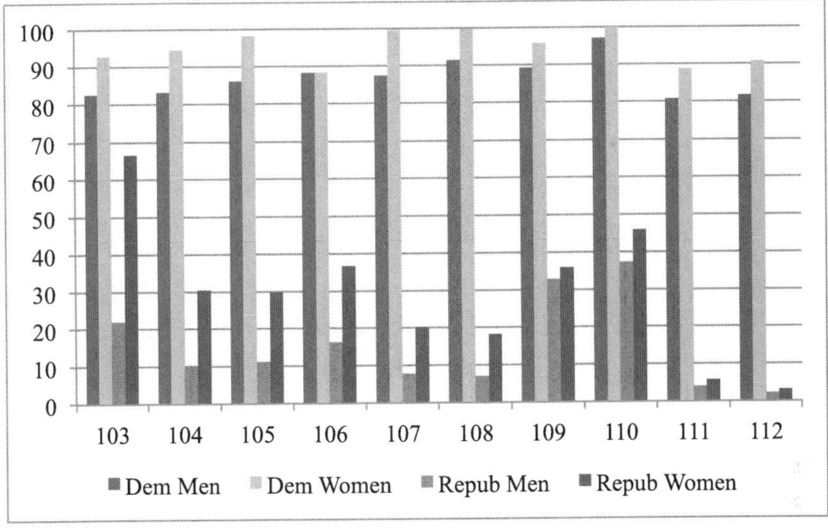

Fig. 8.1. AAUW Recorded Vote Scores by Congress, 1995–2011. (Data from http://www.aauwaction.org/voter-education/congressional-voting-record/. Includes First Session of the 112th Congress.)

at the White House signing ceremony. The bill amended the Civil Rights Act of 1964, which among other things had banned sex discrimination in employment. The bill mandated that the 180-day statute of limitations for filing an equal-pay lawsuit regarding pay discrimination resets with each new discriminatory paycheck. The law was a direct answer to the *Ledbetter v. Goodyear Tire & Rubber Co.*, 550 U.S. 618 (2007), a U.S. Supreme Court decision holding that the statute of limitations for presenting an equal-pay lawsuit begins at the date the pay was agreed upon, not at the date of the most recent paycheck, as a lower court had ruled.

The U.S. House voted 250–177 at the beginning of the 111th Congress to pass the Lilly Ledbetter Fair Pay Act in a party-line vote. All of the Republican female members voting cast "no" votes, all of the female Democrats voted "yea." In the Senate, however, all of the Democratic and the Republican women members voted "yea." This legislative remedy to a Supreme Court decision came nearly 50 years after the Equal Pay Act of 1963 and the Civil Rights Act of 1964 banning sex discrimination in employment had been enacted. The female votes in the House highlight the contemporary division of female members across party lines.

Effecting the Legislative Process beyond Roll Call Votes

Roll call voting, while of great importance to representation, stands at the end point of a long process of initiation, deliberation, and aggregation called the legislative process. Many points in the legislative process allow an individual legislator or a group of legislators to affect what gets on the agenda, how it is framed, what solutions are considered and put into bill form, and what makes it to the floor of the legislature for ultimate debate, vote, and enactment into law. The presence of female lawmakers may affect representation and lawmaking in many ways at many points in the legislative process. They have brought new issues to the agenda and articulated distinct perspectives on issues by explaining how specific policies being considered will affect particular groups of women (Mansbridge 1999). Even if female members no longer vote differently from their male colleagues in a polarized Congress, many examples exist of women using their new power positions to affect legislation on behalf of women by continuing to bring identity politics to the fore and making it matter in the legislative process.

Rep. Rosa DeLauro illustrates this distinctive position of female members in recent sessions in her power post as an Appropriations Committee "cardinal" to promote women's interests. As noted earlier, she became chair of the Appropriations Committee Subcommittee on Agriculture in the 110th Congress. Traditionally farm state lawmakers have coveted membership on this committee. But DeLauro, who represents New Haven, Connecticut, used her role as subcommittee chair to challenge Food and Drug Administration (FDA) actions affecting women's health. The FDA is an agency within the executive branch that falls under jurisdiction of this subcommittee. In May 2007 she introduced the Scientific Fairness for Women Act, which she portrayed as a way of blocking the FDA from making decisions that put corporate or ideological interests above the interests of women's health. Among other things, the bill would ban silicone breast implants until scientific studies proved their long-term safety, require the FDA to study scientific data on women under 18 use of emergency contraception, and make the FDA's Office on Women's Health a funding priority. This act has not become law.

Rep. Carolyn Maloney's action as chair of the Joint Economic Committee in the 111th Congress offers another illustration. In this role, on July 23, 2009, she convened a hearing to examine the current recession's impact on recent trends in workplace policies that help employees meet the dual commitments of work and family life. The hearing was titled "Balancing

Work and Family in the Recession: How Employees and Employers Are Coping." Leading researchers examined the effects of the recession on employer provision of work-life balance policies, the effects on employees and their families, and the role of unions and public policy. Then, too, Republican Rep. Kay Granger took the lead in working with Iraqi women to help them gain skills to run for election in that country's parliamentary elections. These examples illustration ways women have exhibited a distinctive voice in Congress on behalf of women.

Further research has shown that women "have mattered" in Congress in a variety of other ways. Political scientists have found that women in Congress have made a difference throughout the legislative process. They have affected the agenda and sponsorship of legislation; they have influenced the committee decision-making process and floor debate. The chapters of *Women Transforming Congress* prominently describe and analyze these varied aspects of female legislators making a difference in the legislative process. The context of different congresses has constrained distinctive roles they have played, however (Dodson 2006; Swers 2002).

These research efforts have involved careful analysis of male and female members' bill sponsorship and cosponsorship, use of committee positions, floor rhetoric, and work on conference committees. Scholars have categorized issues into women's rights legislation, social welfare, and antifeminist proposals to determine whether women have been more engaged than their male colleagues in promoting concerns of special interest or particular effect on women within the legislature.

For example, Michele Swers (2005) found in the 103th and 104th Congresses that female legislators were more likely than their male colleagues to cosponsor legislation on education, children and family, women's health, and general health issues, all social welfare areas that reflected a gender gap among the public. Only on welfare issues, a fifth area she analyzed, were there no gender differences in cosponsorship. After controlling for a variety of institutional and constituency-related factors that would seemingly affect interest in particular legislative matters, female members, both Democrats and Republicans, showed greater interest in these issues as reflected in their cosponsorship activities. Her research also concluded that

> [t]he close examination of the importance of institutional position . . . [shows] that when women gained access to strategic positions of power, they became even more active advocates of policy initiatives on education, children and families, women's health, and general health than similarly situated men. Thus, Democratic and

> Republican women were more likely to take the lead in cosponsoring legislation on gender gap issues when they were in the majority party. Therefore, in addition to electing more women to office, expanding the representation of women in strategic positions of power, including as members of the majority party and important committees, will enhance the quality of representation by increasing the diversity of viewpoints with a real influence on the congressional agenda. (2005, 427)

Further, Wolbrecht (2000, 2002) and Swers (2002) have demonstrated that female members of Congress are more likely to support bills dealing with feminist or women's rights issues such as domestic violence and abortion and to introduce legislation dealing with new women's issues. Wolbrecht's research, for example, covering congressional sessions from 1955 to 1992, shows that while women constituted an average of 4 percent of the membership they placed 44 percent of new women's rights concerns on the House agenda and proposed a full 43 percent of the new policy solutions (2002).

Most of this research on women "transforming" Congress examined behavior in the U.S. House and Senate during the 1990s, sometimes including earlier time frames in longer trend patterns, and was published in 2002 in *Women Transforming Congress* together with a number of other books in which these authors expanded on their research questions, methodology, and findings (see, for example, Swers 2002; Dodson 2006; and Wolbrecht 2000). Female members' more systematic attention to issues of particular concern to women may have been era specific although I have highlighted some recent instances of female members using their positions of influence to spotlight legislative concerns of women but the more contemporary era also suggests the heightened partisan nature to female representatives' work on behalf of women.

One piece of research has systematically carried the descriptive-substantive nexus of women's representation into the postmillennium congresses although the bulk of their data are from the congresses of the 1990s. Jessica Gerrity, Tracy Osborn, and Jeanette Morehouse Mendez (2007) employed a natural experiment design to determine whether women and men of the same political party represent the same congressional district differently with respect to women's issues. Using bill sponsorship and floor remarks during the 104th to the 107th sessions of the U.S. House of Representatives as measures of legislative behavior, they found that female legislators who replace men in the same district and same party introduce more women's issues bills in Congress although they were found not to speak about such legislation more in their remarks on the House floor than men did.

The extent to which female members have continued to make a difference for women in the postmillennium congresses requires more systematic research especially examining the linkage between their growing institutional influence and attention to women's issues. As women have moved into more leadership positions their attention may have been distracted from issues of special concern to women. Plus, the continued polarization of the House may keep its female members from introducing and addressing such issues and speaking in a distinctive voice on public policy matters. I have provided some anecdotes of women using their leadership to bring attention to problems women face in recent congresses, but the question of whether women matter deserves renewed research attention to continue building a body of knowledge, both challenging myths about the differences women make and finding empirical support for ways in which they do matter. Examining the dynamics of the 35-year-old Congressional Caucus for Women's Issues in recent years provides one lens on the extent of continued concern about women's issues on the part of female House members.

The Congressional Caucus for Women's Issues

The first Congressional Women's Softball Game, a bipartisan and bicameral event with both senators and representatives participating, was held on July 14, 2009, at Guy Mason Field in Washington. Proceeds from the game were to be contributed to the Young Survival Coalition's campaign to educate and support young women living with breast cancer. Roxanne Roberts and Amy Argetsinger vividly described the game in "Not Just Another Girls' Night Out" (2009):

> It is a measure of progress in the quest for equality: There are now enough women in Congress to field a softball team. Well, technically they passed that threshold years ago—heck, the Senate alone technically now has enough ladies for a starting lineup and a nearly complete second-string! Somehow, though, no one ever got around to organizing a game until last night, when a congressional women's team suited up for a charity game against female staffers on a Glover Park field.

A Title IX-generation thing? Not really. In six weeks of practice, one of the standouts was 72-year-old Rep. Grace Napolitano (D-Calif.) "I saw her hit last night," marveled Marcia Stein, head of the Young Survival Coalition, the breast cancer charity that benefited from the match. "But they're all pretty good hitters."

Rep. Grace Napolitano practiced fielding before the game. "We've got a pretty good group of women," said the team captain, Rep. Debbie Wasserman Schultz (D-Fla.), who cooked up the idea last year. She played varsity softball in high school, though others copped to a little less playing time: "Like, for a hot minute in seventh and eighth grade!" confessed Rep. Donna Edwards (D-Md.).

"Oh, Donna is a very good catcher!" gushed Rep. Chellie Pingree (D-Maine). The vibe was both bipartisan-bonding and you-go-girl: Sen. Susan Collins (R-Maine) gamely stepped onto the field with a skirt and pumps below her pink team shirt; Rep. Linda Sánchez (D-Calif.) gave a pep talk to nervous pitcher Rep. Jo Ann Emerson (R-Mo.): "It's really all on us in the outfield!"

Well, sometimes nerves are there for a reason: Emerson walked the first batter. The umpires stopped the first inning—"mercy rule!"—after the mostly 20- and 30-something staffers scored five runs before the congresswomen could notch an out. Soon the staffers led 12–0. And then—the rally. Edwards drew a bases-loaded walk, and the team swarmed Rep. Kathy Castor (D-Fla.) like a home run queen as she strolled home. Sen. Kirsten Gillibrand (D-N.Y.) doubled in the seventh, kicking off a white-hot hitting streak. In the end: a respectable loss, 14–8.

And naturally, speeches: Schultz took the mike to cheer the spirit of bipartisanship and the final fundraising take of $40,000—before she was whisked into an ambulance with the ankle she broke sliding into second.

The softball game tradition has continued. This activity characterizes the contemporary nature of the Congressional Caucus for Women's Issues, which was originally organized in the late 1970s and since has undergone a number of organizational transformations. The growing polarization between the female members of the two parties has not meant the demise of the CCWI, however. In the first decade of this century it continued as a bipartisan organization of the female representatives with almost full membership from women in both parties. During the first decade of the 21st century the Caucus continued to put forth a legislative agenda and pursue a variety of issues that affect women (Carney and Bracy, no date). Jan Schakowsky (D-IL) and Cynthia Lummis (R-WY) served as cochairs of the Caucus in the 112th Congress. The Caucus has eight task forces: Women's Health, Women in the Military/Veterans, Women in the Economy/Business, Violence against Women, International Women's Issues, Education, Women of Color, and Young Women. Each task force is supposed to have a cochair from each party. Three of the newly elected Republican women in the 112th Congress served as cochairs, which suggests continued surrogate representation across the aisle, softening the harsh rhetoric employed around budget issues in this Congress. But two of the task forces had a Democratic chair only (Education and Women in the Economy/Business). Whether this lack is due to indifference or opposition on the part of some of the female Republican members or to the small numbers of Republican female members of the House could use more in-depth research. The current conflict over public policy particularly affecting women described in the next section illustrates the complicated nature of Democratic and Republican female representatives working across the aisle.

A Woman's Place Is in the House chronicled the legislative agenda of the CCWI since its inception and noted its successes and failures regarding the implementation of legislation on behalf of women. After the Republicans gained control of the U.S. House in the 1994 election, Speaker Gingrich disbanded all of the legislative service organizations. The Caucus had to reconstitute itself as a different entity. In addition, as Gertzog points out in his extensive longitudinal analyses of the CCWI (1995, 2002, 2004), female members' gaining of seniority and movement into positions of more substantive leadership lessened the incentive to put their efforts into legislation of particular concern to women through Caucus work rather than in the more general committee system.

The Caucus's task forces seem to provide a means of highlighting areas of special concern to women that might require legislative attention in addition to and perhaps more so than writing specific bills. For example, in July of the first session of the 111th Congress CCWI and Women's Policy, Inc. cosponsored a lunch briefing on "Maternal Health in Afghanistan: How Can We Save Women's Lives?" Organizers included the Republican and Democratic cochairs of the Caucus's Task Forces on International Women's Issues and Women's Health. Earlier in the year, CCWI, the Office of Women's Health, and Women's Policy, Inc. held a similar lunch briefing celebrating the publication of *The Healthy Woman*. In October 2007, Rep. Lois Capps led a Caucus delegation to represent the United States at the Women Deliver Global Conference on Maternal Mortality in London. The United States ranked 41st in the world in maternal mortality rates and as Rep Capps stated in a press release her office issued at that time, "I am honored that my colleagues and I will be representing our country at the Women Deliver Conference as we work with nations from around the world to address the serious issue of maternal mortality. This is why the Women's Caucus was founded—to be leaders on issues that affect women and children." In the very polarized 112th Congress, the Caucus sponsored two briefings, one on women's preventive health and one on the "The Gender Wage Gap: What Is the Impact on Women and Their Families?"

Beyond briefings and social events, what type of legislative effect has the Caucus had over these congresses? Carney and Bracy's research shows that in the 100th through the 103rd Congress most of the legislation the Caucus championed that succeeded in becoming law was substantive legislation that dealt with protection of children, education, environmental issues, and women's health. In the 105th through the 108th Congresses, however, most of the bills that were passed, Carney and Bracy concluded, were largely symbolic legislation, such as honoring women of historical significance or naming post offices. Table 8.3 lists the substantive pieces of legislation the CCWI championed during the nine congresses under consideration in this study that were enacted into law with a comparison to the 103rd Congress that followed the "year of the woman."

CCWI records indicate that the 103rd Congress was a particularly successful session for women's issues. Its legislative action summary lists 66 measures aimed at improving the lives of women and their families as having been enacted. Table 8.3 includes only the major substantive pieces of legislation that became law in that Congress.

The 104th Congress was a particularly difficult session for the CCWI as it was defunded as part of the Republican leadership's centralization efforts, which eliminated all of the congressional service organizations. Thus, its focus was on survival as an organization rather than initiating legislative priorities. Since then the Caucus has had some success especially in the 106th Congress. Unfortunately, it was followed by the 107th Congress, a lost time for those advocating legislation affecting women and children in the aftermath of the September 9, 2001, terrorist bombing. In the following congresses the CCWI lists a few legislative successes through the 110th Congress but none were achieved in the 111th Congress. Although the CCWI continued into the 112th Congress with a gala event celebrating 35 years of existence, task forces in place, and at least a couple of briefings, it is hard not to expect that it will continue to become even less effec-

TABLE 8.3. CCWI Championed Legislative Enactments

103rd Congress
Violence Against Women Act
Family and Medical Leave Act
National Institutes of Health Revitalization Act, Women's Health Provisions
Freedom of Access to Clinic Entrances Act
Gender Equity in Education Act
104th Congress (1995–96): No Legislative Enactments
105th Congress (1997–98)
Federal Employee Health Benefits Program: Inclusion of Contraceptive Coverage for Participants
The Mammography Quality Standards Act
The Commission on the Advancement of Women and Minorities in Science, Engineering, and Technology Development Act
106th Congress (1999–2000)
Reauthorization of the Violence Against Women Act
Breast and Cervical Cancer Prevention and Treatment Act
Medicare Coverage for Medical Nutrition Therapy Services
Lupus Research and Care Amendments of 1999
United Nations Population Fund Funding Act
Folic Acid Promotion and Birth Defects Prevention Act
Right to Breastfeed Act
Child Abuse and Prevention Enforcement Act
Stalking Prevention and Victim Protection Act
Hillory J. Farias Date-Rape Prevention Drug Act
Battered Immigrant Women's Protection Act
Child Care Services for Federal Employees
Military Dependents Communications Confidentiality Act
Veterans Millennium Health Care Act
Program for Investment in Microentrepreneurs (PRIME) Act
Women's Business Sustainability Act
107th Congress (2001–2): No Legislative Enactments
108th Congress (2003–4)
Prevention of and Response to Sexual Assault and Domestic Violence in the Military Act (provided funding for rape-testing kits for women in the military; established a national standard and provided funding for the collection of DNA evidence in backlogged rape cases.)
109th Congress (2005–6)
Reauthorization of the Violence Against Women Act
Reauthorization of the National Breast and Cervical Cancer Early Detection Program
110th Congress (2007–8)
Genetic Information Nondiscrimination Act
Military Family and Medical Leave Act: Gives a Family Member up to 26 Weeks a Year off to Care for a Service Member with Serious Duty-Related Injuries.
111th Congress (2009–10): No Legislative Enactments

tive given the formation by Republican female representatives of their own caucus and the heightened, highly publicized polarized rhetoric between the two parties' female members, and seemingly few policy perspectives to bring them together.

"The War on Women" and the 112th Congress

I end this chapter with a return to the "war on women" debate that raged between the Democrats and Republicans in the 112th Congress and in the 2012 presidential election and conclude by considering its impact on representational perspectives. Once the 112th Congress commenced, the female members used their distinctive "gendered" position to highlight the ideological distance between the parties. The controversies that centered on women's access to reproductive health care and economic position and female officials' leadership in these debates affect how we theorize about the relationship between descriptive, substantive, symbolic, and surrogate representation.

Two events in 2011 showcased this new gendered aspect of partisanship the "war on women" represented. On April 8, in the midst of one of the budget showdowns between the parties with a government shutdown imminent, the female Democratic senators and the female GOP representatives held competing press briefings to emphasize how their party's position would help women and how the other party's approach would hurt women.[4] The Democratic senators' theme was that the Republicans would "throw women and children under the bus," a phrase repeatedly used in their briefing.

What stimulated these briefings was that a key sticking point in solving the immediate budget impasse from the perspective of the female Democratic senators was Republican insistence that no federal money go to Planned Parenthood. As the federal government was about to be shut down, the Republicans wanted any legislation keeping the government operating to bar federal dollars for Planned Parenthood, the country's largest abortion provider but which also offered a wide range of health services to women, especially low income women. The overarching issue, Sen. Barbara Mikulski iterated, was that the Republicans "want to cut funding for prenatal care by $50 million dollars . . . they want to take our mammograms away from us; they want to take prenatal care away from us, take counseling and family planning away from us and we just say 'no.'" Sen. Dianne Feinstein stated that the Republican cuts "hurt women and we women in the Senate will not let it happen. What is at stake is about the ability of poor American women to get health services."

In response, 14 Republican female U.S. House members held a press event that same day with the dominant theme that sound fiscal policy and cutting spending would help their children and their grandchildren. As Rep. Shelley Moore Capito of West Virginia put it, "the argument is about spending and there is nothing more important to the health of my granddaughter who is going to be one next week, my daughter and every woman in America is good sound fiscal policy and that the women of America are not swallowed up by a huge debt and deficit . . . that is about healthy women." Each of the speakers repeated this theme, relating spending cuts to creating a healthy future for children and grandchildren. The April 8 opposing events spotlighting a major public policy dispute in terms of its effect on women, argued by GOP and Democratic female representatives and senators, was the first of a series of such policy conflicts throughout that Congress that the female legislators led.

Chapter 7 described the second event in which Republican congresswomen went to the floor of the U.S. House to explain why they were "Republican women." This event was stimulated by an earlier statement that U.S. Rep. Debbie Wasserman Schultz, chair of the Democratic National Committee, had made at a breakfast roundtable with reporters in which she called the GOP agenda "anti-women" and "a war on women" (Bedard 2011).

As the 112th Congress continued, the "war on women" broadened, becoming even more combative with the female members of each party active participants and spokespersons in the battle. Reproductive issues were one central component of these partisan conflicts. On January 20, 2012, the Obama administration issued a policy statement that would require that most health insurance plans cover contraceptive care for women free of charge and rejected a broad exemption the Catholic Church had sought for insurance provided to employees of Catholic hospitals, colleges, and charities. The administration gave faith-based groups an extra year to comply with the mandate, instead of the August 1, 2012, deadline all secular employers were facing.

Making the announcement, Health and Human Services secretary Kathleen Sebelius said that all "FDA-approved" contraceptive measures should be available to every woman nationwide, free of charge—so everyone will have a share of bearing the cost of subsidizing them, regardless of moral or religious beliefs. The only exception would be for religious organizations that employ and treat only members of their own faith. "Women will not have to forego these services because of expensive co-pays or deductibles, or because an insurance plan doesn't include contraceptive devices," Sibelius said. "This decision was made after very careful consideration, including the important concerns some have raised about religious liberty. I believe this proposal strikes the appropriate balance between respecting religious freedom and increasing access to important preventive services." The administration had debated the rule for months, weighing the competing claims of religious leaders and advocates of women's rights. The rule's announcement set off loud protests from conservatives and religious groups and a major debate ensued that led to some administration modifications to the rule. It also stimulated congressional action on the issue.

A picture of the all-male U.S. Senate Judiciary Committee hearing on Clarence Thomas's appointment as a Supreme Court justice in October 1991 and its treatment of Anita Hill's charge of sexual harassment made against him illustrated the anger that swept through the women's rights community. This anger contributed to women's candidacies in the 1992 election resulting in its being named the "year of the woman." On February 16, 2012 , another picture, this time of the all-male panel called to testify before Rep. Darrell Issa's Oversight and Government Reform Committee hearing on the Obama administration conceptive mandate stirred the ire of women's rights activists once again. Chairman Issa invited five clergymen but not a single woman to testify. Rep. Issa would not allow supporters of the rule to participate as witnesses. In particular, he refused to allow testimony from Sandra Fluke, a Georgetown University law student who supported the policy. Women's health groups responded with outrage. The Democratic female members of the committee walked out of the hearing after loudly asking "where are the women?" House minority leader Nancy Pelosi (D-Calif.) led a protest on Capitol Hill. "Imagine they're having a panel on women's health, and they don't have any women on the panel—duh!" she intoned at a press briefing. EMILY's List quickly created an ad featuring the picture of the five clergymen before the panel to raise money for its candidates. The controversy was further inflamed when controversial conservative political commentator Rush Limbaugh referred to Ms. Fluke as "a slut."

The Republican female House members joined the debate. Rep. Marsha Blackburn led them in a press event objecting to the mandate as violating First Amendment free speech rights. They declared it was not a women's health issue, as Rep. Ellmers among others stated: "This is not about women's health care, this is about the overreach of government."

"As you can see, women are fierce defenders of freedom," Rep. Blackburn concluded at the end of the press statements.[5]

The Senate, too, became embroiled in the issue. At the end of February Republican Senator Roy Blunt brought to the Senate floor an amendment to a transportation funding bill that would have repealed this administration rule. His amendment would have allowed employers and insurers to deny coverage for health care services beyond birth control if those companies had either religious or moral objections. Democratic Senator Patty Murray argued, "It would simply give every boss in America the right to make health care decisions for their workers and their families" (Cohen and Merica 2012). Democrats argued that under the amendment, employers could have cited moral objections to cutting off coverage of immunizations, prenatal care for children of unmarried parents, and other standard procedures. Senator Blunt's office issued a press release stating that "[t]his bill would just simply say that those health care providers don't have to follow that mandate if it violates their faith principles. This is about the First Amendment. It's about religious beliefs. It's not about any one issue." The amendment was tabled on a mostly party line vote of 51–48. Only Sen. Olympia Snowe, among the Republicans, voted against the Blunt amendment.

The battle continued with GOP female lawmakers holding a March 28 press conference and on April 12 a press conference call. The first event focused on health care as the Supreme Court began its hearings on the Affordable Care Act. Rep. Cathy McMorris Rodgers and nine other House Republican female members held the press event to highlight what they viewed as the negative impact of President Obama's health care law on American women. "With Democrats continuing to advance the myth that Republicans are waging a 'War on Women,'" Vice-Chair McMorris Rodgers and the other House Republican women announced that what really scares American women were the president's policies, particularly ObamaCare. As they stated, "As women look at this entire controversy more closely, what they see isn't Republicans trying to undermine women's health, it's that Democrats are trying to scare American women. But what American women really find scary are the President's policies. Republican women are going to continue to focus on the issues that truly matter to women and men—jobs, the economy, the national debt, and repealing ObamaCare" (Congressional Documents and Publications 2012).

Obama supporter Hilary Rosen's comment that Republican presidential candidate Mitt Romney's wife had "not worked a day in her life" precipitated the second press event in April. Senator Kelly Ayotte and Reps.

Cynthia Lummis and Cathy McMorris Rodgers held an "Obama Economy Isn't Working for Women" press conference call. Their thrust was that "American women are tremendously concerned about our debt, our deficit, jobs and the economy. They want better lives for their children and their grandchildren, and we are piling a mountain of debt on our children and grandchildren when we refuse to reform entitlement programs in order to save them and when we refuse to cut spending in a manner that creates a soft landing for our economy and will spur job growth. The Obama policies have failed. In fact, they've made the economy worse, and they've made it worse particularly for women" (State News Service 2012).

Even renewal of what had been a bipartisan piece of legislation, the Violence Against Women Act, became mired in partisan wrangling as Democrats proposed protection expansions for lesbians, Native American women on tribal lands, and female immigrants facing abuse. Democratic representative Gwen Moore and Republican representative Sandy Adams, both victims of abuse earlier in their lives, took the lead on the competing versions of the bill. All but two of the female House Republicans (Reps. Judy Biggert and Ileana Ros-Lehtinen) voted for the Republican version, not including these specific expansions, and all of the Democratic women voted against this version.[6]

Once again, on May 15, 14 Republican female U.S. House members convened a press event to proclaim that the "Republican Party is the real party of American women" after President Obama gave a commencement address at Barnard College in which he touted his administration's efforts to help women (Fourteen GOP House Women 2012). In May the GOP women in the House also formed a women-only caucus named the Women's Policy Committee. According to news stories, its aim was to "raise the stature of female GOP lawmakers and bring a greater woman's touch to the party more commonly associated with men" (Goad 2012). They released a video as part of the announcement that featured all 24 female legislators, listing their credentials as family women, professionals, and conservative lawmakers, with a combined emphasis on their shared desire to "make America great again."

At this point it is too soon to know what form "raising their stature" will take, what the substance of "a greater woman's touch" will be, how it will affect the future of the Congressional Caucus for Women's Issues, and to what extent it will be the focus of articulating a distinctive Republican brand of surrogacy representation for women. No mention of specific policy measures they supported or opposed or initiatives they planned to take was made in the video.

The Women's Policy Committee did send a letter to Secretary of State

Hillary Clinton on October 25, 2012, regarding the Taliban's shooting of 14-year-old Malala Yousufzai in Pakistan who had been speaking out for human rights and girls' education. The committee in its letter urged the Department of State to work with the Pakistani government to "ensure that Malala and all girls throughout Pakistan can safely attend school in the coming months" (Bono 2012). This letter is the only media reference to a formal action of this group during the 112th Congress.

One also needs to ponder that while Speaker Boehner has made it a point to have either Rep. Cathy McMorris Rodgers or Renee Ellmers in press pictures during the 112th Congress it is unclear the extent to which they were part of the leadership team across domains of policy issues beyond being point persons on women's issues. If one were to survey insiders and knowledgeable observers regarding the "real voices" a picture differing from the one Speaker Boehner promotes in his press visuals might quite likely, but not necessarily, be drawn. Speaker Boehner did laud the female representatives for forming the caucus, stating, "Make no mistake, these aren't just leaders on so-called 'women's issues,' these are women leaders on all issues. I am confident the Women's Policy Committee will offer a fresh, new perspective on a vast array of challenges confronting Congress and be an important voice for the Republican conference" (Smith 2012).[7]

While the Republican female members have banded together as a group to present the GOP policy positions as they affect women and disparage the Democratic policy perspectives, female Democrats in the House have been as vocal but have acted in a more individual manner. The Democratic Caucus in the U.S. House has more female members and more with greater seniority. It has a woman at its helm and one of their members, a strong feminist, Debbie Wasserman Schultz, heads the Democratic National Committee. They can individually articulate the Democratic policies from many different positions: in hearings, in speeches and media presentations, as well as protests such as the walkout by Rep. Carolyn Maloney and Eleanor Holmes Norton (the nonvoting delegate for Washington, DC) of the Oversight Committee's hearing on the Obama contraceptive policy rule. The Democratic women of the House do have a formal Democratic Women's Working Group under the auspices of the Democratic Caucus but as an entity it has not achieved or been active to gaining news coverage in recent congresses.

Conclusion

From a descriptive perspective the U.S. Congress as a representative institution is a long ways from equality. The structure of the institution and our elections minimizes the ability of previously excluded groups to achieve a numerically represented presence. Congress has become a more diverse body demographically in the past few decades. It is now an institution in which Muslims and openly gay and lesbian individuals can be elected (at least in some districts). Individuals from more diverse racial and ethnic backgrounds are representatives and senators, and the presence of female members is commonplace but a long way from any sense of a critical mass. It is still primarily an institution of white men. At the same time, young girls visiting the institution, peering inside a committee room or watching the action on the floor of the House (and the Senate), now see women engaged in and leading the process and shaping legislation and not just white women but women of different colors and ethnic backgrounds.

The female members still come together to publicize "women's issues" through a caucus of their own although that group has faded as a substantive policy leader. What is most outstanding in recent congresses is the heightened division between Democratic and Republican female members. Few moderate Republican women are present to stand with Democratic female members in setting a legislative agenda on behalf of women. The parallel chapter on representation in *A Woman's Place Is in the House* concluded that "Women in national leadership positions today tend to be articulate feminists." Writing nearly 20 years later, one can only make that comment about the Democratic female contingent of U.S. House members.

"Acting for women," the substantive aspect of the concept of representation, has become more complex from the lens of whether and how female members are transformative agents in Congress or matter in the legislative process. It seems puzzling that in many congresses after the major legislative enactments affecting women's social and economic position in American society, from the Equal Pay Act of 1963 through the Violence Against Women Act of 1994, were passed, that women's issues were at the center of legislative debate in 2012 with the female members of each party articulating contrasting positions on what policies are best for women.

Certainly the parties would be taking polarized stands on these issues regardless of a female membership, but one has to consider whether if women were not present among the legislators would the differences have turned into "battles." Although only an anecdote, a relevant illustration is a Reuters profile of Rep. McMorris Rodgers that commented that the "war on women" charge by the Democrats "was a call to action [to her] at a time when her male colleagues seemed reluctant to fire back at Democrats. I felt compelled to stand up and try to counter this myth" of a Republican "war on women," she stated (Ferraro 2012). Women's presence has certainly mattered but not in one direction.

In a *Woman's Place Is in the House*, I provided a series of quotes from *The American Woman 1990–91* in which women in the 101st Congress articulated their activities and priorities for women. In 1993 and 1995 researchers at the Center for American Women and Politics conducted a series of interviews with female members of the House and Senate. Among the many subjects on which they interviewed the lawmakers were their perspectives on whether in addition to representing their constituents, they felt they had a further responsibility to represent women outside of their district. Interviews with these female lawmakers showed that they believed they had a special obligation to serve the needs of American women (Hawkesworth et al, 2001; Carroll 2002). Having a responsibility to represent women outside their district was the norm, not the exception, among these women. "Being a surrogate representative for women is . . . part of what it means to be a woman member of Congress at this particular historical moment," Susan Carroll determined from these interviews (2002).

I would suspect that we would find the same commitment to representing women resonating if conversations with the female representatives were held today and they were asked about this responsibility as we move into the second decade of the millennium with ever greater numbers of female lawmakers, although not yet a critical mass and a long way from numerical parity. The "Why I Am a Republican Woman" speeches of the GOP female House members on the floor of the House in June 2011 showed that surrogate representation was part of their congressional vision. How they articulate that surrogacy in terms of public policy could not be more different, however, from the ideological perspective of female Democratic legislators. Descriptive representation and substantive representation for women is now more complex, complicated, and confounding than ever. Women's rights and women's political leadership also continue to be a dynamic part of contemporary political life.

NINE

The 2012 Election and Summary Ideas

Since the analysis of gender and the quest for national legislative office in contemporary elections presented in this study has been completed another election has passed. Therefore, prior to presenting some concluding thoughts about women's quests for membership in the U.S. House and gender in these campaigns, I provide an introductory assessment of women's candidacies in the 2012 election paralleling themes of earlier chapters. The campaigns and election of female contenders for a seat in the U.S. House in the 2012 election was substantially different from the 2010 election cycle. The decline in female membership in the House was reversed and the Democratic partisan advantage increased once again. The numbers of women elected to both the Senate and the House rose to their highest levels ever. Winning the votes of women and debates over women's issues were central features of the presidential election. The "war on women" in the 112th Congress as described in chapter 8 was also prominent in the presidential campaigns with debates over which party was better for women.

The 2012 Election

For women and politics scholars, gender equity proponents, and a public attentive to gender gap politics, the course of the 2012 presidential and congressional elections and the politics of the 112th Congress leading up to them provided an exciting and challenging addition to women's political involvement. Numerical records were broken at all stages of the election process. A record 298 women candidates entered primaries for a seat in the U.S. House of Representatives in the 2012 election, breaking the previous record of 262 female candidates set in 2010.[1] A record number of 163 women were general election nominees, 116 Democrats and 47 Republicans. The previous record had been 141 women (88 Democrats and 53 Republicans) set in 2004. Then in November 78 women won a seat in the House, another record.

The reversal of the slight decline in membership as a result of the 2010 election was a positive step for women, continuing their slow incremental progression as a share of the membership in both the House and the Senate since the historical "year of the woman" in 1992. Nineteen women won election as new members to the U.S. House including three former representatives who won back their seats. Fifteen of the 19 won open seats. Nineteen was the second highest number of first-term female House members of any Congress. The 103rd Congress (1993–94), which had 24 new female members, still holds the record for the highest number of first-term female representatives as a result of the 1992 "year of the woman" election. Five new women also won seats in the U.S. Senate in 2012. Twenty women, 16 Democrats and 4 Republicans, would serve in the Senate in the 113th Congress, 20 percent of its membership. The reelection of 59 female incumbents and 19 newcomers increased the proportion of U.S. representatives who were women to 18 percent of the membership.[2]

As a percentage of the overall membership in these two bodies these gains may seem modest, but given the structural impediments described throughout this work it was a very good year for women, particularly Democratic women. Indeed, another "year of the woman" frame dominated media stories about women's candidacies in 2012.[3] Stories mainly had a positive spin. None suggested caution. For example, Susan Davis writing in *USA Today* led off 2012 with a piece titled "Upward Trend of Female Candidates for Congress: Both Parties Making Efforts to Field Women" (2012). She began her piece with the following statement: "The roster of congressional candidates for this year's elections is taking shape and one trend is emerging: 2012 could be another 'Year of the Woman' in American politics." *Hotline* suggested that "women candidates are playing a starring role in the 2012 Senate landscape (Hotline 2012) while *Roll Call* noted that "[f]emale lawmakers are raising money and the political stakes (Shiner 2012). EMILY's List in promoting its endorsed candidates took to calling the election "W.H.Y. (Women's Historic Year) 2012." Several articles pointed out that the parties were making efforts to field women as candidates although details on those efforts remain elusive.

The concept of opportunity structure has been important for this study of men's and women's contemporary campaigns for a seat in the U.S. House of Representatives. The presence of women based on candidate status has been one aspect of that emphasis. Figures 9.1 and 9.2 show the numbers of women by candidate status and party affiliation for the 2012 election.

Figure 9.1 provides a breakdown by party of the numbers of women entering primaries as incumbents, incumbent challengers, opposition party challengers, and open seat contenders. Figure 9.2 then shows the breakdown of nominees by candidate status and party. Seven female incumbents chose not to seek reelection so just to maintain the status quo seven women would need to be newly elected. As described in previous chapters the opportunity structure has been such that even the number of newcomers has not always been large enough to maintain parity. The record number of female candidates primarily was a factor of Democratic women entering open seat contests and opposition party primaries to challenge Republican incumbents.

Opportunities

The 2012 election was a once-in-a-decade reapportionment election. Congressional reapportionment as a consequence of the 2010 census resulted in eight states gaining seats in the U.S. House and ten states losing seats. In addition, the drawing of new district lines within the states, always a political process, most often controlled by the party in power in the state legislature, affected opportunities for newcomers and in some cases challenges for incumbents. The redistricting process for the 2012 election resulted in 11 races with incumbents of the same party running against each other in a primary (seven Democratic and four Republican). In an additional two races, one in Iowa and one in Ohio, incumbents from opposing parties ran against each other in the general election.

A total of 12 new districts were created in the eight states gaining representation in the U.S. House. Texas gained four additional seats, Florida gained two, and the others gained one each. Overall, once the redistricting process was completed and incumbents had decided whether to run for reelection, retire, or to seek a Senate or governor position, 53 districts had open seats during the primary season. Only ten of these districts were rated as being at all competitive, while 21 and 22 districts were safe for the

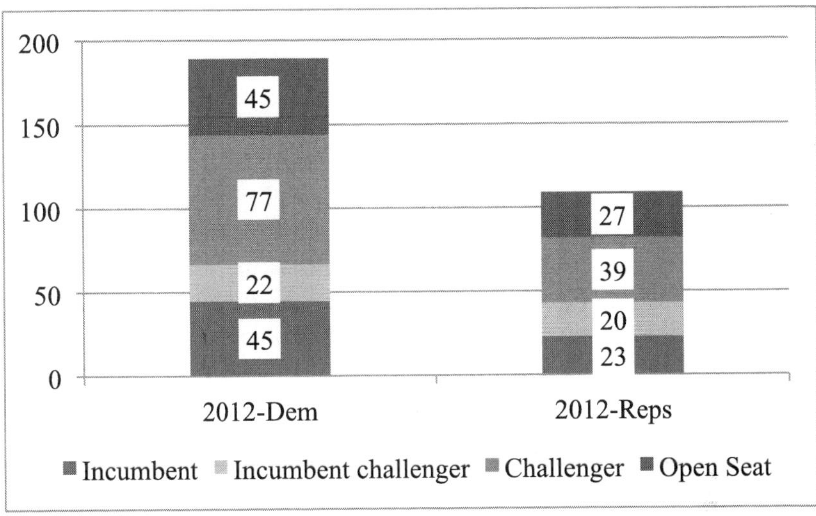

Fig. 9.1. Female Candidates, Primary Elections, 2012 by Party. (Data compiled by the author from the Center for American Women and Politics.)

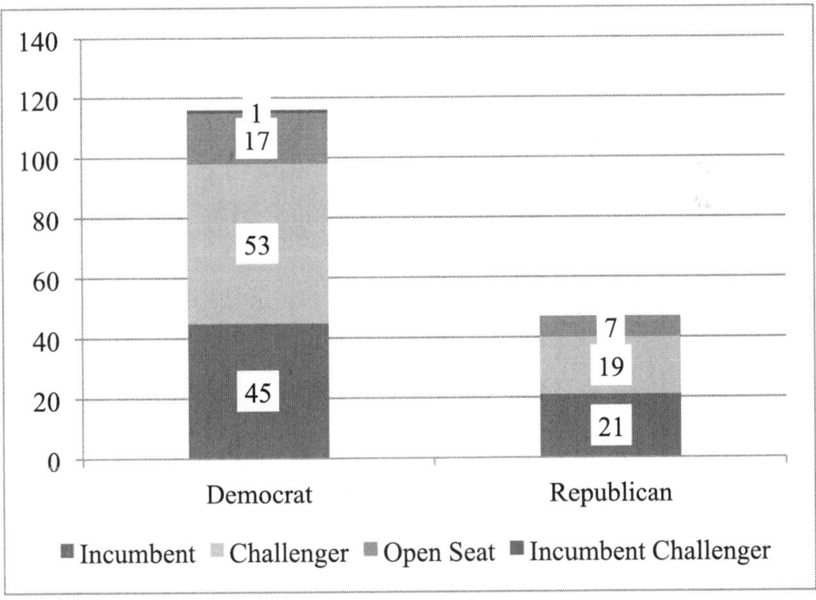

Fig. 9.2. Female Candidates, General Election, 2012. (Data compiled by the author from the Center for American Women and Politics. The incumbent challenger in fig. 9.2 is Democratic state senator Gloria McLeod, who ended up challenging Democratic Rep. Joe Baca after coming in second in California's jungle primary.)

Democrats and Republicans, respectively. Although Texas gained four seats it did not increase its female representation in the House. No new women were elected from that state. Female representatives did increase their numbers in four states, gaining representation: Florida, Arizona, Nevada, and Washington.

A total of 27 Republican women entered the open seat primaries, 12 percent of all of the candidates. At least one female Republican was a candidate in 21 of the 53 contests, 40 percent. That presence increased, however, to 59 percent in safe Republican open seats. Women were candidates in 13 of those 22 opportune seats. They won two of those primaries and went on to win the general election along with one primary victor in a district that leaned Republican.

On the Democratic side, 44 women entered an open seat primary, 29 percent of all of that party's open seat primary contenders. At least one female candidate ran in 29 of the 53 contests, 55 percent. A woman was among the candidates in 67 percent or 14 of the 21 safe Democratic districts. They won 18 of the contests including five of the safe Democratic districts.

The record-setting number of female candidates primarily resulted from the number of Democratic women vying for open seat nominations and as opposition party primary contenders, as figure 9.1 indicates. The larger number of Democratic women running in opposition primaries compared with Republican women is in part a reflection of the minority status of the Democratic Party in the House in the 112th Congress, giving it more opportunities to challenge incumbents. Also, in part 2012 was a more favorable context for Democrats than 2010 and the debate over women's health care energized (and perhaps angered) their female partisans to become engaged.

Gendered Moments

Even given the so-called war on women, this election encountered few gendered moments. Gendered moments are defined as instances in which a candidate disparaged or ridiculed an opponent using a reference based on the opponent's sex. It does not include sexist remarks in the media nor does it include the notorious remarks of male candidates about rape. Rep. Todd Akins of "legitimate rape" fame did engage in an additional gendered moment when he accused his opponent, Senator Claire McCaskill, of acting like a dog fetching expansive government policies and accused her of not acting ladylike in their first debate but acting in a aggressive manner.

His words were "She goes to Washington, D.C., it's a little bit like one of those dogs, 'fetch.' She goes to Washington, D.C., and get all of these taxes and red tape and bureaucracy and executive orders and agencies and brings all of this stuff and dumps it on us in Missouri." The remark was made at a fund-raiser. Then he told the Kansas City Star, "I think we have a very clear path to victory, and apparently Claire McCaskill thinks we do, too, because she was very aggressive at the debate, which was quite different than it was when she ran against Jim Talent. She had a confidence and was much more ladylike (in 2006), but in the debate on Friday she came out swinging, and I think that's because she feels threatened." There did not appear to be any other such comments from candidates at least as far as media attention was concerned. On the other side, Susan Brooks, running in the Republican primary in an open seat in Indiana against six men, began her first commercial with the words "I'm running against some good guys but they are career politicians," drawing attention to her being the only female candidate in the race. This comment also illustrates the advantage theme highlighted in chapter 3. But overall few of these types of gendered moments appeared in the 2012 campaign.

The women newly elected to the U.S. House expanded the diversity of the body in a number of ways. Three were Asian American. The youngest woman ever was elected when Democrat Tulsi Gabbard won Hawaii's 2nd district seat at age 31. Still no woman has broken the thirty year age barrier. Tulsi Gabbard also joined Tammy Duckworth, who won the 8th congressional district seat in Illinois, in having military backgrounds. All of New Hampshire's congressional delegation in the 113th Congress is female and three of Hawaii's four congressional members are female.

Summary Thoughts

This study has analyzed many aspects of contemporary elections to the U.S. House of Representatives, comparing the experiences of male and female candidates in their quests for and retention of seats in that body. In conclusion I present some summary thoughts about the contemporary nature of women's quests for membership and leadership in the U.S. House of Representatives and what the findings say about the gendered nature of these elections.

The gendered nature of campaigns for national legislative office in the United States has declined to near invisibility in the last nine congressional elections. What this decline means is that men's and women's campaigns are much more similar than different. Empirical analyses presented in this study of nine elections between 1994 and 2010 found few differences in female candidates' experiences and performance on the campaign trail from that of male candidates. I have examined differences based on sex throughout the campaign process, both in broad strokes and more nuanced investigations of the electoral process, to reach this conclusion.

Occasionally gendered moments have appeared in campaigns in which one candidate, sometimes a male contender and sometimes a female contender, has faulted his or her opponent for acting in a certain manner or having certain characteristics, which commentators call playing the "gender card." These moments continue to receive attention because they have become unusual, appear to be unseemly, create controversy, and thus are attractive to media personnel. There can still be "hair, hemline, and husband" commentary on the part of journalists. But they are increasingly uncommon in legislative races. Media commentators also continue to look for "years of women" and follow how well women seem to be doing in diverse electoral contexts, raising a type of gender perspective for readers to consider.

But it is the variation in opportunity structure that most explains the number and performance of female candidates in legislative contests and not some "gender" feature of a particular election. The opportunities have not been expansive and women have tended not to take advantage of the available opportunities, which is the main gender factor of contemporary congressional elections. Women and politics scholar Gary Moncrief also endorses this conclusion, stating in a news report, "[t]he electoral system is stacked toward incumbents to the point that gender has become essentially meaningless. It's not relevant in the calculus for most people anymore" (Russell 2004).

Voters have come to respond quite similarly to male and female candidates. It is also not that women are not recruited to run. Party organizations and other groups are increasingly looking for viable female candidates. Neither are female candidates held to some higher standard. They do not have less access to campaign resources. But they continue to choose not to run in a context of limited opportunities. We need more candidates in general and a greater interest in the campaign process. Unfortunately, the political atmosphere has become so negative that potential political leaders, male and female, are loath to engage in the process (see chap. 7 of Fox and Lawless *It Still Takes a Candidate*, 2010). Unfortunately, in addition, the women who have joined the campaign process and entered elected office have done little to change the political environment although they have been shown to approach leadership differently from men.

I offer here some concluding thoughts about the candidacies and election of women to national office and make some suggestions for future research. My contention of a declining gender context to congressional elections does not lessen a concern with the inability of the United States to reach a more critical mass of women in political leadership positions. Women's presence and influence in the U.S. House and Senate continues to be important for their substantive effect on the policy agenda, for affecting the legislative process more generally, and for enhancing its legitimacy. As Norris and Krook have stated:

> [M]ore inclusive parliaments also have the capacity to strengthen civic engagement and democratic participation among the general electorate; female leaders serve as role models who mobilize women as citizens, party members, and political activists. The empowerment of women in elected office can thus strengthen democracy and provide a more effective voice for articulating women's interests. (2011, 6)

Still a Feminist Era?

Readers will have noted that in references to my initial book on men's and women's campaigns throughout this updated study I most often abbreviated the formal citation using only the first half of the title "A Woman's Place Is in the House." Certainly this study of campaigns in the nine elections and the 2012 election postscript have shown that ever more women have established their place in the U.S. Congress and have assumed leadership positions within it although they are far from being numerically represented. But what about the second half of that earlier title "Campaigning for Congress in the Feminist Era"? Readers will also note that my most frequent reference to the group of elections that have followed has been in the context of "the contemporary era." In using this neutral term, these elections have not become contextualized in some more historically substantive fashion centering on equality and rights as the "Feminist Era" highlighted. Feminism is about challenging and changing women's subordination to men.

If "gender" has become less meaningful in national legislative elections, does it necessarily follow that feminism and activism focusing on women's rights are also no longer relevant, that perhaps we have entered into a new age? I doubt we would call these decades a "postfeminist era" in terms of political leadership. Equality has not been reached, organizational efforts to promote women's candidacies have expanded, academic studies of women and politics are robust, and the idea of a woman as president, not yet attained, intrigues us and has stimulated debates about continued sexism in our political system. I also would doubt that we would call it an "antifeminist" era, although the backlash regarding some women's issues, especially abortion policy, might suggest a rise in negativity.

It continues to be a women's rights era. The ten election cycles of the years 1993 through 2012 have occurred in a continuing context of women's rights advocacy, expansion, and backlash. Certainly the current potency of the "war on women" and debate and confrontation surrounding it on both sides indicate the continued relevance of women's equality and rights, although the extent to which women are leading the battle makes one pessimistic about any ideas of female membership changing the nature of Congress. A complex economic system remains in which some women have made gains but deep economic divisions have hindered advancement for women across class and race lines. Female leaders offer a diverse range of visions of public policy solutions many decades after women first formed the second women's rights movement. Women's rights and equality are not just about political leadership but about substantive representation.

In the 1990s the women's rights movement in the United States was challenged as having died or perhaps having entered into a postfeminist era. Further, younger advocates of equality established what has loosely been called "third wave feminism." More attention has been paid to the status and perspectives of a broader range of women across economic and racial groups in advocating for women's rights. Yet, few citizens today think of themselves as feminists when asked in national surveys "do you consider yourself to be a feminist, or not?" According to an ABC/Washington Post 2009 poll, only 23 percent of the respondents answered yes (29 percent of women and 17 percent of men), while 73 percent said no.[4] Rather intriguingly, however, much different results were obtained when the question was posed in the context of a positive definition of a feminist, "One dictionary definition of a feminist is 'someone who believes in the social, political, and economic equality of the sexes.' As you think about that definition, do you think of yourself as a feminist or not?" In this 2005 national CBS survey, 62 percent responded yes and 35 percent said no.[5]

In addition, in the 2010 Pew Research Global Attitudes Project Poll,

64 percent of U.S. respondents agreed that "the country needs to continue making changes to give women equal rights with men," while 33 percent agreed with the alternative statement that "the country has made most of the changes needed to give women equal rights with men." Seventy-two percent of women and 55 percent of men agreed with the former statement of a continuing need to make changes.[6] Thus, it seems that the general public is not of the mind that the movement for equal rights for women is passé. Hillary Clinton's campaign for the presidency in 2008 and Sarah Palin's vice-presidential nomination that year awakened a societal sexism that was stunning. Whether former senator and secretary of state Clinton decides to run for president in 2016 is the political question of the post-2012 election.

Feminism is a pejorative term to political and social conservatives, yet conservative women's groups have expanded notions of equality in their own way although they would restrict the ability of women to control their own bodies, the ultimate goal in freedom and equality for many in the women's rights movement (see Schreiber 2012). In addition, as chapter 8 has emphasized, conservative women have taken to political leadership. For example, four of the five female governors in office in 2013 lead with a conservative philosophy. Conservative female activists no longer see a separate sphere for men and women in the social, economic, and political life of the nation. They relate their motherhood to political leadership as the idea of "mama grizzlies" has so graphically illustrated.

So the feminist era continues in terms of the movement of equal rights for women and advocacy for women as political leaders. Both political parties see it in their interest to publicly announce efforts to recruit women to run for public office and showcase them as leaders in public policy advocacy. Advocacy efforts do not always seem to be expansive in improving the lives of all women across the social and economic spectrum, as the debate over expanding the Violence Against Women Act in 2012 illustrated. Democrats advocated expanded explicit sections of that law aimed at Native American women, lesbian and bisexual women, and illegal immigrant women. Republicans argued against this necessity and focused instead on accountability and austerity in debates. The parties differ over expansion of the Equal Pay Act, discrimination claims under the Civil Rights Act, and funding of Planned Parenthood.

These debates provide evidence of a continued women's rights movement but it is a movement taking place on a new plane with women in some aspects of American life moving ahead of men such as in higher education. A number of "glass ceilings" have been broken. Women have made strides in the military, one of the major bastions of masculinity. But not all women have shared equally in economic advances. If, for example, we examine poverty and access to health care statistics women disproportionately bear the ills of our society. As a society we still have not come to grips with the difference of childbearing being incorporated into a world of similarity between the sexes. Women's rights activism is still a major feature of American politics and quests for political leadership are part of that movement.

Creating a Critical Mass: Obstacles and Opportunities

Just as the conventional perspective based on scholarly research states that when women run for public office they win, the other side of the conventional perspective states that women are less politically ambitious than men and less likely to seek public office. The basis of this latter conclusion, now widely accepted, has primarily been responses regarding running for public office of a national sample of men and women with the occupational credentials to be credible candidates in Lawless and Fox's *It Still Takes a Candidate* (2010). The statistic that is at the base of this belief about ambition differences and their impact is that 57 percent of women in their study compared to 41 percent of men when asked responded that they have never thought about running for office. The female respondents were also more than twice as likely to say that they were not at all qualified to run (28% to 12%). At the same time, 10 percent of the female and 19 percent of the male respondents reported that they had seriously considered running for public office. Thus, only a minority of both sexes appeared to be politically ambitious in terms of pursuing a political career. Overall, the women in that survey may be professionally ambitious but not about holding public office.

Two contemporary aspects of politics, contradictory in nature, frame the prospect of increasing women's interest in running for and holding public office. On the negative side is the nature of contemporary politics that dissuades both men and women who would make good public officials from engaging in the campaign process. On the more positive side is the increase in capacity-building initiatives aimed at women to provide them with the encouragement, skills, and resources to seek elective positions.

Congress: An Uncivil Institution

Although perhaps in many aspects as ambitious as men, mounting campaigns for the U.S. House of Representatives may not be attractive to many women because it has become such an incredibly unpleasant institution from which to exercise leadership and influence in the political system. Further, campaigns for those positions are mean and nasty and extraordinarily expensive undertakings. Both potential male and female candidates have been opting out of such campaigns. In a special report for the *New York Times* in 1998, Richard Berke noted:

> In interviews throughout the country, people who chose not to run in 1998—many for what appeared to be winnable seats—offered many reasons. But the explanations were similar: would-be members of Congress complained that the rigors of fund-raising and of being away from home exacted too much of a personal toll. And even if they could be assured of being elected to the $136,700-a-year position . . . many people said that serving in the House was no longer an enticing calling. Several said they could make more of a difference serving in their state legislatures than in the United States Congress.

To invest in a campaign for a seat in the national legislature an individual concerned with effecting national policy making and being a political leader must have a vision of these institutions as viable and positive places to achieve their goals. The image of the contemporary Congress is definitely not as a place where meaningful policy deliberation and effective lawmaking takes place. These negative perceptions about Congress as a place to work surely have an effect on more women running. Recent congresses have been viewed quite negatively. In the summer of 2009, contempt for members of Congress was exhibited in ugly town meeting protests and even death threats around the nation. Accusations of being anti-American and un-American have been hurled around the floors of Congress regarding Democratic and Republican policies. The intensity of the negative response to efforts of the Obama administration to reform the health care system that substantial numbers of Americans have said is in a state of crisis would certainly not be an inducement for politically ambitious individuals to view Congress as an attractive institution in which to make public policy. The 112th Congress ignominiously achieved a record low approval rating from the general public. Gallup's tracking poll of the public's approval of the job Congress is doing reached an all-time low in November 2011 with an approval rating of 13 percent.[7]

Incivility is not new to the contemporary Congress but a general atmosphere of negativity does appear to be especially notable compared with the Congress at mid 20th century. In "How to Make Congress Popular," John Hibbing noted that "it appears that some quality challengers are dissuaded by a public so disaffected with Congress and its members" (2002, 219). The days of former House Speaker Sam Rayburn's "going along to get along" have disappeared, according to Barbara Sinclair, based on her years of close observation of Congress and interviews with key players in that institution. She writes that "[t]he cocoon of good feeling had been replaced by overt partisan hostility [in the 1990s]. Republicans accused Democrats of tyranny and corruption, of having created a 'corrupt legislative process,' of 'trampling on minority rights . . . and stifling dissent'" (2006, 5). In the preface to *Congress Behaving Badly* Sunil Ahuja writes that "the U.S. Congress has become a bitter place. The last few decades have seen an enormous rise in hostility and confrontation. Many in the new crop of members from both sides of the aisle, are intensely partisan in their political orientation, who often engage in acrimonious and uncivil behavior and readily question the motives of their colleagues" (2008, xiii). The Annenberg Public Policy Center's *Civility in the House of Representatives: The 105th Congress* emphasized the heightened rate of "name calling" and "vulgarity usage" (Jamieson 1999). (See also Milbank and Broder 2004.)

Attempts have been made to instill a more civil environment within Congress. In the later 1990s, a group of members organized a series of bipartisan "civility retreats." They were held in 1997, 1999, and 2001. The initial retreat organized by the Bipartisan Congressional Planning Committee was designed to "seek a greater degree of civility, mutual respect and, when possible, bipartisanship among Members of the House of Representatives in order to foster an environment in which vigorous debate and mutual respect can coexist." For the first two retreats the Annenberg Public Policy Center prepared background reports analyzing such examples of incivility as uses of vulgarity, words taken down and ruled out of order, and calls for the House to be in order. The third retreat ended in acrimony, however, as the close division in the House between Democrats and Republicans led to anger over the division of resources and committee seats. Democratic minority leader Richard Gephardt vowed that he would never attend another one because "they have yet to produce any results, and so there's no point in being there" (Wolfensberger 2007).

In 2006 Democratic Rep. Emanuel Cleaver and Republican Rep. Shelly Moore Capito tried again to reinstall a sense of comity in that institution by initiating a "Civility Hour" on the floor of the House. They were to conduct a "civil debate on the issue of taxation," according to a news release from Rep. Cleaver's office.[8] It is uncertain whether any other civility hours ensued. No media accounts suggest any follow-up activities or impact. In the wake of the shooting of Congresswoman Gabrielle Giffords in January 2011, some attempts were made to be more civil in Congress with gestures such as having a seatmate of the opposite party at presidential addresses, but at the same time Republican Rep. Joe Wilson of South Carolina deeply offended the traditional air of respect of presidential congressional addresses when he shouted "you lie" at President Obama during a State of the Union address.

In 2006 congressional scholars Thomas Mann and Norman Ornstein wrote *The Broken Branch* in which they asserted that Congress was failing America. Deliberation was disappearing, rules were being broken, and harsh partisanship was on display, resulting in bad public policy and little oversight of the executive branch. In 2012, they wrote a follow-up work titled *It's Even Worse Than It Looks: How the American Constitutional System Collided with the New Politics of Extremism*. As they state, "As bad as the atmospherics were, the new and enhanced politics of hostage taking, of putting political expedience above the national interest and tribal hubris above cooperative problem solving, suggested something more dangerous, especially at a time of profound economic peril" (2012, 4).

Polarization is exampled by the increasing ideological distance between the parties in the House and Senate as measured through median DW-nominate scores[9] or ideological voting scores as measured by the *National Journal* and the increase in the extent to which a majority of Democrats vote against a majority of Republicans on roll call votes (Sinclair 2006, 6–9). Little overlap in the voting scores of Democrats and Republicans exists in contemporary congresses. The most liberal Republican is to the right of almost all Democrats and the most conservative Democrat is to the left of almost all Republicans, Sinclair tells us in 2006 (13). Polarization has continued into the most recent Congress. I noted in chapter 8 the extreme distances between the vote rating scores of Democrats and Republicans in the first session of the 112th Congress. The party unity score for Democrats in the U.S. House in 2011 was 87 percent. Their highest level was 92 percent in 2008. The Republican unity score was 91 percent. Their highest score was 94 percent in 2003 (Zeller 2011).[10]

Thus, we should ask why women (and men) would want to run for public office in the first place given the contemporary atmosphere of scandal, incivility, and polarization. Potential candidates, both men and women, may ask for what purpose should they run for a position in these institutions if their concern is to make a positive contribution to public policy making. In a recruitment study of the 2006 election that Brian Frederick and I undertook (discussed earlier) that explored the extent to which male and female potential candidates were taking advantage of windows of opportunity by running in open seat primaries for the U.S. House, we found that 49 percent of the women surveyed who decided not to run when asked about their decision-making process regarding seeking election in a open seat district checked that "the ineffectiveness of the U.S. House as policy-making institution" was a "very important" or an "important" factor in their decision not to become a candidate and 56 percent checked that "the inability of members of the U.S. House to work together" was a "very important" or "important" factor (2007).

Institutional problems such as these provide a counterbalancing and sobering perspective on incentive structures and on questions about the role of ambition in women's quests for equal numbers in political leadership positions at the same time that those women who have sought such positions are increasingly successful. These problems suggest that it may not just be a question of lower levels of ambition that account for the scarcity of female candidates for national office but the negativity surrounding the institutions and the political process one must engage in to get there. Fewer male and female community and political leaders may be turning their efforts to influence public policy elsewhere. Here is a significant political science question ripe for future systematic empirical research.

Women's candidacies for the state legislature declined in the initial elections of the millennium before increasing slightly in the more recent elections. Although women have been shown to be less politically ambitious than men (Lawless and Fox 2005, 2010), this factor cannot alone account for *a drop* in women seeking and gaining state level lawmaking positions in the early elections of the millennium. Would we expect that women were becoming less ambitious? It may be more a matter of the nature of campaigns for these offices that has not stimulated women to continue to seek them in ever increasing numbers and why term limits have not advantaged women. The number of candidates running for local office has dropped and elections have been canceled because of a lack of candidates (Macedo et al. 2005, 66), suggesting a larger societal problem than women simply not being ambitious. The role that the civil nature of institutions plays on women's career ambitions and elective office candidacies is an area calling for more research from both an ambition perspective and an institutional perspective. And we do need to keep in mind that more women than ever sought a seat in the U.S. House in the 2012 election.

In a 2012 Leadership Connection blog piece titled "Parity in Politics—Why Women Don't Want It," Kathleen Schafer provided a number of thoughts paralleling these ideas about women possibly turning away from quests for political leadership. Although the piece expresses only one person's thoughts, Schafer has a long career in political leadership training. The articulation of her ideas deserves consideration in line with the perspective I present here. The following is a quote from her piece.

> Woman are not running for office because they are choosing to spend their time and energy in ways other than engaging in the senseless, and all too often futile, act of policy making in contemporary politics. No amount of preparation is going to change the pragmatic nature of women who will choose to focus their energy and attention on real world solutions, rather than engage in politics that rarely creates meaningful change and when it does at a very high personal cost to one's quality of life.

Campaign Financing as an Issue

One other negative factor that must also be taken into consideration in reflecting on the likelihood of more women seeking national office is that of the fund-raising aspects of our contemporary campaigns. The amounts of money now required to mount viable campaigns for national office and even in some cases for state legislative office are daunting, and obscene to some observers. It is not that women are not formidable fund-raisers, as this study has shown, but the distaste for engaging in this activity may be a significant factor in decisions to take one's ambitions in other directions. The rise of super-PACs only makes matters worse. It is in this context that the lack of campaign finance reform becomes a serious issue for those who would advance the numbers of women in electoral office. Changing the nature of financing our campaigns for public office may be at least a necessary condition, if not a sufficient one, to increase the number of women running for and winning these positions.

The emphasis on money may also discourage potential male candidates, but given the underrepresentation of women in political office it has greater significance for them. The amount of money a candidate needs to raise to run a viable campaign has grown with each election season. And among other things, the more money one has the more one can run ads criticizing opponents, thereby increasing the negativity of campaigns. In the conclusion to their study of candidate perspectives on negative campaigning discussed earlier, Herrnson and Lucas (2006) asked whether negative campaigning, and the different constraints the political context places on the strategies and tactics available to male and female candidates, discourage potential female candidates from running for public office more than it discourages potential male candidates. Ambitious women may have little incentive to seek public office. They can use their ambition in other ways. It is important to consider whether "clean campaigns" enhance women's entrance into the political fray. It should be incumbent upon research scholars to examine this other side of the "coin" in studying the reasons why more women are not seeking public office.

At the conclusion to *It's Even Worse Than It Looks* Mann and Ornstein call for changing the country's poisonous culture. They offer a number of suggestions to move in that direction such as restoring public shame, creating a shadow Congress, and recreating a public square. What they do not suggest, curiously, is a call for greater political leadership among the citizenry through seeking public office. Getting more community leaders to put themselves forward as candidates for elective office would seem to be an imperative for improving the poisonous environment. The liberal feminist community and the conservative feminist community have undertaken such efforts on the part of women a major part of their contemporary call to action.

Broadening the Campaign World of Women

Capacity-building efforts to increase women's candidacies and their effectiveness has become a central and growing undertaking of women's groups engaged in the political process from the Girl Scouts to the American Association of University Women, from the National Federation of Republican Women to EMILY's List and various university programs.

The growing number and diversity of groups aimed at counteracting "the encouragement gap" that has affected women's lower levels of public office seeking than men's is a positive counterpoint the elements of the poisonous political culture. The plethora of such activity is a positive feature of women's contemporary quests to achieve a critical mass among our political leaders. Norris and Krook's concept of "capacity building" captures this movement (2011).

Under the auspices of the Organization for Security and Cooperation in Europe, Pippa Norris and Mona Lena Krook have developed a six-step action plan involving a series of fast-track strategic interventions to contribute to the attainment of gender equality in elected office (2011). Capacity development is one of their six interventions. It involves strengthening "the skills and resources of women in the pipeline for elected office, with initiatives by parties, the media and NGOs, including knowledge networks, mentoring programs, skills training and funding for women candidates." Norris and Krook include a range of activities under capacity development. As they state:

> A diverse range of initiatives are designed to build the capacity of the pool of potential women leaders in the pipeline, to strengthen the skills, experience, and knowledge of women once they enter elected office, as well as to address broader issues of institutional capacity-building. These interventions can be categorized in terms of three distinct but overlapping threads: *equal opportunity initiatives* (candidate training, recruitment initiatives, and knowledge networks), *initiatives to combat stereotypes and raise awareness* (media campaigns and citizen education), and *political party initiatives* (women's sections, fundraising, and women's parties). (8)

Even within a negative and expensive environment, capacity development programs of all kinds aimed at boosting the number of women running for public office have been initiated within the United States in the past two decades. Capacity development programs have been a popular strategy among advocates of increased female political leadership in this country especially since institutional changes such as the adoption of quota systems or movement to a proportional representation system, parts of Norris and Krook's six-step plan, are unlikely to even be considered let alone adopted in the United States.[11]

Proponents of gender equality in U.S. elective offices have developed a wide variety of such capacity-building initiatives to bring women into the electoral area. In the past two decades these initiatives have expanded both downward and outward. By downward I am referring to age and to activities to encourage young women and girls to gain public confidence and become political leaders. The Center for American Women and Politics has run the NEW Leadership summer institute since 1991. The summer institute is an intensive residential program that educates college women about politics and policy making and encourages their participation in the political process.[12] In 1999, it expanded this program to colleges and universities across the country. A more recently initiated effort of this sort is Running Start. American University in Washington, DC, hosts Running Start, which is an annual women's political leadership retreat begun in 2007. The program brings together over 50 high school girls from across the country with the goal of encouraging them to enter political office. A third young women's program is Future Frontrunners, a segment of LIFETIME Networks nonpartisan Every Woman Counts campaign. The 2008 Future Frontrunners Summit took the winners of its high school and college leadership contest to the 2008 Democratic and Republican national conventions where they participated in leadership training workshops with women elected officials. Contestants submitted written or video essays answering the question "What would you do if you were president?" The AAUW initiated the Elect Her program in 2011. Elect Her workshops train women to run for and assume leadership positions in campus-based elections. The workshop instructs female students to carry out their ideas and initiatives while raising a voice to unaddressed problems in their community.

Further, the Girl Scouts of the USA has developed a Ms. President Patch Program in cooperation with the White House Project. This program is a participation project as opposed to the traditional badges that Girl Scouts work to earn. Girls must participate in at least one project centered on learning about women in leadership positions historically, get involved in a school election campaign, look for female leaders in their community, and write about and follow them to obtain a Ms. President patch.

Then there is *What's Your Point, Honey?* which premiered in 2008. This documentary created by Amy Sewell and Susan Toffler tells the story of seven young women who participated in the White House Project and a CosmoGirl program aimed at starting them on the road to the presidency. It aims to create a pipeline so that many women will be ready to run for the highest office in the land. The seven women featured in *What's Your Point, Honey?* were all leaders on college campuses or local communities and in 2006 they participated in Project 2024. The idea of the project is that by 2024—the year when the magazine's youngest readers will reach 35 and be eligible to run for U.S. president—one CosmoGirl from each year of the program will stand on the presidential debate floor as a real candidate.

In addition to working with younger women, capacity development programs have rapidly expanded outward from national efforts to state and local initiatives. Indeed, CAWP itself is engaged in such an activity with it Ready to Run campaign training. Held annually by CAWP, Ready to Run is a bipartisan program for women who want to run for office, work on a campaign, get appointed to office, become community leaders, or learn more about the political system. EMILY's List, too, launched its Political Opportunity Program after the 2000 election, a training and support program for pro-choice Democratic women seeking state legislative, constitutional, and key local offices. EMILY's List boasts of holding 180 trainings in 36 states, training more than 6,300 people between 2001 and 2010 (www.emilyslist.org). In July 2007, the Women's Campaign Forum launched the She Should Run campaign. By September 2008 more than 1,000 women had been nominated to run by having their names submitted to an online database the Women's Campaign Forum had constructed.

CAWP has also conducted a national survey to identify campaign training programs within the 50 states.[13] They identified training programs for women in 35 states in 2013. These programs are run by an assortment of organizations including the political parties, universities, and progressive and conservative groups. On the Republican side, the Richard C. Lugar Excellence in Public Service Series begun in Indiana in 1993 and mentioned in chapter 6 is the longest-running state training program. Up to 20 Republican women are selected annually to participate in eight monthly daylong sessions covering issues in government, campaigns, and leadership development. The series culminates with a four-day summit in Washington, DC. Republican organizations in 14 other states currently have adopted this model to advance women's political leadership skills through running similar programs. On the Democratic side, Emerge America is its most prominent state training program. Started in California in 2002 it now is active in nine states. It runs a 7-month, 70-hour training program in these states.

From the perspective of students of the political process it is important to theorize about the impact of these capacity development programs, to examine the extensiveness and durability of these efforts across the country, and to study the outcomes of all of these diverse undertakings to stimulate women's political leadership and develop their leadership skills across the age spectrum and across the country. Our charge should be to learn how people become aware of these efforts, who is attracted to them, who goes on to run and to win public office, and to assess their effectiveness and the determinants of that effectiveness. What have the winners done once elected to promote women's interests? Are they transforming our public institutions? This domain of gender politics is a fascinating one for future research, for connecting academic enterprises with activism on behalf of women's political leadership, and for achieving a critical mass and moving beyond it to real equality.

The question remains, however, which will be the stronger force regarding expanding the numerical representation of women in public office. Will it be the increasing organizational capacity-building programs to encourage the efficacy and engagement of girls and young women in politics and their recruitment and training programs to provide women with resources to run for political office and achieve political leadership? Or will it be the incivility and polarization of political institutions and the angry reaction of some Americans to the efforts of policy makers to solve public problems or their inaction that discourage people with ideas and skills to be political leaders from seeking public office? My hope is that capacity building will be the stronger force. But that will be a great challenge.

Notes

CHAPTER 1

1. The designation of a nation as an electoral democracy is based on Freedom House measurements. See www.freedomhouse.org.

2. The Beijing Platform can be found at http://www.un.org/womenwatch/daw/beijing/platform/decision.htm.

3. Regarding the critical mass, I am not focusing here on the implications of having at least a certain number of women in the legislative body; rather, my concern is solely with numerical representation. (See the discussion regarding "Rethinking the Critical Mass Debate" in *Politics & Gender*, December 2006.)

4. In 1972, Democratic presidential candidate George McGovern appointed Jean Westwood chair of the Democratic National Committee. She was not elected to the position.

5. A new research initiative of Kathleen Dolan seeks to address this lack of individual-level data that have as their primary focus the examination of the impact of gendered attitudes on American elections. "The Impact of Gender Stereotypes on Voting for Women Candidates for the U.S. House and Senate in 2010," presented at the 2011 annual meeting of the Midwest Political Science Association, is a first look at her findings.

6. The 2008 Pew Research Center's Social & Demographic Trends Report survey found little change in the distribution of responses on perceived obstacles to female leadership. (See "A Paradox in Public Attitudes, Men or Women: Who's the Better Leader?" http://pewresearch.org.)

CHAPTER 2

1. A systematic statistical analysis of trends in media stories is difficult to conduct. Election media related sources have grown over this time period. Selecting

only a subset of sources that have been consistently present across all elections for analysis would diminish the variety of media stories about women's candidacies, constraints, and prospects and exclude guest commentaries by activists and knowledgeable others.

2. Since individual women mounted multiple campaigns over these election cycles, I often use the term "candidacies" rather than "candidates."

3. The database of candidates presented in this study consists of all individuals listed in primary election reports available at state websites and CQ's *America Votes* series. The Center for American Women and Politics *Election Watch* listing of women candidates was used to denote the sex of candidates in each of the election cycles. Candidates who dropped out during or after a district primary are not included.

4. This report can be found at http://www.cqpolitics.com/wmspage.cfm?docID =weeklyreport-000002997734.

5. The numbers of newly election female representatives in this chapter in each election cycle includes women who won special elections during the cycle as well as those who won in the 1994 general election.

6. Blanche Lincoln (D-AR) was also one of the women newly elected to the House in 1992 who left the House and then successfully ran for the U.S. Senate in 1998 but, as noted in this chapter, she was defeated in 2010.

CHAPTER 3

1. State Senator McLeod did win a seat in the U.S. House. Once the new districts were finally configured, U.S. Rep. Joe Baca decided to run in the district State Senator McLeod was eyeing rather than in his former district, which was no longer "so friendly" toward him. In California's "jungle primary" the top two candidates regardless of party go on to the general election. McLeod came in second to Rep. Baca. She then beat him in the general election.

2. Special election candidacies are not included in the analyses of this chapter. Its focus is on primary elections and special elections have not always included a primary stage. Analysis of women's presence and success in special elections of this time period is incorporated into chapter 4, which investigates the general election stage of the campaign process.

3. Differences were statistically significant within both parties; the Republican difference at the .03 level, the Democratic difference at the .000 level.

4. A systematic accounting of Tea Party–backed candidates in the 2010 primaries is not available but a New York Times listing of such general election candidates lists 17 (13%) of Tea Party House candidates to be women. See http://www.nytimes.com/interactive/2010/10/15/us/politics/tea-party-graphic.html.

5. In 2008, the open seat primary winners in two districts dropped out and their party selected a replacement after the primary. These two replacements are not included in this analysis.

6. It is possible that the rating of the competitive nature of a primary may have varied over the course of the election cycle; however, most movement would have been in the "competitive" domain, from leans and toss-up, than movement from a "safe" category to a competitive one. All three competitive categories are grouped

together in this analysis. In 2010, the competitive ratings of districts most dramatically moved in races involving incumbents, not the open seats.

7. Indeed, looking ahead in time, Republican Susan Brooks employed this strategy in her open seat primary campaign in Indiana's 5th district in the 2012 election. She was the lone female candidate running against six men. Her first TV commercial began with the words "I'm running against some good guys but they are career politicians," drawing attention to her being the only female candidate in the race. She won the primary and the general election.

8. Denise Majette, who had won the seat in 2002, opted to run for the U.S. Senate in 2004 rather than to retain her House seat. She lost her Senate bid in the general election.

9. For example, Lawless and Pearson (2008) make this argument in "The Primary Reason for Women's Underrepresentation" yet they do not construct an empirical indicator of "better."

10. Previous office-holding experience was obtained for the elections through 1998 from CQ Weekly Reports, which included such information in their tables of primary election results. Information for the subsequent elections was obtained from a Lexis-Nexis search and Google searches. Information on frivolous candidates (those receiving 5 percent or less of the vote) was difficult to obtain. I have erred on the side of coding them as not having had previous office-holding experience.

11. The difference is statistically significant based on a chi-square test (X^2 = 25.97, p < .000). However, since we are comparing the total population this analysis is for descriptive purposes.

12. During some of the election cycles included in this analysis Washington State (1994–2000) and California (1998–2000) used a distinctive primary election system that affected the calculation of the percentage of the vote candidates received. These elections were conducted under a "blanket primary rule" in which candidates of both major and minor parties ran in a single primary for a seat with the top two vote-getters moving on to the general election. In 2000, the Supreme Court ruled such electoral systems unconstitutional in that they violated the parties' right to association. In these cases, I have recalculated the percentage of the vote candidates received to reflect their percentage of the vote they obtained of the total votes candidates running under their party's label received. In most cases, the official reports of the states' Secretary of State Office included both the percentage of all votes the candidates received and the percentage they received of their party's votes. This recalculation allows me to include these races in an analysis of how well women candidates fared in open seat primaries compared with male candidates within parties.

13. The difference was not statistically significant.

CHAPTER 4

1. One might examine a multiple regression model to attempt to explain this discrepancy including various district demographic variables. But the small number of female candidates and the small number of open seat districts precludes a large enough sample size to provide enough variation and power in such an analysis or

the construction of meaningful coefficients to move beyond the qualitative discussion presented in this chapter.

2. The overall difference was statistically significant at the .001 level. The differences within the parties were .04 for the Republicans and .009 for the Democrats.

3. The ad can be seen at http://www.youtube.com/watch?v=bPa8teSoLwg.

CHAPTER 7

1. As I completed this study, actress Ashley Judd was seriously considering a run in the Democratic primary in the 2014 Senate contest to oppose incumbent Republican Mitch McConnell in the general election. But she has since declined to run.

2. In 2012, North Dakota elected Democrat Heidi Heitkamp to the U.S. Senate.

CHAPTER 8

1. For a description of feminalism, see Georgia Duerst-Lahti's chapter "Knowing Congress as a Gendered Institution" (2002) in *Women Transforming Congress*.

2. The Democrats call their membership organization a caucus; the Republicans call theirs a conference.

3. Michele Bachmann announced her candidacy for the open position of Republican Conference chair after the 2010 election. Rep. Mike Pence, who had held the position, said he was not seeking reelection to the post. Rep. Bachmann staked her claim to the position as a leader of the Tea Party Caucus. However, it immediately became clear that she would not win a contest to be conference chair. Thus, she withdrew her name from consideration.

4. Videos of the two press events are available at http://www.c-spanvideo.org/program/WomenSena and http://www.c-spanvideo.org/program/Womenon2.

5. A video of the press event can be found at http://www.youtube.com/watch?v=Sa8hOwweRDI.

6. The Violence Against Women Act was renewed in the 113th Congress. It was passed, including most of the Democratic Party's provisions, with slight modifications from the earlier version debated in 2012.

7. Cathy McMorris Rodgers was elected chair of the Republican Conference at the beginning of the 113th Congress, the fourth-ranked leadership position of the conference.

CHAPTER 9

1. This number only includes candidates who competed in primary elections or were nominated by their party to fill a vacancy after the primary season. It does not include candidates who dropped out along the way even after a primary victory. Nor does it include contenders in party conventions who did not compete in a primary after losing a convention endorsement. It does include Nancy Cassis who

ran a write-in campaign in Michigan's 11th district Republican primary after Rep. McCotter dropped out past the filing deadline. Party leaders endorsed her candidacy but she ultimately failed to win the nomination.

2. Several weeks after the election, however, Rep. Jo Ann Emerson announced her resignation from Congress, lowering the number to 77. But then Democrat Robin Kelly won the special election to replace Jesse Jackson Jr. to bring the number back up to 78.

3. This conclusion is based on a search of media stories about women's candidacies in Lexis-Nexis from January 2011 through November 2012 using the key words "women candidates" and "election."

4. This poll is the most recent one asking this question in the Roper Center's archive of poll questions. It can be found at ABC News/*Washington Post* poll, July 2009. Retrieved May 29, 2012, from the iPOLL Databank, Roper Center for Public Opinion Research, University of Connecticut. http://www.ulib.niu.edu:4939/data_access/ipoll/ipoll.html.

5. CBS News poll, May 2005. Retrieved May 29, 2012, from the iPOLL Databank, Roper Center for Public Opinion Research, University of Connecticut. http://www.ulib.niu.edu:4939/data_access/ipoll/ipoll.html.

6. Pew Global Attitudes Project poll, April 2010. Retrieved May 29, 2012, from the iPOLL Databank, Roper Center for Public Opinion Research, University of Connecticut. http://www.ulib.niu.edu:4939/data_access/ipoll/ipoll.html.

7. This poll can be found at http://www.gallup.com/poll/150038/Congress-Approval-Ties-Time-Low.aspx.

8. The news release can be found at http://www.house.gov/list/press/mo05_cleaver/FirstCiviliyHour.html.

9. DW-NOMINATE scores are calculated from all nonunanimous roll call votes in the House and provide an estimate of each House member's ideology along a unidimensional Left-Right continuum ranging from −1.0 to 1.0, with higher scores signifying a more conservative voting record. This technique was developed by Keith Poole and Howard Rosenthal. See their *Congress: A Political-Economic History of Roll Call Voting* (Oxford: Oxford University Press, 1997).

10. The 2011 scores can be found at http://media.cq.com/media/2011/votestudy_2011/graphics/.

11. The Six-Step Action Plan of Norris and Krook (2011) consists of: (1) *Constitutional Rights:* guarantee equal rights for women and men, including rights to the suffrage and to candidate nomination; (2) *Electoral System:* reform the type of electoral system; proportional representation with large district magnitudes maximizes opportunities for women; (3) *Legal Quotas:* review laws regulating candidate recruitment processes for all parties; the use of reserved seats for women members or gender quotas for candidates generally expand women's representation; (4) *Party Rules and Recruitment Procedures:* review internal candidate recruitment processes within each party; adopt fast track strategies in party rulebooks and regulations to achieve gender equality for nominated candidates; (5) *Capacity Development:* strengthen the skills and resources of women in the pipeline for elected office, with initiatives by parties, the media and NGOs, including knowledge networks, mentoring programs, skills training and funding for women candidates; (6) *Parliamentary Reform:*

reform the rules and internal procedures within parliament, including the facilities and working conditions, hours of sitting, principles for leadership recruitment, and provision of childcare facilities.

12. More information about this program can be found at www.cawp.rutgers.edu/education_training/New Leadership.

13. This list can be found at http://www.cawp.rutgers.edu/education_training/trainingresources/index.php.

References

Abzug, Bella. 1984. *The Gender Gap: Bella Abzug's Guide to Political Power for American Women.* Boston: Houghton Mifflin.

Acker, Joan. 1992. "Gender Institutions: From Sex Roles to Gendered Institutions." *Contemporary Society* 21:565–69.

Ahuja, Sunil. 2008. "Preface." *Congress Behaving Badly: The Rise of Partisanship and Incivility and the Death of Public Trust.* Westport, CT: Praeger.

American National Election Studies. 1990–99, 2008. "Guide to Public Opinion and Electoral Behavior." http://www.electionstudies.org/nesguide/nesguide.htm.

Anzia, Sarah, and Christopher Berry. 2011. "The Jackie (and Jill) Robinson Effect: Congresswomen and the Distribution of Federal Spending." *American Journal of Political Science* 55, 3 (July): 478–93.

Atkeson, Lonna Rae. 2003."Not All Cues Are Created Equal: The Conditional Impact of Female Candidates on Political Engagement." *Journal of Politics* 65:1040–61.

Atkeson, Lonna Rae, and Nancy Carrillo. 2007. "More Is Better: The Influence of Collective Female Descriptive Representation on External Efficacy." *Politics & Gender* 3, 1 (March): 79–103.

Ayres, B. Drummond, Jr. 1992. "Campaign Trail; Tips for Young Politician-in-the-Making." *New York Times*, October 24.

Bar-Lev, Abby. 2006. "Year of the Woman Begins Tuesday." *Minnesota Daily*, November 2; www.mndaily.com/articles/2006/11/02/69686.

Beckel, Michael. 2011. "Political Donors' Gender Disparity." http://www.opensecrets.org/news/2011/08/political-donors-gender-disparity.html.

Bedard, Paul. 2011. "New DNC Boss Calls GOP 'Anti-Women.'" USNEWS.com, May 26.

Berch, Neil. 2004. "Women Incumbents, Elite Bias, and Voter Response in the 1996 and 1998 U.S. House Elections." *Women & Politics* 26, 1: 21–33.

Berke, Richard. 1998. "Skipping the Race—A Special Report; Run for Congress? Parties Find Rising Stars Are Just Saying No." *New York Times*, March 15, 1:1.

Bernstein, David S. 2010. "GOP's Glass Floor?" thephoenix.com/BLOGS/talking-politics, July 9.

Biersack, Robert, and Paul S. Herrnson. 1994. "Political Parties and the Year of the Woman." In *The Year of the Woman: Myths and Realities*, edited by Elizabeth Adell Cook, Sue Thomas, and Clyde Wilcox. Boulder: Westview Press.

Blake, Aaron. 2007. "House Republicans Aim for More Recruitment of Women in 2008." *The Hill*, January 22.

Blake, Aaron. 2012. "Elizabeth Warren and the Red Sox Test." *Washington Post*, April 12.

Bono, Mary. 2012. "Women's Policy Committee Ask State Department to Seek Justice for Pakistani Girl Shot by Taliban Terrorists." *Congressional Documents and Publications*, October 12.

Branton, Regina. 2009. "The Importance of Race and Ethnicity in Congressional Primary Elections." *Political Research Quarterly* 62 (September): 459–73.

Brewer, Mark D., and Jeffrey M. Stonecash. 2007. *Split: Class and Cultural Divides in American Politics*. Washington, DC: CQ Press.

Broder, David. 1994a. "Key to Women's Political Parity: Running." *Washington Post*, September 8, A17.

Broder, David. 1994b. "Women Candidates on Crime Issue." *Times-Picayune*, June 14, B7.

Broder, David. 2006. "Narrowing the House's Gender Gap." *Washington Post*, April 9, B7.

Brown, Carrie Budoff. 2008. "Obama Camp Adds Women to Top Ranks." *Politico*, June 20.

Burns, Nancy, Kay Schlozman, and Sidney Verba. 2001. *The Private Roots of Public Action: Gender, Equality, and Political Participation*. Cambridge, MA: Harvard University Press.

Burrell, Barbara. 1985. "Women's and Men's Campaigns for the U.S. House of Representatives, 1972–1982: A Finance Gap?" *American Politics Quarterly* 13, 3: 251–72.

Burrell, Barbara. 1994. *A Woman's Place Is in the House: Campaigning for Congress in the Feminist Era*. Ann Arbor: University of Michigan Press.

Burrell, Barbara. 2005. "Campaign Financing: Women's Experience in the Modern Era." In *Women and Elective Office: Past, Present and Future*, 2nd ed., edited by Sue Thomas and Clyde Wilcox, 26–40. New York: Oxford University Press.

Burrell, Barbara. 2006. "Political Parties and Women's Organizations: Bringing Women into the Electoral Arena." In *Gender and Elections: Shaping the Future of American Politics*, edited by Susan J. Carroll and Richard L. Fox, 143–68. New York: Cambridge University Press.

Burrell, Barbara. 2008a. "Likeable? Effective Commander-in-Chief? Polling on Candidate Traits in the 'Year of the Presidential Woman.'" *PS: Political Science and Politics* 41, 4: 747–52.

Burrell, Barbara. 2008b. "Political Parties, Fund-raising, and Sex." In *Legislative Women: Getting Elected, Getting Ahead*, edited by Beth Reingold, 41–58. Boulder: Lynne Rienner.

Burrell, Barbara. 2010. "Political Parties and Women's Organizations: Bringing Women into the Electoral Arena." In *Gender and Elections: Shaping the Future of*

American Politics, 2nd ed., edited by Susan J. Carroll and Richard L. Fox, 210–38. New York: Cambridge University Press.

Burrell, Barbara, and Brian Frederick. 2007. "Political Windows of Opportunity: Recruitment Pools, Gender Politics, and Congressional Open Seats." Paper presented at the Annual Meeting of the Southern Political Association, New Orleans.

Burton, Michael, and Daniel Shea. 2002. *Campaign Mode: Strategic Vision in Congressional Elections*. Lanham, MD: Rowman and Littlefield.

Byrne, Carol. 1994. "Female Democrats Go on the Road to Reelect Each Other; Legislators United as 'Ultimate Outsiders' in Male Bastion." *Minneapolis Star Tribune*, June 1, 4a.

Bystrom, Dianne G., Mary Christine Banwart, Lynda Lee Kaid, and Terry A. Robertson. 2004. *Gender and Candidate Communication*. New York: Routledge.

Campbell, David, and Christina Wolbrecht. 2006. "See Jane Run: Women Politicians as Role Models for Adolescents." *Journal of Politics* 68, 2 (May): 233–47.

Canon, David. 1990. *Actors, Athletes, and Astronauts: Political Amateurs in the U.S. Congress*. Chicago: University of Chicago Press.

Carney, Kate, and Leslie Bracy. 2007. "Do Women Still Work Together? Evidence from the 100th–108th Congress." Paper presented at the Annual Meeting of the Southern Political Science Association, New Orleans.

Carroll, Susan. 2002. "Representing Women: Congresswomen's Perceptions of Their Representational Roles." In *Women Transforming Congress*, ed. Cindy Simon Rosenthal, 50–68. Norman: University of Oklahoma Press.

Carroll, Susan, and Richard Fox. 2006. "Introduction: Gender and Electoral Politics into the Twenty-First Century." In *Gender and Elections: Shaping the Future of American Politics*, edited by Susan J. Carroll and Richard L. Fox. New York: Cambridge University Press.

Carroll, Susan, and Richard Fox. 2010. "Introduction: Gender and Electoral Politics into the Twenty-First Century." In *Gender and Elections: Shaping the Future of American Politics*, 2nd ed., edited by Susan J. Carroll and Richard L. Fox, 1–12. New York: Cambridge University Press.

Catalyst. 2011. *Statistical Overview of Women in the Workplace*. http://www.catalyst.org/publication/219/statistical-overview-of-women-in-the-workplace.

Catalyst. 2012. "Women in the Law: Quick Takes." http://www.catalyst.org/publication/246/women-in-law-in-the-us.

Chaddock, Gail Russell. 2004. "The Rise of Women Candidates." *Christian Science Monitor*, October 19, 1.

Cogan, Marin. 2011. "GOP Freshmen Women Go on Offense." *Politico.com*, June 20.

Cogan, Marin, and Richard E. Cohen. 2010. "The GOP's Gender Gap." *Politico.com*, November 9.

Cohen, Tom, and Dan Merica. 2012. "Senate Kills Controversial 'Conscience' Amendment." *CNN Wire*, March 1.

Congressional Documents and Publications. 2012. "McMorris Rodgers and GOP Women Hold Presser on ObamaCare's Impact on Women." March 28.

Congressional Record. 2011. "Republican Women on Job Growth." June 21. http://www.c-spanvideo.org/program/HouseSessionPart313.

Connolly, Ceci. 1994a. "A Political Novelty No More, Women Test Endurance." *Congressional Quarterly Weekly Report*, May 7, 1139–41.

Connolly, Ceci. 1994b. "Despite Pubic Ire, Insiders Still Have Winning Ways." *Congressional Quarterly Weekly Report*, August 6, 2274–75.

Conrad, Dennis. 2008. "Halvorson: From Cosmetics Sales to Congress." Associated Press, December 5.

Cooperman, Rosalyn. 2001. "Party Organizations and the Recruitment of Women Candidates to the U.S. House since the 'Year of the Woman'." Paper presented at the Annual Meeting of the American Political Science Association, San Francisco.

Crespin, Michael H., and Janna L. Deitz. 2010. "If You Can't Join 'Em, Beat 'Em: The Gender Gap in Individual Donations to Congressional Candidates." *Political Research Quarterly* 63, 3: 81–593.

Dabelko, Kirsten La Cour, and Paul Herrnson. 1997. "Women's and Men's Campaigns for the U.S. House of Representatives." *Political Research Quarterly* 50, 1 (March): 121–35.

Dahl, David, and Jennifer S. Thomas. 1994. "Women Candidates Hope to Hold Their Own in Elections." *St. Petersburg Times*, July 10, 10A.

Davidson, Roger. 2009. "Partisan Surge and Decline in Congressional Elections in 2008." In *The American Elections of 2008*, edited by Janet Box-Steffensmeier and Steven Schier. Boulder: Rowman and Littlefield.

Davis, Susan. 2006. "GOP Keeps Team, Promises Changes." *Roll Call*, November 20.

Davis, Susan. 2012. "Upward Trend of Female Candidates for Congress; Both Parties Making Efforts to Field Women." *USA Today*, January 30, 4A.

Day, Christine L., and Charles D. Hadley. 2005. *Women's PACs: Abortions and Elections*. Upper Saddle River, NJ: Pearson Prentice Hall.

Democratic Congressional Campaign Committee. 2006. "DCCC Announces Red to Blue Program for Strong Candidates for Change across the Country." February 28. http://dccc.org/newsroom/entry/Red_to_Blue/.

Dettmer, Jamie. 2004. "Senator Dole Is Eyeing Leadership of Key Senate Committee, GOP Post." *New York Sun*, November 12.

Dobbin, Muriel. 2002. "Women Advance, But Path to Power Still Steep." *Sacramento Bee*, February 22, A20.

Dodson, Debra. 2006. *The Impact of Women in Congress*. New York: Oxford University Press.

Dolan, David. 2004. "Dole to Lead GOP Senate Efforts; N.C. Senator Will Raise Money for 2006 Campaigns, Recruit Candidates." *Herald-Sun*, November 17.

Dolan, Kathleen. 2004. *Voting for Women: How the Public Evaluates Women Candidates*. Boulder: Westview Press.

Dolan, Kathleen. 2005. "How the Public Views Women Candidates." *In Women and Elective Office: Past, Present, and Future*, edited by Sue Thomas and Clyde Wilcox, 41–59. New York: Oxford University Press.

Dolan, Kathleen. 2008. "Symbolic Mobilization? The Impact of Candidate Sex." *In Legislative Women: Getting Elected, Getting Ahead*, edited by Beth Reingold, 85–100. Boulder: Lynne Rienner.

Dolan, Kathleen. 2010. "The Impact of Gender Stereotyped Evaluations on Support for Women Candidates." *Political Behavior* 32:69–88.

Dolan, Kathleen. 2011. "The Impact of Gender Stereotypes on Voting for Women Candidates for the U.S. House and Senate in 2010." Paper presented at the 2011 Annual Meeting of the Midwest Political Science Association, Chicago.

Duerst-Lahti, Georgia. 2002. "Knowing Congress as a Gendered Institution." In *Women Transforming Congress*, edited by Cindy Simon Rosenthal, 20–49. Norman: University of Oklahoma Press.

Duerst-Lahti, Georgia. 2006. "Presidential Elections: Gendered Space and the Case of 2004." In *Gender and Elections: Shaping the Future of American Politics*, edited by Susan J. Carroll and Richard L. Fox, 12–42. New York: Cambridge University Press.

Edmonds, Patricia, and Richard Benedetto. 1994. "Angry White Men/Their Votes Turn the Tide for GOP/Men Want to Torch Washington." *USA Today*, November 11.

Elder, Laurel. 2008. "Whither Republican Women: The Growing Partisan Gap among Women in Congress." *The Forum* 6, 1, Article 13, April 3. The Berkeley Electronic Press. DOI: 10.2202/1540-8884.1204.

Ellperin, Juliet. 2000. "For Women, a Crucial Role; Democratic Candidates May Help Regain Hill." *Washington Post*, August 15, A01.

Espo, David. 2006. "In Wake of Senate Loss, Republicans Turn Anger on Campaign Committee Led by Elizabeth Dole." Associated Press, December 23.

Ezzard, Martha. 2000. "Hear Them Roaring at the Ballot Boxes; Female Candidates Take a Giant Leap to Heights of Power." *Atlanta Journal and Constitution*, November 12, 3C.

Feldman, Linda.2008a. "Hillary Clinton Shattered a Political Glass Ceiling." *Christian Science Monitor*, June 6.

Feldman, Linda. 2008b. "Women Make Modest Gains in Election 2008." *Christian Science Monitor*, November 16.

Ferraro, Thomas. 2012. "Top Republican Woman in Congress Becomes a Force." Reuters, May 18.

Fiber, Pamela, and Richard L. Fox. 2005. "A Tougher Road for Women? Assessing the Role of Gender in Congressional Elections." In *Gender and American Politics*, edited by Sue Tolleson-Rinehart and Jyl J. Josephson, 64–81. Armonk, NY: M. E. Sharpe.

Fiorina, Morris. 2005. *Culture War? The Myth of a Polarized America*. New York: Pearson, Longman.

Ford, Lynne. 2006. *Women and Politics: The Pursuit of Equality*. Boston: Wadsworth, Cengage Learning.

Ford, Lynne. 2011. *Women and Politics: The Pursuit of Equality*. 3rd ed. Boston: Wadsworth CENGAGE Learning.

Fortier, John. 2008. "2008 Will Not Be a Banner Year for Women." Politico.com, March 24.

Fourteen GOP House Women. 2012. "GOP Is the Real Party of Women." http://www.politico.com/news/stories/0512/76340.html.

Fowler, Linda L., and Jennifer L. Lawless. 2009. "Looking for Sex in All the Wrong

Places: Press Coverage and the Electoral Fortunes of Gubernatorial Candidates." *Perspectives on Politics* 7, 3: 519–36.

Fox, Richard. 2010. "Congressional Elections: Women's Candidacies and the Road to Gender Parity." In *Gender and Elections: Shaping the Future of American Politics*, edited by Susan J. Carroll and Richard L. Fox, 187–209. New York: Cambridge University Press.

Francia, Peter L., John C. Green, Paul S. Herrnson, Lynda Powell, and Clyde Wilcox. 2003. *The Financiers of Congressional Elections*. New York: Columbia University Press.

Franke-Ruta, Garance. 2010. "Record Numbers of Republican Women Are Running for House Seats." www.washingtonpost.com, May 1.

Frederick, Brian. 2009. "Are Female House Members Still More Liberal in a Polarized Era? The Conditional Nature of the Relationship between Descriptive and Substantive Representation." *Congress and the Presidency* 36:181–202.

Freedom House. 2006. "Freedom in the World 2006." http://www.freedomhouse.org.

Freeman, Jo. 1987. "Whom You Know versus Whom You Represent: Feminist Influence in the Democratic and Republican Parties." In *The Women's Movements of the United States and Western Europe: Consciousness, Political Opportunity, and Public Policy*, edited by Mary Fainsod Katzenstein and Carol McClurg Mueller. Philadelphia: Temple University Press.

Freeman, Jo. 1989. "Feminist Activities at the Republican Convention." *PS: Political Science and Politics* 22 (March): 39–47.

Frommer, Frederic J. 2004. "Republicans Choose Elizabeth Dole to Head 2006 Senate Campaigns." www.sfgate.com, December 3.

The Frontrunner. 2006. "OH13: Primary Eve Sawyer FEC Complaint Claims Sutton Coordinated with EMILY's List." May 5.

The Frontrunner. 2010. "AL2: Women's Group for Roby in GOP Primary Hits Barber for Hosting Nightly Poker Games." June 29.

Fulton, Sarah A., Cherie D. Maestas, L. Sandy Maisel, and Walter J. Stone. 2006. "The Sense of a Woman: Gender, Ambition, and the Decision to Run for Congress." *Political Research Quarterly* 59, 2 (June): 235–48.

Gaddie, Ronald Keith, and Charles S. Bullock. 1997. "Structural and Elite Features in Open Seat and Special U.S. House Elections: Is There a Sexual Bias?" *Political Research Quarterly* 50, 2 (June): 459–68.

Gaddie, Ronald Keith, and Charles S. Bullock III. 2000. *Elections to Open Seats in the U.S. House*. Boulder: Rowman and Littlefield.

Gaddie, Ronald Keith, Charles S. Bullock III, and Scott E. Buchanan. 1999. "What Is So Special about Special Elections?" *Legislative Studies Quarterly* 24, 1 (February): 103–12.

Gerrity, Jessica, Tracy Osborn, and Jeanette Morehouse Mendez. 2007. "Women and Representation: A Different View of the District?" *Politics & Gender* 3, 2: 179–200.

Gertzog, Irwin. 1995. *Congressional Women: Their Recruitment, Integration, and Behavior*, 2nd ed. Westport, CT: Greenwood Press.

Gertzog, Irwin. 2002. "Women's Changing Pathways to the U.S. House of Representatives: Widows, Elites, and Strategic Politicians." In *Women Transforming Congress*, edited by Cindy Simon Rosenthal, 95–118. Norman: University of Oklahoma Press.

Gertzog, Irwin. 2004. *Women and Power on Capitol Hill: Reconstructing the Congressional Women's Caucus*. Boulder: Lynne Rienner.

Giroux, Gregory. 2007. "Democratic-Led 110th Congress Is Old Boys' Club with a Twist as Women, Blacks Gain Clout." www.cqpolitics.com/2007/02/democraticled_110th_congress_i.html.

Goad, Ben. 2012. "CONGRESS: GOP Women Seek to Raise Their Profile." *Press Enterprise (Riverside, CA)*, May 9.

Goldmacher, Shane. 2011. "Negrete McLeod to Run for Congress: 'I'm in, I'm in, I'm in, I'm in'." http://latimesblogs.latimes.com/california-politics/2011/06/negrete-mcleod-to-run-for-congress-im-in-im-in-im-in-im-in.html.

Goodman, Ellen. 2002. "Post-Gender Politics and Cautionary Tales: Women Candidates Are in a Double Bind, but Some Manage to Wriggle Free." *Boston Globe*, November 13, A17.

Goodman, Ellen. 2004. "Little Mention of Woman for VP." *Boston Globe*, July 8, A11.

Goodrich, Lawrence. 1998. "It Looks Like Good (Election) Year for Women in Politics." *Christian Science Monitor*, January 12, 1.

Groppe, Maureen. 2012. "Election Could Send More Women to Congress." Gannett News Service, March 16.

Gwaltney, John Langston. 1980. *Drylongso, a Self-Portrait of Black America*. New York: Vintage.

Hannagan, Rebecca J., Jamie Pimlott, and Levente Littvray. 2010. "Does an EMILY's List Endorsement Predict Electoral Success, or Does EMILY Pick the Winners?" *PS* (July):503–8.

Harrell, Peter E. 2004. "A Florida Democrat Poised to Succeed Her Political Mentor in the House." *Congressional Quarterly Today*, June 25.

Hawkesworth, Mary. 2003. "Congressional Enactments of Race-Gender: Toward a Theory of Raced-Gendered Institutions." *American Political Science Review* 97 (November): 529–50.

Hawkesworth, Mary, Kathleen Casey, Krista Jenkins, and Katherine Kleeman. 2001. "Legislating by and for Women: A Comparison of the 103rd and 104th Congresses." New Brunswick, NJ: Center for American Women and Politics, Eagleton Institute of Politics, Rutgers, State University of New Jersey.

Herrick, Rebekah. 1995. "A Reappraisal of the Quality of Women Candidates." *Women & Politics* 14, 4: 25–38.

Herrick, Rebekah. 1996. "Is There a Gender Gap in the Value of Campaign Resources?" *American Politics Quarterly* 24, 1 (January): 68–80.

Herrnson, Paul. 2008. *Congressional Elections: Campaigning at Home and in Washington*. 5th ed.. Washington, DC: CQ Press.

Herrnson, Paul, J. Celeste Lay, and Atiya Kai Stokes. 2003. "Women Running 'As Women': Candidate Gender, Campaign Issues, and Voter-Targeting Strategies." *Journal of Politics* 65, 1 (February): 244–55.

Herrnson, Paul, and Jennifer C. Lucas. 2006. "The Fairer Sex? Gender and Negative Campaigning in U.S. Elections." *American Politics Research* 34:69–94.

Hershey, Marjorie Randon. 1997. "The Congressional Elections." In *The Election of 1996*, edited by Gerald Pomper, 205–40. New York: Chatham House.

Hibbing, John. 2002. "How to Make Congress Popular." *Legislative Studies Quarterly* 95, 1: 219–44.

Hoffman, Kim U., Carrie Palmer, and Ronald Keith Gaddie. 2001. "Candidate Sex and Congressional Elections: Open Seats before, during, and after the Year of the Woman." In *Women and Congress: Running, Winning, and Ruling*, edited by Karen O'Connor, 37–58. New York: Haworth Press.

Holland, Judy. 2006. "Big Election Year Predicted for Women Candidates: Seen as Honest Outsiders, They Could Have Best Showing since '92." *San Francisco Chronicle*, A13.

The Hotline. 2010. "You Hit Like a Girl." August 2. www.nationaljournal.com.

The Hotline. 2012. "The Meaning of Deb." May 17. www.nationaljournal.com.

Hunt, Karen. 2010. "S. Dakota Race Has Pelosi-Palin Focus." www.politico.com, November 1.

Interparliamentary Union. 2007. "Women in National Parliaments." http://www.ipu.org/wmn-e/world.htm.

Isenstadt, Alex, 2010. "Barber Draws Scrutiny for Poker Tourneys." www.politico.com, June 25.

Jacobson, Gary. 1989. "Strategic Politicians and the Dynamics of U.S. House Elections, 1946–1986." *American Journal of Political Science* 83:773–93.

Jacobson, Gary. 1990. "The Effects of Campaign Spending in House Elections: New Evidence for Old Arguments." *American Journal of Political Science* 34, 2 (May): 334–62.

Jacobson, Gary. 1997. "The 105th Congress: Unprecedented and Unsurprising." In *The Elections of 1996*, edited by Michael Nelson, 143–66. Washington, DC: CQ Press.

Jacobson, Gary. 2001. "Congress: Elections and Stalemate." In *The Elections of 2000*, edited by Michael Nelson, 185–209. Washington, DC: Congressional Quarterly Press.

Jacobson, Gary. 2003. "Terrorism, Terrain, and Turnout: Explaining the 2002 Midterm Elections." *Political Science Quarterly* 118, 1: 1–22.

Jacobson, Gary. 2007. "Referendum: The 2006 Midterm Congressional Elections." *Political Science Quarterly* 122, 1: 1–24.

Jacobson, Gary. 2009. *The Politics of Congressional Elections*. 7th ed. New York: Pearson Longman.

Jamieson, Kathleen Hall. 1995. *Beyond the Double Bind*. New York: Oxford University Press.

Jamieson, Kathleen Hall. 1999. *Civility in the House of Representatives: The 105th Congress*. Philadelphia: Annenberg Public Policy Center, University of Pennsylvania.

Kathlene, Lyn. 1994. "Power and Influence in State Legislative Policymaking: The Interaction of Gender and Position in Committee Hearing Debates." *American Political Science Review* 88:560–76.

Kathlene, Lyn. 1995. "Alternative Views of Crime: Legislative Policymaking in Gendered Terms." *Journal of Politics* 57:696–723.

Kenny, Sally. 1996. "New Research on Gendered Political Institutions." *Political Research Quarterly* 49, 2 (June): 445–66.

Kernell, Samuel, and Gary C. Jacobson. 2003. *The Logic of American Politics*. Washington, DC: CQ Press.

Khan, Naureen. 2012. "Can She-PAC Help Republicans Solve Their Woman Problem?" *National Journal*, February 24.

Knickerbocker, Brad. 1998. "Women's March to Political Equality Marked by Short Steps." *Christian Science Monitor*, November 30, 3.

Koch, Jeffrey. 1997. "Candidate Gender and Women's Psychological Engagement in Politics." *American Politics Quarterly* 25:118–33.

Kornblut, Anne E. 2010. "Primaries Push More Women into General Elections, but Most Fresh Faces Now Belong to Republican Party." www.washingtonpost.com, September 15.

Kraushaar, Josh. 2011. "Democrats Bet the Senate on Women." *National Journal Daily AM*, November 29.

Kronholz, June. 2007. "Women's March into Office Slows." *Cook Political Report*, August 15.

Kropf, Martha E., and John A. Boiney. 2001. "The Electoral Glass Ceiling: Gender, Viability, and the News in U.S. Senate Campaigns." In *Women and Congress: Running, Winning, and Ruling*, edited Karen O'Connor, 37–58. New York: Haworth Press.

Kunin, Madeleine. 2004. "U.S Women Lag in Elected Office." *Boston Globe*, May 31.

Larserud, Stina, and Rita Taphorn. 2007. *Designing for Equality: Best-Fit, Medium-Fit and Non-favourable Combinations of Electoral Systems and Gender Quotas*. Stockholm, Sweden: International Institute for Democracy and Electoral Assistance (IDEA).

Lawless, Jennifer. 2004. "Politics of Presence? Congresswomen and Symbolic Representation." *Political Research Quarterly* 57:81–99.

Lawless, Jennifer. 2009. "Sexism and Gender Bias in Election 2008: A More Complex Path for Women in Politics." *Politics & Gender* 5, 1 (March): 70–80.

Lawless, Jennifer, and Richard Fox. 2005. *It Takes a Candidate: Why Women Don't Run for Office*. New York: Cambridge University Press.

Lawless, Jennifer L., and Richard L. Fox. 2010. *It Still Takes a Candidate: Why Women Don't Run for Office*. New York: Cambridge University Press.

Lawless, Jennifer, and Katherine Pearson. 2008. "The Primary Reason for Women's Underrepresentation? Reevaluating the Conventional Wisdom." *Journal of Politics* 70, 1: 67–82.

Lawless, Jennifer L., and Sean M. Theriault. 2006. "Women in the U.S. Congress: From Entry to Exit." In *Women in Politics: Outsiders or Insiders?* edited by Lois Duke Whitaker, 164–81. Upper Saddle River, NJ: Pearson Education.

Lawrence, Regina, and Melody Rose. 2010. *Hillary Clinton's Race for the White House: Gender Politics and the Media on the Campaign Trail*. Boulder: Lynne Rienner.

Layton, Lindsey. 2007. "Moms in the House, with Kids at Home." *Washington Post*, July 19, A01.

Leonard, Mary. 1998. "For Women Candidates, a New Tack." *Boston Globe*, October 18, A1.

Leonard, Mary. 2000. "Women Candidates Fierce, Financed." *Boston Globe*, November 5, A37.

Leonard, Mary. 2002. "Political Landscape Becomes Foreboding for Women Candidates." *Boston Globe*, March 21, A3.

Lovley, Erika. 2009. "GOP Women: A Minority in a Minority." www.politico.com, May 10.

Lugar, Richard., 1983. "A Plan to Elect More GOP Women." *Washington Post*, August 21.

Macedo, Stephen, et al. 2005. *Democracy at Risk: How Political Choices Undermine Citizen Participation and What We Can Do About It*. Washington, DC: Brookings Institution Press.

Maisel, Louis Sandy. 1982. *From Obscurity to Oblivion: Running in the Congressional Primary*. Knoxville: University of Tennessee Press.

Mann, Thomas, and Norman Ornstein. 2006. *The Broken Branch: How Congress Is Failing America and How to Get It Back on Track*. New York: Oxford University Press.

Mann, Thomas E., and Norman J. Ornstein. 2012. *It's Even Worse Than It Looks: How the American Constitutional System Collided with the New Politics of Extremism*. New York: Basic Books.

Mannies, Jo. 1996. "This Election Year 'Politics as Usual' Means That Women Are Everywhere." *St. Louis Post-Dispatch*, October 23, 5B.

Manning, Jennifer E. 2011. *Membership in the 112th Congress: A Profile*. Washington, DC: Congressional Research Service.

Mansbridge, Jane. 1999. "Should Blacks Represent Blacks and Women Represent Women? A Contingent 'Yes.'" *Journal of Politics* 61:628–57.

Marcus, Ruth. 2010. "Fallin Plays the 'Mommy Card.'" *Tulsa World*, October 28, A17.

Mascaro, Lisa. 2010. "Women in Washington, Your Seats Are at Risk." LATimes.com, August 29.

Matland, Richard. 1993. "Institutional Variables Affecting Female Representation in National Legislatures: The Case of Norway." *Journal of Politics* 55, 3: 737–55.

Matland, Richard, and David C. King. 2002. "Women as Candidates in Congressional Elections." In *Women Transforming Congress*, edited by Cindy Simon Rosenthal, 119–45. Norman: University of Oklahoma Press.

Matland, Richard, and Michelle Taylor. 1997. "Electoral System Effects on Women's Representation: Theoretical Arguments and Evidence from Costa Rica." *Comparative Political Studies* 30, 2: 186–210.

McCormick, Erin, and Marc Sandalow. 2006. "Pelosi Mines 'California Gold' for Dems Nationwide." *San Francisco Chronicle*, April 3.

Milbank, Dana, and David Broder. 2004. "Hopes for Civility in Washington Are Dashed; in Bush's Term, Tone Worsened, Partisans Say." *Washington Post*, January 18.

Milyo, Jeffrey, and Samantha Schosberg. 2000. "Gender Bias and Selection Bias in House Elections." *Public Choice* 105:41–59.

Morin, Richard, and Claudia Deane. 2000. "Sex in Elections: It's Not What You Think." *Washington Post*, April 9, B01.

Nagourney, Adam. 1996. "A Good Year for Running; More Women, Fewer Causes." *New York Times*, April 28, Section 4, 4.

Nelson, Candice. 1994. "Women's PACs in the Year of the Woman." In *The Year of the Woman: Myths and Realities*, edited by Elizabeth Adell Cook, Sue Thomas, and Clyde Wilcox. Boulder: Westview Press.

Nichols, Bill. 2006. "Women Look to Gain More Ground in the Senate; Numbers Could Reach New High after the Election." *USA Today*, October 16, A5.

Niven, David, and Jeremy Zilber. 2001. "'How Does She Have Time for Kids and Congress?' Views on Gender and Media Coverage from House Offices." In *Women and Congress: Running, Winning, and Ruling*, edited by Karen O'Connor, 37–58. New York: Haworth Press.

Nixon, David, and R. Darcy. 1996. "Special Elections and the Growth of Women's Representation in the U.S. House of Representatives." *Women & Politics* 16, 4: 99–108.

Norris, Pippa, and Mona Lena Krook. 2011. *Gender Equality in Elected Office: A Six Step Plan*. Vienna, Austria: OSCE Office for Democratic Institutions and Human Rights.

Norton, Noelle. 1999. "Uncovering the Dimensionality of Gender Voting in Congress." *Legislative Studies Quarterly* 24, 1: 65–86.

O'Connor, Karen. 2001. *Women in Congress: Running, Winning, and Ruling*. New York: Haworth Press.

Ondercin, Heather L., and Susan Welch. 2005. "Women Candidates for Congress." In *Women and Elective Office: Past, Present, and Future*, 2nd ed., edited by Sue Thomas and Clyde Wilcox, 60–80. New York: Oxford University Press.

Ondercin, Heather L., and Susan Welch. 2009. "Comparing Predictors of Women's Congressional Success: Candidates, Primaries, and the General Election." *American Politics Research* 37, 4 (July): 593–613.

Page, Susan. 2010. "In Congress, a Step Back for Women Is Looming; Elections Are Likely to Trim Their Numbers." *USA Today*, October 4, A1.

Palmer, Barbara, and Dennis Simon. 2001. "The Political Glass Ceiling: Gender, Strategy, and Incumbency in U.S. House Elections, 1978–1998." In *Women and Congress: Running, Winning and Ruling*, edited by Karen O'Connor, 59–78. New York: Haworth Press.

Palmer, Barbara, and Dennis Simon. 2004. *Breaking the Political Glass Ceiling*. New York: Routledge.

Palmer, Barbara, and Dennis Simon. 2005. "When Women Run against Women: The Hidden Influence of Female Incumbents in Elections to the U.S. House of Representatives from 1952–2002." *Politics & Gender* 1, 1: 39–63.

Palmer, Barbara, and Dennis Simon. 2006. *Breaking the Political Glass Ceiling: Women and Congressional Elections*. New York: Routledge.

Palmer, Barbara, and Dennis Simon. 2008. *Breaking the Political Glass Ceiling*. 2nd ed. New York: Routledge.

Palmer, Barbara, and Dennis Simon. 2012. *Women and Congressional Elections: A Century of Change*. Boulder: Lynne Rienner.

Peters, Ronald, and Cindy Simon Rosenthal. 2008. "Assessing Nancy Pelosi." *The Forum* 6, 3: Article 5, http://www.bepress.com/forum/vol6/iss3/art5.

Phillips, Anne. 1998. "Democracy and Representation: Or, Why Should It Matter Who Our Representatives Are?" In *Feminism and Politics*, edited by Anne Phillips, 224–40. Oxford: Oxford University Press.

Pimlott, Jamie. 2010. *Women and the Democratic Party: The Evolution of EMILY's List*. Amherst, NY: Cambria Press.

Politico.com. 2010. "2010: The Year of GOP Women." December 15. http://www.politico.com/news/stories/1210/46374.html.

Poole, Keith. 2008. "Nominate Data." http://voteview.com/dwnl.htm.

Reingold, Beth. 2008. "Introduction." In *Legislative Women: Getting Elected, Getting Ahead*, edited by Beth Reingold. Boulder: Lynne Rienner.

Riskind, Jonathan. 2002. "Deborah Pryce." *Columbus Dispatch*, December 23.

Rivers, Caryl. 2008. "Anti-Hillary Message Says 'Women Go Home.'" www.womensenews.org, May 27.

Roberts, Roxanne, and Amy Argetsinger. 2009. "Not Just Another Girls' Night Out." www.washingtonpost.com, July 15.

Romney, Ronna, and Beppie Harrison. 1988. *Momentum: Women in America Politics Now*. New York: Crown.

Roper Starch Worldwide. 1999. *Virginia Slims' American Women's Opinion Poll*. Storrs, CT: Roper Center.

Rosenthal, Cindy Simon. 1998. *When Women Lead: Integrative Leadership in State Legislatures*. New York: Oxford University Press.

Rosenthal, Cindy Simon. 2002a. *Women Transforming Congress*. Norman: University of Oklahoma Press.

Rosenthal, Cindy Simon. 2002b. "Introduction." In *Women Transforming Congress*, edited by Cindy Simon Rosenthal, 3–19. Norman: University of Oklahoma Press.

Rosenthal, Cindy Simon. 2008. "Climbing Higher: Opportunities and Obstacles within the Party System." In *Legislative Women: Getting Elected, Getting Ahead*, edited by Beth Reingold, 197–220. Boulder: Lynne Rienner.

Rosin, Hanna. 2011. "Good Ol' Girl." *The Atlantic*, February. http://www.theatlantic.com/magazine/archive/2011/01/good-ol-8.

Rozell, Mark. 2000. "Helping Women Run and Win: Feminist Groups, Candidate Recruitment, and Training." *Women & Politics* 21:101–16.

Rubin, Alissa J. 1994. "1994 Elections Are Looking Like the 'Off Year' of the Woman." *Congressional Quarterly Weekly Report*, October 13, 2972–74.

Rucker, Philip. 2010. "In South Dakota, Democrats' Own 'Mama Grizzly' vs. 'the Next Sarah Palin." *Washington Post*, August 23.

Russell, Betsy Z. 2004. "Attitudes Favor Female Candidates, Study Says; But BSU Analyst Says Incumbency Pivotal and Gender 'Not Relevant' for Most Anymore." *Spokesman Review*, July 22.

Sanbonmatsu, Kira. 2005. *When Women Run*. Ann Arbor: University of Michigan Press.

Sapiro, Virginia, and Pamela Conover. 1997. "The Variable Gender Basis of Electoral Politics: Gender and Context in the 1992 Election." *British Journal of Political Science* 27:497–523.

Sapiro, Virginia, Katherine Cramer Walsh, Patricia Strach, and Valerie Hennings. 2011. "Gender, Context, and Television Advertising: A Comprehensive Analysis of 2000 and 2002 House Races." *Political Research Quarterly* 64, 1: 107–19.

Schafer, Kathleen. 2012. "Parity in Politics—Why Women Don't Want It." http://leadershipconnection.net/blog/parity-politicswhy-women-dont.

Schreiber, Ronnee. 2012. *Righting Feminism: Conservative Women and American Politics*, paperback ed., with a New Epilogue. New York: Oxford University Press.

Schwindt-Bayer, Leslie A. 2009. "Making Quotas Work: The Effect of Gender Quota Laws on the Election of Women." *Legislative Studies Quarterly* 34, 1: 5–28.

Scott, Austin. 1974. "Democratic Women See Gains in 1974." *Washington Post*, March 31.

Seltzer, Richard A., Jody Newman, and Melissa Vorhees Leighton. 1997. *Sex as a Political Variable: Women as Candidates and Voters in U.S. Elections*. Boulder: Lynne Rienner.

Shiner, Meredith. 2012. "Female Lawmakers Are Raising Money and the Political Stakes." *Roll Call*, April 19.

Shiner, Meredith, and Glenn Thrush. 2009. "The GOP's Women Problem." www.politico.com, November 9.

Sigelman, Lee. 1981. "Special Elections to the U.S. House: Some Descriptive Generalizations." *Legislative Studies Quarterly* 6, 4 (November): 577–88.

Sinclair, Barbara. 2006. *Party Wars: Polarization and the Politics of National Policy Making*. Norman: University of Oklahoma Press.

Slevin, Peter. 2004. "For Women, a Year to Make History; Number of Candidates on National, State Ballots Reflects a Rise in Aspirations." *Washington Post*, October 14, A04.

Smith, Jada. 2012. "Forming a Caucus, Republican Women Send a Message." *New York Times*, May 22.

Smith, Steven S., Jason M. Roberts, and Ryan J. Vander Wielen. 2007. *The American Congress*. 5th ed. New York: Cambridge University Press.

Spillius, Alex. 2010. "Grizzly Phenomenon: The Rise of a New Politics in America; 2010 Midterm Elections." *Daily Telegraph* (London), October 30.

State News Service. 2012. "Kelly Ayotte: Obama's Policies Have Failed Women." April 12.

Steinhauser, Paul, and Amy Livingston. 2010. "Anti-Pelosi Ads Break Record." *CNN Politics*, http://politicalticker.blogs.cnn.com/2010/11/08/anti-pelosi-ads-break-records/.

Stevens, Allison. 2002. "Both Parties Say Women's Wallets Ripe for Tapping." www.womensenews.org, January 14.

Stevens, Allison. 2005. "Women Stake Out Leadership Turf in Congress." www.womensenews.org, March 29.

Stevens, Allison, 2006a. "Anti-incumbent Mood May Aid Women in 66 Primaries." www.womensenews.org, August 26.

Stevens, Allison. 2006b. "Female Dark Horses Surge to Election's Finish Line." www.womensenews.org, November 2.

Stevens, Allison. 2006c. "Tuesday Promises to Be 'Year of the Woman' Part II." www.womensenews.org, November 5.

Stevens, Allison. 2008. "Clinton's Legacy Leaves Light on for Other Women." www.womensenews.org, June 6.

Stolberg, Sheryl Gay. 2004. "Partisan Loyalties and the Senate Women's Caucus." *New York Times*, April 28.

Swers, Michele. 2002. *The Difference Women Make: The Policy Impact of Women in Congress*. Chicago: University of Chicago Press.

Swers, Michele. 2005. "Connecting Descriptive and Substantive Representation: An Analysis of Sex Differences in Cosponsorship Activity." *Legislative Studies Quarterly* 30, 3: 407–33.

Swers, Michele L. 2008. "Policy Leadership beyond 'Women's Issues.'" In *Legisla-*

tive Women: Getting Elected, Getting Ahead, edited by Beth Reingold, 117–34. Boulder: Lynne Rienner.

Swers, Michele L., and Carin Larson. 2005. "Women in Congress: Do They Act as Advocates for Women?" In *Women and Elective Office: Past, Present and Future*, 2nd ed., edited by Sue Thomas and Clyde Wilcox, 110–28. New York: Oxford University Press.

Tate, Katherine. 2003. *Black Faces in the Mirror: African Americans and Their Representatives in Congress*. Princeton: Princeton University Press.

Taylor, Paul, Rich Morin, D'Vera Cohn, April Clark, and Wendy Wang. 2008. "A Paradox in Public Attitudes: Men or Women: Who Is the Better Leader?" Washington, DC: Pew Research Center.

Thomas, Sue. 2005. "Introduction." In *Women and Elective Office: Past, Present and Future*, 2nd ed., edited by Sue Thomas and Clyde Wilcox, 3–25. New York: Oxford University Press.

Toeplitz, Shira. 2010. "Where Are the Women GOP House Candidates?" www.cqpolitics.com, March 11.

Toner, Robin. 2006. "Women Wage Key Campaigns for Democrats." *New York Times*, March 24, A1.

Tumulty, Karen. 2012. "Twenty Years On, 'Year of the Woman' Fades." *Washington Post*, March 24.

U.S. Census Bureau. 2007. *Survey of Business Owners*. www.census.gov/econ/sba.

Vaida, Bara, and Jennifer Skalka. 2008. "Can EMILY's List Get Its Mojo Back? *National Journal*, June 28.

Walsh, Debbie. 2006. "Election 2006: Many New Women Expected in U.S. House." CAWP Election Watch Press Release, September 27.

Whitman, Christie. 2008. "The Plight of Women Seeking Elective Office." *Record* (Bergen County, NJ), March 3, 7.

Wolbrecht, Christina. 2000. *The Politics of Women's Rights: Parties, Positions, and Change*. Princeton: Princeton University Press.

Wolbrecht, Christina. 2002. "Female Legislators and the Women's Rights Agenda: From Feminine Mystique to Feminist Era." In *Women Transforming Congress*, ed. Cindy Simon Rosenthal, 170–239. Norman: University of Oklahoma Press.

Wolbrecht, Christina, and David Campbell. 2006. "See Jane Run: Women Politicians as Role Models for Adolescents." *Journal of Politics* 68, 2 (May): 233–47.

Wolfensberger, Don. 2007. "Incivility Is a Symptom of a Larger Problem on Capitol Hill." *Roll Call*, October 1.

Women's Campaign Forum. 2007. *Vote with Your Purse: Harnessing the Power of Women's Political Giving for the 2008 Election and Beyond*. Washington, DC: Women' Campaign Forum Foundation. http://d3n8a8pro7vhmx.cloudfront.net/womenandpolitics/pages/50/attachments/original/1378712514/wcff-vote-with-your-purse-2007.pdf?1378712514.

Women's Campaign Forum. 2009. *Vote with Your Purse: Harnessing the Power of Women's Political Giving for the 2008 Election and Beyond*. www.wcfonline.org.

Yen, Hope. 2011. "In a First, Women Surpass Men in Advanced Degrees." Associated Press Online, April 27.

Zeller, Shawn. 2011. "The Staying Power of Partisanship." *CQ Weekly*, January 3.

Index